A Garden of
Herbs

HERB GARDEN, MISSION HOUSE, STOCKBRIDGE, MASSACHUSETTS

A Garden of
Herbs

by
Eleanour Sinclair Rohde

REVISED AND ENLARGED
EDITION

Dover Publications, Inc., New York

This Dover edition, first published in 1969, is an unabridged republication of the revised and enlarged edition, as published by Hale, Cushman & Flint in 1936.

The publisher is grateful to the Director of the Oberlin College Library for making a copy of this work available for reproduction.

Standard Book Number: 486-22308-6
Library of Congress Catalog Card Number: 75-81736

Manufactured in the United States of America
Dover Publications, Inc.
180 Varick Street
New York, N.Y. 10014

CONTENTS

xvi

ILLUSTRATIONS

PREFACE

"Were it not for the sake of Custom, which has made it as unfashionable for a Book to come abroad without an introduction as for a Man to appear at Church without a Neckcloth or a Lady without a Hoop-petticoat, I should not have troubled you with this."—E. SMITH, *The Compleat Housewife*, 1736.

NOWADAYS every one who writes a book, especially a small book, offers an apology for doing so. But this book is so unpretentious that an apology for writing it would be absurd. There is an immense wealth of literature, both learned and charming, on the subject of herbs, but there is no small practical handbook for those who are going to create an old-fashioned herb garden, and who want to know how to use these herbs as our great-grandmothers did. The fashion for " blue," " grey," " white " or Japanese gardens has died out ; the rock garden still fascinates, but, unless made and maintained by skilful hands, it is apt to look ridiculous, so let us hope that the herb garden is to be restored to its former pride of place. Even those of us with the smallest suburban plots can make a delightful herb garden, and, no matter how tiny, it is a perpetual joy. Herbs ask so little and they give so much. All that the majority of our common herbs want is a fairly poor soil (the poorer the better for the aromatic herbs) and plenty of sunlight. People who know nothing of herbs imagine that it might be a dull garden consisting of only foliage plants. But there is no blue more beautiful than that of borage, whilst bergamot, valerian, mallows, marigold, and the stately mullein (to mention only a few examples) make lovely splashes of colour. There need be no limit to the size of the garden, for, as one eminent herbalist tells us, there are on an average about seven hundred different remedies for most of the common ailments, but it is undoubtedly the moderate-sized garden which is the most attractive. This little book deals only with the few well-known English wild and garden herbs which every one can grow and use.

No mention is made of the purely medicinal uses of herbs, the receipts being merely for the excellent old herbal teas, the syrups and conserves, the herbal drinks and home-made wines, the candied flowers and leaves, the sweet waters, washing-balls, pomanders, etc., which our great-grandmothers were so skilful in preparing. I have included just a few recipes, which are, alas, of no use in our sadly unimaginative age! One of these will be found under the heading "Thyme": "To enable one to see the Fairies," and I can only trust it will not fall under the eye of any severely practical person, but as William Coles says of some of the things in his *Art of Simpling* : "if there be any that are not true yet they are pleasant."

ELEANOUR SINCLAIR ROHDE.

CRANHAM LODGE,
 REIGATE, SURREY.

PREFACE TO THE THIRD EDITION

THIS edition has been revised and enlarged, recipes for the old-fashioned elder rob, elder cream, mint pasties, mint butter, may-blossom flavouring, mulled claret, raspberry wine, cherry wine, ginger wine, etc., being added, as well as the most commonly used of the French *tisanes*. I am indebted to Mr. Simpson of Dunsfold, Godalming, for the very kind loan and permission to reproduce from a MS. book written by a butler in his family over 200 years ago—May, 1719. I quote the butler's introductory letter in full on page 245. The most interesting receipts from this book will be found in the chapter " Additional Receipts."

E. S. R.

A GARDEN OF HERBS

CHAPTER I

OF HERB GARDENS

" The worship of Demeter belongs to that older religion, nearer to the Earth, which some have thought they could discern behind the more definitely national mythology of Homer. She is the goddess of dark caves. . . . She knows the magic power of certain plants cut from her bosom to bane or bless. . . . She is the goddess of the fertility of the earth in its wildness."—WALTER PATER.

" Talke of perfect happiness or pleasure and what place was so fit for that as the garden place where Adam was set to be the Herbarist."—JOHN GERARD.

" Then there are some flowers, they always seem to me like over-dutiful children : tend them never so little and they come up and flourish and show as I may say their bright and happy faces to you."
—DOUGLAS JERROLD.

" A GARDEN of herbs, a vineyard, a garden enclosed— all these have the gravity of use and labour, and are as remote as memory, and as familiar, secluded and secret." But what do we know of herb gardens ?—for we use so few herbs, and those we have relegated to an obscure corner of the kitchen garden. It is a little difficult even to imagine a time when " vegetables " occupied only an insignificant part of the herb garden, and a still earlier time when both the flower garden and the vegetable garden were non-existent, and the herb garden reigned supreme. Even in Tudor days only very wealthy men had separate gardens merely for pleasure, whilst all the small manors and farm-houses throughout the country still retained the old herb garden.

For over seven centuries before that time, all the gardens in England were herb gardens, and very beautiful they must have been, for roses, lilies, gilly-flowers, lavender, rosemary, fennel, poppies, marigolds, honeysuckle, periwinkles, peonies and violets were all used as herbs. Our ancestors ate such enormous quantities of meat, that for " vegetables," as we understand them, they would have had very little use, and what they needed in large quantities were all sorts of herbs, for stuffings and stewings, for decorations, for perfume and for medicine. Indeed, " vegetables " are quite newcomers in England. They declined in favour throughout Europe with the fall of the Roman Empire, and though they were reintroduced after the Renaissance, they were not in common use till at least a hundred years later. We were far behind our continental neighbours in our knowledge of them, and vegetables which figured in the old Roman menus were considered luxuries in this country in the days of the later Stuarts. Though potatoes were introduced into England in Elizabeth's reign, they were not grown to any extent, and the working people did not eat them for another two hundred years. Gilbert White, writing late in the eighteenth century, says of them : " They have prevailed by means of premiums within these twenty years only, and are much esteemed here now by the poor, who would scarcely have ventured to taste them in the last reign." Of Jerusalem artichokes we knew nothing till we learnt about them from the Red Indians ; and they were only introduced into England in Tudor days. It was about the same time that French beans were first cultivated in this country, but scarlet runners were unknown till Stuart times. The wild carrot is an indigenous plant in the British islands, but of the cultivated carrot we were ignorant till the Flemish immigrants in the early seventeenth century introduced them. To them also we owe our present garden spinach, which has had a long journey to reach us, for it is said to have come from Asia through Spain. The wild cabbage was used by our ancestors from Saxon days, and one of the Saxon names for March was " sprout-kale month " ; but otherwise the whole *brassica* tribe were unknown to us till the late sixteenth and seventeenth centuries.

Sir Anthony Ashley, of Wimborne St. Giles, Dorset, who died in 1627, has always had the reputation of being the first to introduce the modern cabbage into England, and on his tomb there is a cabbage portrayed at his feet. His monument was seriously damaged by a fire a few years ago, but fortunately the cabbage was saved ! Mrs. Earle, in her *Pot-pourri from a Surrey Garden*, pointed out that even as late as 1824 there were no strawberries in our sense of the word. Samuel Hartlib, writing in 1659, says : " About fifty years ago this art of gardening began to creep into England, into Sandwich and Surrey, Fulham and other places. Some old men in Surrey, where it flourisheth very much at present, report that they knew the first gardeners that came into those parts to plant cabbages, colleflowers and to sow turneps and carrots and parsnips, and raith-rape peas, all which at that time were great rarities, we having few or none in England but what came from Holland and Flanders. These gardeners with much ado procured a plot of good ground and gave no lesse than eight pounds per acre ; yet the gentleman was not content, fearing they would spoil his ground because they did use to dig it. So ignorant were they of gardening in those days."

The kitchen garden, therefore, as we know it, is quite modern, and during the many centuries when "vegetables" were almost unknown, our ancestors relied on the health-giving properties of herbs. Even as late as the middle of the last century the herb garden retained an honoured place, and the old-fashioned herbs were still cherished for their rare virtues. Like the wise man, described by Solomon, our forefathers did not despise the God-given virtues of these humble plants. Much of the old lore has been lost, and patent medicines have been allowed to usurp the place of the herbal teas ; but at last herbs are coming into their own again, and we are beginning to realise our folly in making so little use of them, and especially of the sun-loving aromatic herbs. The mere scent of them is a tonic, and even in winter their leaves give one a delicious reminder of sunshine and joyous vitality. Why waste their virtues, which since Chaldæan days have been extolled by the wisest men of all ages ? We have come to look upon health as the mere absence of disease—with us it is a negative thing ; but the word "health," with its cognates "holy,"

"The Lord hath created medicines out of the earth; and he
that is wise will not abhor them."—Ecclesiasticus xxxviii, 4

" whole," " wholesome," has a positive sense, and the old herbalists were never weary of preaching the use of herbs, not only to cure, but also to keep one in perfect health. Just because it is the custom, we make use of all the showier " herbs," which now fill our kitchen gardens, not only because they are pleasant, but also because of their health-giving properties ; but why neglect the older herbs—sage, thyme, yarrow, wild strawberry leaves, violet and primrose leaves, angelica, balm, rosemary, fennel, agrimony, borage, betony, cowslip flowers and leaves, elder, tansy and many others ? The old herbal teas are wonderful tonics, and some of them—balm tea, for instance—are delicious. Why have modern house-wives abandoned making rose-petal conserve ? (This is far too delicate and fairy-like a concoction to be called " jam.") Why do we never make strawberry wine, which was Sir Walter Raleigh's favourite cor-dial ? Why are our salads such dull affairs compared with the salads of Tudor and Stewart days ? Why do we not flavour vinegar with gillyflowers, rosemary and many other herbs ? Why do we never serve syrups made from flower-petals—for example, roses, or violets, or cowslips—with sweet dishes? Recipes for these and many other concoctions will be found in the pages following.

With the substitution of foreign spices for our own English herbs in flavouring, the old herbalists have little patience. " As for fiery spices," said Sir John Hill, " God designed those for the countries where they grow ; with us they have continually disagreed." Like all herbalists, he was equally severe with those who preferred foreign drugs to our own medicinal herbs. " Nature has in this country and doubtless also in all others provided in the Herbs of its own growth the remedies for the several diseases to which it is most subject, and although the addition of what is brought from abroad should not be supposed super-fluous, there is no occasion it should make the other neglected." Tea is described by Tryon as a " pretty, innocent, harmless liquor " ; but he continues, " its great esteem is chiefly for Novelty's sake, and because 'tis outlandish and dear and far fetcht, and therefore, admired by the multitude of ignorant people, who have always the greatest esteem for those things they know not."

For fruits and vegetables unnaturally forced, and all other " improvements " on Nature's methods, the old herbalists had nothing but censure. " Whether men should attempt the forcing of Nature," wrote one, " may best be judged by observing how seldom God Almighty does it Himself." " The foreign plants brought into our stoves with so much expense and kept there with so much pains may fill the eye with empty wonder ; but it would be more to the honour of the possessor of them to have found out the use of one common herb at home than to have enriched our country with an hundred of the others. Why should he who has not yet informed himself thoroughly of the Nature of the meanest Herb which grows in the next Ditch ransac the earth for foreign wonders ?- Does he not fall under the reproach with the generality of those who travel for their Improvement, while they are ignorant of all they left at home, and who are ridiculous in their In-quiries concerning the Laws and Government of other Countries, while they are not able to give a satisfactory answer to any question which regards their own ? "

But apart from the use to be made of the herbs, how beautiful an old herb garden is, and how altogether lovable. Instead of the restless activities needed in a modern garden, the very name " herb garden " suggests rest and tranquillity, a quiet enclosure full of sunlight, and delicious scents, and plants whose peace is never disturbed ; and where the humblest of new-comers can always find its own niche, and a welcome from the older inhabitants. If ever we revive the beautiful old English herb garden, it is to be hoped that it will be the garden of the fourteenth and fifteenth centuries which will claim its old place in our affections, for at no time were herb gardens more beautiful.

They were rectangular enclosures surrounded by a wall or a very thick hedge, and all round was a bank of earth planted with sweet-smelling herbs. At intervals recesses were cut to serve as seats, and they were covered with turf, " thick yset and soft as any velvet," or camomile. This idea of a bank of earth thrown up all round was borrowed from the thirteenth-century monastic gardens, nearly all of which had them, and they were soon copied in all the gardens. How thick the hedges were may be gathered from the old poem, " The Flower and the Leaf."

> " The hegge as thicke as a castle wall,
> That who that list without to stond or go
> Though he would all day prien to and fro,
> He should not see if there were any wight within or no."

Sometimes there was a pergola or covered way

round three sides of the wall, but more commonly only on one side. Illustrations of these covered ways may be seen in the old missals. The covered-in alley of the Dutch garden in Kensington gardens is just like an illustration from *The second booke of Flowers*, *Fruits*, *Beastes*, *Birds and Flies* (1650), and would be a very good model for any one wishing to make one of the old covered ways. There was usually a cistern or simple fountain in some part of the garden, and nearly always a " herber." This herber, one hastens to add, bore little or no resemblance to that modern atrocity the summer-house, for herbers consisted merely of poles with rosemary or sweetbriar or dog-roses growing over them. As in Chaucer's day the herber might have a medlar tree growing by it, and for seats inside the low-growing camomile, or just turf. Hyle suggested that herbers should be covered with plants " of a fragrant savoure," such as rosemary, and that they should be so constructed " that the Owner's friends sitting in the same may the freelier see and beholde the beautie of the garden to theyr great delyght."

What they grew in the fifteenth-century herb gardens can easily be ascertained. The earliest original English treatise on gardening extant is a manuscript now in the Library of Trinity College, Cambridge. It is called *The Feate of Gardening*, and was written by Mayster Jon Gardener in 1440, and his list of the herbs includes strawberries (wild strawberries, of course), hyssop, woodruff, betony, borage, henbane, lavender, southernwood, tansy, thyme, violets, waterliles, hollyhocks, yarrow, mint, rue, roses, saffron, camomile, foxgloves, centaury, agrimony, Herb Robert,

lily candidum, wormwood, sage, horehound, groundsel,
hart's tongue fern, pimpernel, clary, comfrey, valerian
and cowslips, besides many others.   There is in the
British Museum a fifteenth-century manuscript (Sloane
MS. 1201) which is a book of cookery receipts, and
this gives a complete list of herbs used in cooking, and
in addition to those mentioned in Mayster Jon Gardener's enumeration, this list includes Alexanders,
mugwort, basil, bugloss, burnet, chervil, caraway,
chives, daises, dittany, dandelion, dill, elecampane,
eyebright, agrimony, fennel, marigold, gillyflowers,
germander, borage, mercury, mallow, mint, marjoram, nettles, orage, parsley, primroses, rocket, savory,
smallage, sorrel, sow-thistle, vervain, rosemary and
roses.   These two lists give a very fair idea of the herbs
grown in an ordinary fourteenth or fifteenth-century
garden, and the vision of the sweet, homely flowers
with their delicious scents rises before one, when
one reads Chaucer's description in the *Romaunt of
the Rose.*

> " Ful gay wis al the ground, and queynt
> And poudred as men had it peynt,
> With many a fresh and sundry flour
> That casten up a ful good savour."

Of the earlier herb gardens we have, alas ! very little
definite knowledge.   We know from Pliny that the
Druids used large numbers of medicinal herbs, and
we gather from his account that the knowledge of
herbal medicine was confined to the priesthood.   He
tells us, moreover, that they gathered herbs with such
striking ceremonies that it might seem as if the British
had taught them to the Persians, whose country was

supposed to be the home of superstitious medicine. All the written lore on herbs previous to Alfred's reign has been lost, and any books there were, were probably destroyed during the terrible Danish invasion, when so many valuable monastic libraries were burnt. That these books on herbs existed is almost certain, for we know that in the eighth century, Boniface, " the Apostle of the Saxons," received letters from various persons in England asking him for books on simples. The oldest herbal in England is an MS. in the British Museum which was written under the direction of one, Bald, who, if he was not a personal friend of King Alfred's, had at any rate access to the king's correspondence, for he gives certain prescriptions sent by Helias, Patriarch of Jerusalem, to the king. In a lecture delivered before the Royal College of Physicians in 1903, Doctor J. F. Payne commented on the remarkable fact that this and several other Saxon manuscripts on herbs were written in the vernacular, and thus they were unique in Europe at that time. " In no other European country was there at that time any scientific literature written in the vernacular. The Saxons had a much wider knowledge of herbs than the doctors of Salerno, the oldest school of medicine in Europe and also the oldest European university. No treatise of the school of Salerno contemporaneous with the Leach book of Bald is known, so that the Anglo-Saxons had the credit of priority. . . . The Leach book of Bald was the first medical treatise written in Western Europe which can be said to belong to modern history, that is produced after the decadence and decline of the classical medicine. . . . In fact it is the earliest medical treatise produced by any of the modern

nations of Europe." This old manuscript to which
Doctor Payne referred is supposed to have been
written under the direction of some one called Bald,
who is described in the manuscript[1] as the owner of
the book, the name of the actual scribe being Cild. It
is evident that Bald was a leech, and he was probably
a monk, for at that time very few books were written
except in monasteries. Bald had a remarkably wide
knowledge of native plants and garden herbs, but
though he gives exact prescriptions for the giving of
these herbs in drinks, with ale, vinegar or milk and
honey, and how to make them into ointments with
butter, it is quite impossible to ascertain exactly what
cultivated and wild herbs were included in the herb
gardens of those days. We only know that they called
their herb gardens wyrtzerd, or wyrttun, and that they
certainly grew peonies, gillyflowers, marigolds, violets
and periwinkles, to which last they gave the delightful
name " Joy of the Ground."

In Norman days the principal herb gardens were
those attached to the monasteries, and it is interesting
to remember that the present little cloister of Westminster Abbey and the College garden once formed
part of the old Infirmary garden, where the herbs for
the healing of the sick and for Church decorations

---

[1] At the end of the second part of the MS. is written in Latin
verse :—

" Bald is the owner of this book which he ordered Cild to write,
Ernestly I pray here all men, in the name of Christ
That no treacherous person take this book from me,
Neither by force nor by theft nor by any false statement.
Why ? Because the richest treasure is not so dear to me
As my dear books which the grace of Christ attends."

were grown. But if the monks maintained the knowledge of herbs in one way, it must also be remembered
that, on the other hand, they were largely responsible
for the loss of what remained of the Druidical knowledge of plants, which was discountenanced by the
Church, because much of it had become associated with
witchcraft. The seventh book of Alexander Neckham's
poem, " De laudibus divinæ Sapientiæ " (*circa* 1200)
is on herbs, and in his *De Naturis Rerum* he gives a
description of what a " noble garden " should be. His
list of herbs includes roses, lilies, violets, mandrakes,
parsley, fennel, southernwood, coriander, sage, savory,
hyssop, mint, rue, dittany, smallage, lettuce, garden
cress, peonies, onions, garlic, leeks, beets, herb mercury, orach, sorrel and mallows. But it is not till we
come to the fourteenth or fifteenth centuries that we
have any definite knowledge of what the gardens
looked like and what they grew in them.

From the Tudor days onwards began the separation
of the flowers from the herbs. As new vegetables were
introduced, the modern kitchen garden was gradually
established, and the herb garden decreased in size ;
but in importance not for another two centuries at
least. It became the special province of the housewife, and in it she grew all the herbs she needed for
the kitchen : for teas, ointments and simple medicines,
for making distilled waters, for sweet bags to scent the
linen, for washing-balls and pomanders. The post of
still-room maid in those days was not a sinecure.
There was no lack of books to guide the housewife of
Tudor and Stewart days : the most notable being
Hyll's *Proffitable Art of Gardening*, Gerard's *Herball*,
William Lawson's *The Country Housewife's Garden*,

Parkinson's *Paradisus*, and Gervase Markham's various works. William Lawson gives a delightful description of the ideal gardener who should be " religious, honest and skilful." " Religious," he proceeds to explain (" because many thinke religion but a fashion or custome to goe to Church "), to be one " who cherishes above all God's word and the Preachers thereof " (so much as he is able), and by " honest " he means " one who will not hinder your pleasures in the garden," and he adds that he must not be a " lazy lubber." When he comes to gillyflowers (why have we given up this delightful name for carnations ?) in his list of herbs he gives one of those personal touches, which are so irresistibly charming in the old writers. With a childlike faith in his readers' sympathy he tells us, " I have of them nine or ten severall colours and divers of them as bigge as Roses. Of all flowers (save the Damaske Rose) they are the most pleasant to smell. Their use is much in ornament and comforting the spirits by the sense of smelling." Biographies full of facts and dates sometimes leave one cold, but those few words bridge the centuries in a flash, and one sees the old gardener in the glory of the July sunshine working happily amongst his gillyflowers. It is Lawson also who gives the sage advice to the housewife, that if her maids help her with the weeding she must teach them the difference between herbs and weeds. Thomas Hyll (who adopted the *nom de plume* of " Didymus Mountain " for one of his books !) is in some ways the quaintest of these three writers ; but one cannot help feeling that like most Tudor authorities on gardening he did not mean to be taken quite literally, and it is pleasant to find that in those days, as now, between book gardening and practical gardening there was a great gulf fixed ! It is doubtful whether any one could suggest a more appropriate hedge for the herb garden than his idea of young elder trees at intervals. There should, of course, be an elder tree in every herb garden ; for have not herbs since time immemorial been under the protection of the spirit of the elder tree ? A hedge of briars, as Hyll truly observes, " within three years would well defend out both thefe and beaste, nor would it be in danger of the wanton wayfairing man's firebrand passinge by, although he should put fire to it." Time apparently was of no object, for he suggests that the briars should be grown from seed. Like the majority of gardeners and herbalists in those days, Hyll believed firmly that the sowing of seeds should be done whilst the moon was waxing, and all cutting back when the moon was waning. He also gives us this astonishing secret, " That many savours and tastes may be felte in one herb : take first of the lettuce two or three seeds, of the endive so many, of the smallage the lyke, of the Basil, the Leek and the Parsley. Put altogether into a hole and there will spring up a plant having so many savours or tastes." He cautions one to pay respect to the stars, " whose Beames of lighte and influence boothe quicken, comforte, preserve and mayntayne or ells nippe, drye, wyther, consume and destroye by sundrye ways the tender seedes." After a lengthy and confusing astrological discourse, he adds apologetically that perchance " the most part of the common sort of his readers will think these things above their capacity, but his conscience bounde him somewhat to put such matter into their heades."

When one reads the curious instructions in these

old books one cannot help wondering whether any anxious learner took them seriously. Did they ever sprinkle seeds with wine to strengthen them, and drag speckled toads about the garden to safeguard the young herbs ? Did they hang hyena and crocodile skins in the alleys to protect them from lightning, and hippopotamus' skins or owls' wings outspread against tempests ? Were eagles' feathers planted in the four corners and in the middle to ward off mists and frosts ? And to avert disease in the plants did they burn the left horn of an ox ? Was any one ever seen creeping stealthily into his neighbour's garden to purloin caterpillars, in order to seethe them with the herb dill and sprinkle the mixture in order to abolish caterpillars for ever from his own garden ? (" Take very dilegent hede," Hyll thoughtfully adds, " that none of this water fall neither on your face, nor hands.") Did they put a solitary mole into a pot so that when " he crieth out the others minding to help him forth will also fall into the pot " ? Were mice frightened away by the beds being sprinkled with water in which the cat had been washed, or by a mixture of wild cucumber, henbane and bitter almonds ? " No adder," says Hyll, " will come into a garden in which grow wormwood, mugwort and southernwood, and therefore it should be aptly planted in the corners or round about the garden." Did any one follow the advice to run after adders and throw green oak leaves on them that they might die forthwith ? Adders it seems love fennel " as toads love sage and snakes rocket." And if after a strenuous day the croaking of the frogs disquieted the gardener, did he go and hang up lanterns to make them think the sun was shining ?

In the sixteenth century the fashion for growing herbs in " knots " and " mazes " came in, and, though artificial, at least they are not so ugly as the survivals one still sees of the geometrical flower-beds of Victorian days. The Tudor garden of any pretension also included a wild part where the herbs could be trodden on, and of such a garden there is the well-known description in Bacon's essay. The idea of a wild garden where the sweet-smelling herbs might be trodden on survived into the eighteenth century. In the *English Housewife of the Seventeenth and Eighteenth Centuries*, there is a description of one of the few genuine old herb gardens still to be seen in England. It is at St. Anne's Hill near Chertsey-on-Thames, originally the home of Charles James Fox, and now the property of Sir Albert K. Rollit, and the herb garden is left very much as it was in Charles James Fox's days. " The herbs are in no particular order and are not raised above the level of the turf walks and offer themselves to be trodden on. There are rosemary, borage, thyme, sage, fennel, mint, parsley, rue, lavender, chives, southernwood, tarragon, savory, hyssop, chervil and marjoram growing in charming confusion enclosed by the thick old-world beech and yew hedges which are probably older than the Georgian house." One eighteenth-century herb garden must have been unique in its fencing, for this was made entirely of sword-blades picked up on the field of Culloden. One of the most famous eighteenth-century herb gardens was Sir John Hill's in Bayswater. This doctor advocated that there should be public herb gardens in various parts of England planted with every herb useful in medicine, in the arts or Husbandry, that they should be open always free of expense to all people, and that there should be " some person present to show what was deserved to be seen and explain what was necessary." Till such gardens were made he generously invited any one who was interested to come to his garden at Bayswater—" let none fear to apply, the plants are there and every one is welcome." At the end of his *Virtues of British Herbs* there is a note : " If any one entertain a doubt concerning the plant he would use after comparing it with the figure and description, the gardener at Bayswater shall give a sample of it for asking, and all persons can command the farther opinion and directions of the author when they please." Sir John Hill's works on herbs are so learned that it is refreshing in the middle of one of them to light on this remark : " I was introduced in Yorkshire to one Brewer, who has contrived a Dress on Purpose for Herbalising, and had a mask for his face and pads to his knees that he might creep into the thickets." This, alas, is all he tells us of this enthusiast.

But whether fashioned on the old-world model or made just according to the fancy of the owner, a herb garden should be essentially a garden enclosed ; a sanctuary of a sweet and placid pleasure ; a garden of peace and of sweet scents, filled with all the humble, lovable old plants one so rarely sees, and which never look really happy in company with showy modern plants. A modern herb garden might be made surrounded by banks (such as one sees round Devonshire cottage gardens), and these could be smothered with herbs—violets, cowslips, borage, wild strawberries, germander, betony, yarrow, centaury, wild thyme, and so on. If there were room on one bank even nettles,

dandelions, lesser celandine, daisies, etc., might be
allowed to grow, not with the abashed furtive air they
assume in the presence of that terribly grand and
merciless person the gardener, but spreading themselves cheerfully and comfortably in the sun, happy in
the knowledge that even if the aforesaid gardener
rejects them, their owner realises they have virtues
not to be found amongst the inhabitants of the largest
and tidiest kitchen garden.   And how beautiful the
garden itself could be with every variety of lavender,
rosemary, bergamot, hyssop, thyme, fennel, rue, marjoram, lad's love, sweetbriar, and all the old sweet-
scented roses ; even if these were the only inhabitants
of the old-fashioned herb garden included in it.   There
should be nothing of the " grand air " in a herb garden.
As Rousseau wisely observed : " The ' grand air ' is
always melancholy in a garden, it makes one think of
the miseries of the man who affects it. . . . The two
sides of the alleys will not be always exactly parallel,
its direction will not be always in a straight line, it will
have a certain vagueness like the gait of a leisurely man
—the owner will not be anxious to open up fine pros-
pects in the distance.   The taste for points of view and
distances comes from the tendency which most men
have to be pleased only where they do not happen to
be : they are always longing for what is far from them,
and the artist who does not know how to make them
sufficiently satisfied with what surrounds them allows
himself this resource to amuse them ; but the man
of whom I speak has not this anxiety, and when he is
well where he is he does not desire to be elsewhere."
As Mrs. Bardswell has already told us, the only possible
addition to a herb garden is a sun-dial.   In the seven-

teenth century it was customary to have a sun-dial surrounded by herbs, and

> " How could such sweet and wholesome hours
> Be reckoned but with herbs and flowers."

There is much to be learned from the old herbalists besides a knowledge of herbs and herb gardens. Could any one give better advice than old Tryon ? " Let not Carking Cares nor Perturbations afflict your Minds about such things as are out of your power to help or remedy, nor abandon yourselves too much to any Passion, be it Love, Hate, Revenge or the like ; avoid envy, strife, violence and oppression either to man or Beast ; Stillness and Complacency of Mind are two main props to support our Adamical Building ; a Chearful heart causeth the countenance to shine, a good conscience is a continual Feast and Content is Nectar to the Spirits, and Marrow to the Bones. Therefore study to be satisfied with your Portion and thank and bless God for his Bounties which you enjoy, and use his creatures for the end they were given thee, and above all, consider that thou art made in the image of God and in thee is truly contained the Properties of all Elements ; therefore thou art obliged to imitate thy Creator and so to conduct thy ways that thou mayest attract the benign influences of the Celestials and Terrestrials and the favourable irradiations of the Superior and Inferior worlds, and on the other side not to awaken the Dragon that is always lurking about the Golden Fruit in the fair Garden of the internal Hesperides, nor irritate the original poisons, nor raise combustions within by falling into Disorders without ; but managing all things in Temperance and Simplicity, and hearkening to the Voice of Wisdom and the Dictates of Reason and Nature, thou shalt transact the days of thy pilgrimage here in Peace and Tranquility and be prepared for the fruition of more compleat and undisturbed as well as endless Felicity."

Perhaps when we revive the old herb garden the herbs will imbue us with more of the spirit of the old herbalists. To read their works is to feel one knows at least something of the minds of the writers ; and widely as their personalities differ, one thing they all seem to have had in common, and that was the spirit of the great Linnæus, who, after seeing a flower open said, " I saw God in His Glory passing near me and bowed my head in worship." " If every herb," says William Coles, " show that there is a God, as verily it doth, the very beauty of plants being an argument that they are from an Intellectual principle ; what Lectures of Divinity might we receive from them if we would but attend diligently to the inward understanding of them ? " " They are to be cherished," says Harrison, " and God to be glorified in them because they are His good gifts and created to do man help and service." The preface to Parkinson's *Paradisus* is so beautiful that I cannot forbear quoting some of it at length. " Although the ancient Heathens did appropriate the first invention of the knowledge of Herbs and so consequently of physicke, some unto Chiron the Centaure, and others to Apollo or Æsculapius his sonne ; yet we that are Christians have out of a better schoole learned that God the Creator of Heaven and Earth, at the beginning when he created Adam, inspired him with the knowledge of all naturall thinges : for as he was able to give names to all the living Creatures,

according to their severall natures ; so no doubt but
hee had also the knowledge, both what Herbes and
Fruits were fit, eyther for Meate or Medicine, for Use
or for Delight, and that Adam might exercise this
knowledge, God planted a garden for him to live in
(wherein even in his innocency he was to labour and
spend his time) which hee stored with the best and
choysest Herbes and Fruits the earth could produce,
that he might have not only for necessitie whereon to
feede, but for pleasure also ; the place or garden
called Paradise importing as much, or more plainly the
words set downe in Genesis the second, which are
these : ' Out of the ground the Lord God made to
grow everie tree pleasant to the sight and good for
meate ' ; . . . But my purpose is onely to show you,
that Paradise was a place (whether you will call it a
Garden or Orchard or both, no doubt of some large
extent) wherein Adam was first placed to abide ; that
God was the Planter thereof, having furnished it with
Trees and Herbes, as well pleasant to the sight, as
good for meate and that hee being to dresse and keepe
this place, must of necessity know all the things that
grew therein, and to what uses they serve or else his
labour about them, and knowledge in them had been
in vain.   And although Adam lost the place for his
transgression, yet he lost not the naturall knowledge
or use of them, but that as God made the whole world,
and all the Creatures therein for Man, so hee may use
all things as well as pleasures as of necessitie, to be
helpes unto him to serve his God.   Let men therefore,
according to their first institution so use their service,
that they also in them may remember their service to
God, and not (like our Grandmother Eve) set their

affections so strongly on the pleasure in them, as to deserve the losse of them in this Paradise, yea and of Heaven also. For truly from all sorts of Herbes and Flowers we may draw matter at all times not only to magnify the Creator, that hath given them such diversities of formes, scents and colours, that the most cunning Workman cannot imitate and such vertues and properties, that although wee know many, yet manye more lye hidden and unknowne, but many good instructions also to ourselves : That as many herbes and flowers with their fragrant sweet smels doe comfort and as it were revive the Spirits and perfume a whole house ; even so such men as live vertuously, labouring to doe good, and to profit the Church of God and the commonwealth by their paines or penne, doe as it were send forth a pleasing savour of sweet instructions, not only to that time wherein they live and are fresh, but being drye, withered and dead, cease not in all after ages to doe as much or more. Many herbes and flowers that have small beautie or savour to commend them, have much more good and vertue : So many men of excellent rare parts and good qualities doe lye unknown and not respected, untill time and use of them doe set forth their properties. Againe many flowers have a glorious shew, yet of no other use ; So many doe make a glorious ostentation, and flourish in the world . . . yet surely they have no other vertue than their outside to commend them or leave behind them. The frailty also of man's life is learned by the soone fading of them before their flowering, or in their pride or soon after, being either cropt by the hand of the spectator, or by a sudden blast withered and parched, or by the revolution of time decaying of its owne nature : as also that the fairest flowers or fruits first ripe, are soonest and first gathered. The mutability also of States or persons, by this, that as where many goodly flowers and fruits did growe in this yeare and age, in another they are quite pulled or digged up, and eyther weedes and grasse grow in their place, or some building erected thereon, and there place is no more known. The Civill respects to be learned from them are many also ; for the delight of the varieties both of formes, colours and properties of Herbes and Flowers, hath ever been powerfull over dull, unnatured, rusticke and savage people, led only by Natures instinct ; how much more powerfull is it, or should be in the mindes of generous persons ? for it may well bee said, he is not human that is not allured with this object."

Name.	Classification.	Hght. in ft.	Colour.	Time of Flowering.
Angelica . .	Perennial	4'–6'	Yellowish	July.
Anise . .	Annual	1½'	Yellowish	July.
Balm . .	Perennial	2'	Foliage	June–October.
Basil (Bush) .	Annual	½'	Foliage	July–August.
Basil (Sweet) .	Annual	3'	Mauve	July–August.
Bergamot .	Perennial	2'	Red	July–September.
Borage . .	Annual	1½'	Blue	May–June.
Caraway . .	Biennial	2'	White	June.
Catmint . .	Perennial	2'	Mauve	July–September.
Chives . .	Perennial	1'	Pink	June.
Clary . .	Biennial	2'–3'	Blue	July.
Coriander .	Annual	1'–3'	Mauve	July.
Cumin . .	Annual	1'	Rose	June–July.
Dill . .	Annual	2'–2½'	Yellow	July.
Fennel . .	Perennial	4'	Yellow	July–August.
Horehound .	Perennial	2½'	White	July.
Hyssop . .	Perennial	2'	Blue	July–August.
Lavender .	Perennial	2'–4'	Lavender	July–September.
Lovage . .	Perennial	4'	Yellow	June–July.
Marigold .	Annual	2'	Yellow	May–October.
Marjoram .	Perennial	2'	Purplish	June–August.
Meadowsweet .	Perennial	2'–4'	Cream	June–September.
Mullein . .	Biennial	4'	Yellow	July.
Parsley . .	Annual	1'	Foliage	
Peppermint .	Perennial	½'	Foliage	
Rosemary .	Perennial	5'	Blue	July.
Rue . .	Perennial	2'	Greenish	June–September.
Sage, red, green	Perennial	2'	Purplish	August.
Savory . .	Winter Perennial	1½'	Pale purple	July.
Savory . .	Summer Annual	1'	Pale lilac	July.
Spearmint .	Perennial	1'	Foliage	
Southernwood .	Perennial	2'–3'	Foliage	
Tansy . .	Perennial	3'	Yellow	Aug.–September
Tarragon .	Perennial	2'	Foliage	
Thyme . .	Perennial	1'	Purplish	May–August.
Valerian . .	Perennial	4'	Pink	June–September.
Water Mint .	Perennial	1½'	Blue	July.
Woad . .	Annual	2'–3'	Yellow	June–September.
Woodruff .	Annual	1½'	White	May–August.
Wormwood .	Perennial	2½'	Foliage	

CHAPTER II

OF SUNDRY HERBS

" Lerne the hygh and marvelous vertue of herbes. Know how inestimable a preservative to the helth of man God hath provyded growying every daye at our handes, use the effects with reverence and give thanks to the maker celestyall. Behold how much it excedeth to use medecyne of eficacye naturall, by God ordeyned, than wicked wordes or charmes of eficacye unnaturall by the divyll invented."—*The virtuose boke of Distyllacion of the Waters of all maner Herbes* . . . by Master Jherom Brunswyke, 1527.

" Who would looke dangerously up at Planets that might safely loke downe at Plants ? "—JOHN GERARD, *The Herball*, 1597.

" There is no question but that very wonderful effects may be wrought by the Vertues which are enveloped within the compasse of the Green Mantles wherewith Many Plants are adorned."— W. COLES, *The Art of Simpling*, 1656.

AGRIMONY

IN many herbals Agrimony is spelt Argemoney, and the name is derived from the Greek " *argemos*," a white speck on the eye which this plant was supposed to cure. English country folk used to call it " Church-steeples," and the plant with its exquisitely delicate spike of yellow flowers is certainly suggestive of a steeple. From the days of our Saxon ancestors Agrimony has been highly esteemed.

A SUGGESTED PLAN

Sweet Briar Hedge
Cabbage Roses
Damask Roses — Valerian

Rosemary Hedge

Sweet Briar Hedge

Edging of Garden-Thyme — Bergamot

Angelica | Marigold | Balm | Meadowsweet
Horehound | Southernwood | Borage

Rosemary

Rue | Tarragon | Meadowsweet | Bush Basil | Coriander | Borage | Sweet Basil | Lavender

Fennel | Borage
Hyssop
Tarragon | Cumin | Bergamot
Lavender

Edging of Garden Thyme
Sage
Edging of Garden Thyme

Hyssop
Calmint | Calmint
Hyssop

Madonna Lilies

Varieties of Wild Thyme between the Flagstones

Lavender
Borage
Cumin | Marigold
Tansy
Fennel

Lavender
Bergamot | Horehound
Clary
Coriander
Mullein | Borage

Madonna Lilies

Wild Marjoram
Hyssop | Hyssop
Wild Marjoram

Edging of Lemon Thyme
Sage
Edging of Lemon Thyme

Garden Thyme — Edging of Bergamot

Anise | Dill | Bush Basil | Marigold
Hyssop | Tarragon | Southernwood

Rosemary Hedge

Sweet Briar Hedge

Sweet Briar Hedge

Sweet Briar Hedge

Damask Roses
Cabbage Roses
Sweet Briar Hedge — Rosemary

FOR A HERB GARDEN

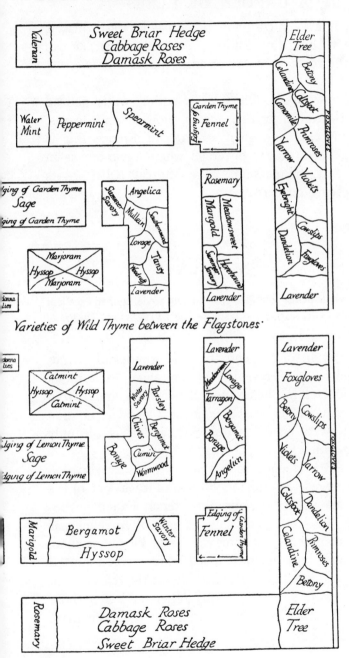

As it is a very common perennial in waste places, any one wishing to include it in their herb garden can obtain the roots in spring or autumn.

AGRIMONY TEA.—One pint of boiling water poured on to a handful of the stems, flowers and leaves. Leave till cold and then strain. In France this is drunk as an ordinary beverage when Agrimony is in flower, and the peasants have a great belief in its health-giving properties.

ANGELICA

" The whole plante, both leafe, roote, and seede, is of an excellent comfortable sent, savour and taste."—JOHN PARKINSON, *Theatre of Plants*, 1640.

There is an old legend that the wonderful virtues of Angelica were revealed by an angel to a monk during a terrible plague, and hence its name. From earliest times Angelica has enjoyed a great reputation for its powers against witchcraft, and it is the only herb for which Gerard claims this quality.

The leaves steeped in hot water were largely used to allay any sort of inflammation, and it was one of the ingredients in the famous old French Eau d'Arquebusade. To " bite and chaw " a root of Angelica was much recommended during the Great Plague of 1660. In Stewart days the best dried roots were imported from Spain, but Sir John Hill tells us that those from Bohemia were superior to any other, and that those English Angelica was second only to the Bohemian.

Amongst the Laplanders Angelica was held in high repute, and they used to crown their poets with it in order that they might be inspired by the scent of it. Formerly they used to make an incision in the stems and crown of the root at the beginning of spring, and collect the musk-flavoured resinous gum which came out.

Angelica is a member of the umbelliferæ order. *Angelica sylvestris* (which grows wild in this country) has a hairy stalk and its flowers are white, whereas *Angelica officinalis* has fluted stalks and yellow or greenish flowers. The scent of Angelica is curiously attractive and even when raw the stems and root have a pleasant taste. Angelica likes moisture, but it is almost as adaptable as forget-me-not in accommodating itself to any fairly good soil. Abercrombie speaks of it as an annual-perennial, i.e. it is best to take it up and replant yearly. The seed is slow and capricious in germinating. It is best to sow the seed in August as soon as it is ripe. Sow thinly, and when six inches high, thin them to at least three feet apart. They flower in June of the second year and must then be cut down, as if allowed to run to seed they soon perish.

To CANDY ANGELICA.—Boil the stalks of Angelica in water till they are tender ; then peel them and put them in other warm water and cover them. Let them stand over a gentle Fire till they become very green ; then lay them on a cloth to dry ; take their weight in fine Sugar with a little Rose-water and boil it to a Candy height. Then put in your Angelica and boil them up quick ; then take them out and dry them for use.—From *The Receipt Book of John Nott*, Cook to the Duke of Bolton, 1723.

To Preserve Angelica Roots.—Wash them, slice them thin, put them to steep in fair Water, and shift the Water every day, for three Days. Then set them all night in a Pot over warm Embers, pour off the water in the Morning, and take two Pounds of Sugar and two Quarts of Water to a Pound of Roots, and boil them in it ; when they are boil'd enough take them out and boil the Syrup gently.—*Ibid*.

Angelica Water.—Take of the Leaves of Angelica four Pounds, Annise-seeds three Ounces, Coriander and Carraway seeds of each four Ounces ; cut the Leaves small and bruise the seeds carefully together in a Mortar, put them into the Still with six Gallons of White Wine, and let them stand all Night, the next Morning put in a Handful of fresh Clove Gillyflowers, the same Quantity of Sage-flowers, and the same Quantity of the Tops and Leaves of Sweet Majoram ; when all are in, stir them well up with a Stick, and then put on the Head of the Still, close it with a paper wetted with Flour and Water Paste, and then distill off the Liquor ; the quantity to be drawn off is three Gallons ; it is excellent.—From *The Receipt Book of Elizabeth Cleland*, 1759.

To Candy Angelica Leaves.—Take the Leaves before they be grown too big, put them into a Skillet of boiling water ; when they are tender, take them out, spread them on the bottom of plates, open them, and lay them one upon another, till the plate be pretty full ; then pour upon them sugar boiled to a pretty thick syrup, and let them stand two or three days, heating them now and then on some coals ; lay them upon glasses, sift sugar on first, lay the leaves on one by one, and dry them in the sun ; when they are dry, lay them in boxes, with paper between each layer of leaves.—From *The Receipt Book of Mrs. Anne Shackleford of Winchester*, 1767.

ANISE

Although a native of Egypt, anise does well in English gardens if given a warm, sunny place, and it was grown, in the old herb gardens as early as the fourteenth century. Anise was one of the chief ingredients of the spiced cake served at the end of a rich feast by the Romans, and it is to this cake our modern bridal cake is supposed to trace its ancestry. Even in the early nineteenth century anise was commonly used for flavouring soups and sometimes bread, but it is rather too aromatic for the modern taste.

ANISE is a half-hardy annual. Sow during April in pots plunged in a hot-bed, and remove to a warm, light border in May. Anise only ripens its seeds in exceptionally hot summers in this country.

ANISEED TEA.—Half a pint of boiling water on two teaspoonfuls of the bruised seed.

ARTICHOKE (GLOBE)

The Globe Artichoke is such a modern-looking plant, yet it is in reality one of the oldest inhabitants of the herb garden. Its name is derived from the Arabic " *Alkharshuf*," and as it is one of the oldest cultivated " herbs " in the world, it should find a place in every herb garden, however tiny. Some herbalists call it the thistle of the garden, and Hyll tells us that " it grew wild in the fields, and came by diligence to be carefully bestowed in the garden, where through travail brought from his wildness to serve unto the use of the mouth." Some of the old instructions for the growing of artichokes are very delightful. " See that the mice haunt not the roots," says one, " for once allured of the pleasant taste of them, they very often resort in great number from far places to the marvellous spoil of the roots." Moles also, it seems, are deadly enemies, and to keep them away you must either " bring uppe and learne a young Catte, or tame a weesell to hunt daily in those places." According to the Neapolitan Rutilius, if the seeds are sown the wrong way down the artichokes will grow crooked, weak and very small. If you desire to grow the heads without prickles you are instructed either to break the sharp ends of the seeds or else to put each seed in a lettuce root with the rind pared off before planting it. To ensure a pleasant flavour the seeds must be soaked in rose or lily water, or the juice of bay leaves mixed with sweet almonds, or new milk and honey, or aromatised wine, and in whatever pleasant liquor the seeds have

(a) Distilling Herbs

(b) An Apothecary's Garden

been steeped the artichokes when ripe will have the flavour of it. Formerly, even the leaves were considered a delicacy, and they were carefully blanched in the late summer. Our English artichokes were so highly esteemed in Tudor days that the plants were exported to Italy, France, and the Low Countries.

PRESERVING OF ARTICHOKES.—Cut off the Stalkes of your Artichokes within two inches of the Apple; and of all the rest of the Stalkes make a strong decoction, slicing them into thinne and small peeces, and keepe them in this decoction: You must lay them first in warme water, and then in colde, to take away the bitternesse of them. This of Mr. Parsons, that honest and painefull Practicer in his profession.

In a mild and warme winter, about a month or three weeks before Christmas, I caused great store of Artichokes to be gathered with their stalkes in their full length as they grew; and, making first a good thick Lay of Artichoke leaves in the bottome of a great and large vessel, I placed my Artichokes one upon another, as close as I could couch them, covering them over, of a pretty thicknesse with Artichoke leaves: those Artichokes were served at my Table all the Lent after, the apples being red and sound, only the tops of the leaves a little faded."—Sir Hugh Platt, *Delights for Ladies*, 1594.

To STEW ARTICHOKES.—First let your artichokes be boyled, then take out the core and take off all the leaves, cut the bottome into quarters splitting them in the middle. Provide a flat stewing pan or dish wherein put thin Manchet tostes, and lay the artichoke on them, the Marrows of two Bones, five or six large blades of mace, halfe pound of preserved plums, with their syrup and sugar (if the syrup doe not make them sweet enough). Let all these stew together. If you stew them in a dish, serve them in it, not stirring them only, lay on some preserves which are fresh, as Barberries or suchlike. Sippit it and serve it up. Instead of Preserves you may stew ordinary Plummes which will be cheaper if you have no old Preserves.—From *The Receipt Book of Joseph Cooper*, Cook to Charles I, 1654.

To Fry Artichokes.—Boyl and sever all from the Bottoms, and slice them in the midst and quarter it, dip them in Batter and fry them in Butter, for the Sauce take Butter and Sugar with the juice of an orange. Dish your Artichokes with this sauce (being fried brown) and lay boyl'd marrow of bones on them. Garnish it with Orange and serve up.—*Ibid.*

Artichoke Pie.—Take your artichokes, boil them and take out the Leaves and the Core, and trim the Bottoms. Cut some in quarters and some whole. To eight Bottoms take the Marrows of four good bones taken out as whole as you can. Toss these in the Yolks of eggs, and season them with Salt, Sugar, Ginger, Cinnamon and Nutmeg. Raise a Pie. Lay in your Bottoms, put Marrow between and your quarters uppermost, lay marrow with them. Put on them the Yolks of eight hard eggs. Lay over them Citron and Dates. Put over Butter, and close it and Bake.—*Ibid.*

RESOLES OF ARTICHOKES OR POTATOES.—Take Artichoke bottoms boiled (or potatoes boiled), and beat them in a Mortar with good marrow from bones, seasoned with Salt, Nutmeg, Ginger, Cinnamon and Sugar, Orange-flower water or Rose-water, some grated citron ; work up with Naples bisket grated, and the Yolks of Eggs, and put it in sweet paste, and either bake it or fry it.

Another way is with the yolks of hard eggs minced, and add to them half as much almonds, finely beaten as eggs, season with the same as before, and work it up with bisket, thick butter, and the yolks of eggs, and put in some plumpt currants, and either bake them or fry them in butter.—*Ibid.*

TO FRY YOUNG ARTICHOKES.—Take young artichokes or suckers, and pare off all the outside as you pare Apples, and boyl them tender, then take them up and slit them thorow the midst, but do not take out the coare, but lay the split side downeward on a dry cloth to draine out the water. Then mix a little Flower, two or three yolks of eggs, beaten Ginger, Nutmeg, Vinegar and Salt, to the thickness of a batter and roule them well in it. Then get a frying-pan with Butter pretty hot, and fry them in it till they be brown ; for the Sauce make a Lear with yolks of eggs, white wine, cinnamon, ginger, sugar, with a great piece of butter, keeping it with stirring on the fire till it be thick. Then dish them on white Bread-Tostes with the Caudle on them, and serve them up.—*Ibid.*

ARTICHOKE PIE.—The bottoms of artichokes with

Marrow and dates with a handful of herbs and baked in a pie.—John Evelyn, *Acetaria*, 1699.

ARTICHOKES BROILED.—Broil them and as the scaley leaves open, baste them with sweet and fresh oyl, but with care extraordinary, for if a drop fall upon the coals all is marr'd : that hazard escaped, eat them with the juice of Orange and Sugar.—*Ibid*.

POTTED ARTICHOKES.—The way of preserving them fresh all winter is by separating the Bottoms from the Leaves and after Parboiling, allowing to every Bottom a small earthern glazed Pot ; burying it all over in fresh melted Butter as they do Wild Fowl, etc. Or if more than one in a larger Pot in the same Bed and Covering Layer upon Layer.

They are also preserved by stringing them on Pack thread, and clean Paper being put between every Bottom to hinder them from touching one another, and so hung up in a dry place.—*Ibid*.

ARTICHOKES, THE BRIGOULE WAY. — Take the middling sort of Artichokes, pare them, and take off the Choke ; put them into a Stew-pan, seasoned with Pepper, Salt, Garlic cut small, some Truffles, Mushrooms, green Onions, and Parsley ; put it all to your Artichokes, add a Glass of Water with a Glass of Oil, and let them stew ; being done, dish them up with their Liquor and Lemon-juice.—From *The Receipt Book of Vincent La Chapelle*, Chief Cook to The Prince of Orange, 1744.

ARTICHOKES, THE ITALIAN WAY.—Take the middling sort of Artichokes, pare and boil them, till you can easily take off the Chokes, and cut small Parsley with a few green Onions and Mushrooms ; put them in a Stew pan over the Fire, with half a Glass of good Oil, Pepper, Salt, and sweet Herbs ; put in a Baking-pan some Slices of Bacon, place over these your Artichokes, put into every Artichoke Mushrooms and green Onions, cover these with Slices of Bacon, and put them into the Oven ; being done, take them out to drain, and dish them up. At another time, serve them up with a White Sauce.—*Ibid.*

BALM

" Balm makes the heart merry and joyful."—*Arabian Proverb.*

" The herb without all question is an excellent helpe to comfort the heart as the very smell may induce any so to believe."—JOHN PARKINSON, *Paradisus,* 1629.

Balm is a favourite herb with every one, for there are few leaves with a more delicious and refreshing scent. Balm tea also, with its delicate lemon flavour, is not only most wholesome, but quite unlike any other summer drink. The plant grows wild nearly everywhere in the south of England, and in a garden it is a rampant grower, but it is impossible to have too much of it. No wonder it was a favourite strewing herb in the days when the delightful custom prevailed of strewing herbs. Gerard tells us that if bee-hives are rubbed with balm " it causeth the bees to keepe together and causeth others to come unto them."

He also tells us that besides being good for toothache, " it is good for those that cannot take breath unlesse they hold their neckes upright." The famous Balm of Gilead in which the Ishmaelites, to whom Joseph was sold, trafficked, and of which Jeremiah speaks, was the true balsam of Judæa, which at one time grew only at Jericho. There is an old legend that it was necessary to pick it whilst instruments of music were played, this being the only way of distracting the attention of the asps who guarded it. When the Turks took the Holy Land they transplanted large quantities of the plant to Grand Cairo, where janissaries guarded it during the time the balsam was flowing. Our English balm has always been extolled by herbalists as " sovereign for the brain." One of them says : " It is an hearbe greatly to be esteemed of students, for by a special property it driveth away heaviness of mind, sharpeneth the understanding, and encreaseth memory."

BALM is a hardy herbaceous perennial, and is a terribly rapid spreader. It likes a clayey soil, but it should never be given manure. Propagate by root division (the smallest pieces will grow) any time during the spring and autumn or by slips taken in May. The latter must be inserted in a shady border in May or June, and removed to permanent quarters in September.

How to make the Water which is usually called BALME-WATER.—To every gallon of Claret wine put one pound of green balme. Keep that which cometh first, and is clearest, by itselfe, and the second and whiter sort, which is weakest and comest last, by itselfe : distill in a pewter Limbeck luted with paste to a brasse pot. Draw this in May or June, when the herb is in his prime.—Sir Hugh Platt, *Delights for Ladies*, 1659.

BALM WINE.—Take twenty pounds of lump sugar and four gallons and a half of water, boil it gently for one hour, and put it into a tub to cool ; take two pounds of the tops of green balm, and bruise them, put them into a barrel with a little new yeast, and when the liquor is nearly cold pour it on the balm ; stir it well together ; and let it stand twenty-four hours, stirring it often ; then bung it tight, and the longer you keep it the better it will be.—From *The Receipt Book of Richard Briggs*, many years Cook at the Globe Tavern, Fleet Street, the White Hart Tavern, Holborn, and at the Temple Coffee House, 1788.

BALM WINE.—Boil ten pounds of moist sugar in four gallons of water for over an hour, and skim it well. Pour into an earthenware vessel to cool. Bruise a pound and a quarter of balm tops and put them into a small cask with yeast spread on toast, and when the above liquor is cool, pour it on the balm. Stir them well together, and let the mixture stand for twenty-four hours, stirring it frequently ; then close it up, lightly at first and more securely after fermentation has quite ceased. When it has stood for six or eight weeks bottle it off, putting a lump of sugar into each bottle. Cork the bottle well and keep it at least a year before putting it into use.—Dr. Fernie, *Herbal Simples*, 1897.

BALM TEA.—Pour one pint of boiling water on two ounces of the young tops and leaves.

BASIL

" This is the herb which all authors are together by the ears about and rail at one another (like lawyers)."—NICHOLAS CULPEPPER, *The English Physitian.*

There are few plants in the herb garden with more contradictory associations than basil. Amongst all European nations it is supposed to be endowed with both beneficent and sinister qualities, whilst in the East there is no herb with more sacred associations. Tulasi (basil) is a holy herb to the Hindoos, and is grown near every temple and dwelling that it may protect those who cultivate it from misfortune, and guide them to Heaven. It is sacred to Vishnu, and " propitious," " perfumed," " devil-destroying," are only a few of the epithets applied to it. De Gubernatis says of it : " Under the mystery of this herb is shrouded without doubt the god-creator himself. The herb tulasi is consecrated to Vishnu ; but it is no less adored by the votaries of Siva. Krishna, the popular incarnation of the god Vishnu, has also adopted this herb for his worship. When an Indian dies they place on his breast a leaf of tulasi ; when he is dead they wash the head of the corpse with water in which flax-seeds and tulasi leaves have been dropped." Good fortune awaits those who build their house on a spot where tulasi has grown freely, and there is no forgiveness in this world or the next for any one who wilfully uproots it. It must never be picked at all except for some worthy purpose, and this prayer is said : " Mother Tulasi, be thou propitious if I gather you with care, be merciful unto me, O Tulasi, Mother of the world." In Malabar sweet basil is very largely cultivated, and tulasi plays an important part when the Maharajah of Travancore performs the Sacred Ceremony of tulabharam. In the Deccan basil is regarded with equal veneration, and is planted on the altar before each Brahmin house.

It is curious that among Western nations one of the oldest associations with basil is hatred and abuse. The ancient Greeks believed basil must be sown with words of abuse or else it would not flourish, and to this day the French have the proverb, " *semer le basilic* "— slandering. Both amongst Western and Eastern nations basil is associated with death, and in Crete the plant is associated with the Evil One. Yet in Western Europe it is regarded as of sovereign power against witches ! The Italians say basil engenders sympathy between those who wear it ; and to Moldavians it is an enchanted flower of such potency, that a man who accepts a sprig from a woman will love her for ever. Bacon records the curious superstition that if basil is exposed too much to the sun it changes into wild thyme, and nearly every old herbalist assures us that rue and basil will never grow near each other. Basil was one of the old strewing herbs. Its clove-like flavour is much prized by good French cooks, but our English cooks do not appreciate it, though they occasionally will use it to flavour soup. Evelyn tells us that it must be used very sparingly, and for salads, only the tender tops. In those days strong flavours were popular.

BASIL (both the bush and the larger sweet basil) should be sown in gentle heat in March, hardened off in May, and planted out at the end of May on to warm borders or beds of light, rich earth. Bush basil is hardier than sweet basil and the former sometimes survives our English winters.

BETONY

" Betony is good for a man's soul or his body."

Saxon Herbal.

" Wood betony is in its prime in May,
   In June and July does its bloom display,
   A fine bright red does this grand plant adorn,
   To gather it for drink I think no scorn ;
   I'll make a conserve of its fragrant flowers,
   Cephalick virtues in this herb remain,
   To chase each dire disorder from the brain.
   Delirious persons here a cure may find
   To stem the phrensy and to calm the mind.
   All authors own wood-betony is good,
   'Tis King o'er all the herbs that deck the wood ;
   A King's physician erst such notice took
   Of this, he on its virtues wrote a book."

JAMES CHAMBERS, *The Poor Phytologist.*

Betony has indeed fallen from its old high estate, for how few now know or care about its virtues ? Yet with the exception of vervain, there was no herb more highly prized in olden times. The Saxon herbal, to which reference is made in the above, is supposed to be an abridged copy of a treatise written by Antonius Musa,

physician to the Emperor Augustus, on the virtues of
this plant, which apparently cured every ill which
could befall one's head, including nightmare. It was
to be gathered " without use of iron, and when thou
have gathered it, shake the mould till naught of it
cleave thereon, and then dry it in the shade very
thoroughly, and with its roots altogether reduce it to
dust, then use it and taste of it when thou needest."
Every old herbalist was loud in its praises, and to-day
any one can prove for themselves the fact that betony
certainly cures a headache with surprising rapidity.
In Italy they say, " may you have as many virtues as
betony," and " sell your coat and buy betony," is a
well-known proverb amongst the peasants. It is still
one of the ingredients in herbal snuffs, but even if you
do not make use of its virtues, you should have betony
in your herb garden, for then no evil spirits nor witches
will come near you ! Gerard tells us that he found the
white-flowered betony " in a wood by a village called
Hampsteed, near unto a worshipfull gentleman's
house, one of the Clarks of the Queen's Counsell,
called Master Wade, from whence I brought plants
for my garden, where they flowered as in their natural
place of growing."

Though betony grows naturally in shady places, it
does equally well in full sunshine, and it loves a bank.

CONSERVE OF BETONY, AFTER THE ITALIAN WAY.—
Betony new and tender one pound, the best sugar
three pound, beat them very small in a stone mortar,
let the sugar be boyled with two quarts of betony
water to the consistency of a syrup, then mix them
together by little and little over a small Fire, and so

make it into a Conserve, and keep it in Glasses.—*The Queen's Closet Opened,* by W. M., Cook to Queen Henrietta Maria, 1655.

BETONY TEA.—Put two ounces of the herb (flowers and leaves) into two quarts of water, and simmer to three half-pints.

GREEN SALVE OR BETONIAN OINTMENT.[1]—Take a handful of each of the following herbs, Balm, Sage, Southern-wood, Rosemary, Wood Betony, Camomile, Lavender, Feverfew, Red rosebuds and Wormwood. Strip all from the stalks and cut fine, then boil in 1¼ lbs. of fresh Lard in the Oven for two or three hours, and squeeze thro' a cloth. For a bruise rub gently, and for an inward bruise take the size of a nut in hot beer at bed-time.

BORAGE

" The vertue of the conserve of borage is especially good against melancholie ; it maketh one merie."—*The Treasurie of Hidden Secrets and Commodious Conceits,* 1586.

Pliny calls borage euphrosynum because it made men joyful, and it was one of the four " cordial flowers "

---

[1] This recipe was kindly given me by Miss C. S. Burne, President of The Folk Lore Society, who appended this note to it :—
Mrs. Mary Goodlad (*née* Haworth, of Bury, Lancashire) born 1788, died 1870, made and prescribed this ointment regularly. I have myself been treated with it in childhood. The recipe is copied from her own handwriting in a MS. book of recipes belonging to her daughter, my mother.

for cheering the heart, the other three being rose, violet and anchusa. Parkinson in his *Paradisus* tells us that its lovely blue flowers were favourites in " women's needlework," and it is curious that it should have disappeared from modern embroidery, for with its effective black eye, it is always so attractive. According to Thomas Hyll the seeds of borage should be gathered when half ripe and then laid in the sun to ripen, but any modern herbalist will tell you that borage needs no care; for it is only too ready to seed itself everywhere. Borage flowers never seem lovelier than when growing in profusion with ragged robin and cow-parsley on the steep banks of Devonshire lanes. Formerly, borage leaves were an esteemed pot-herb, and the young tops were used to flavour soup, a custom which well might be revived, " for they are of an excellent cordial savour." Borage flowers are particularly attractive in potpourri on account of their lovely blue colour. They should be picked when full grown and just before they expand, other-wise they will soon lose their colour. They should be spread out at once to dry, preferably on wire sieves.

BORAGE may be sown in any light soil in April, and again in July, and if left alone it will seed itself. The plants should be well thinned (eighteen inches apart), and it is better not to transplant them.

TO CANDY BORAGE, OR ROSEMARY FLOWERS.—Boil Sugar and Rose-water a little upon a chafing-dish with coales : then put the flowers (being thorowly dried, either by the Sun or by the Fire) into the Sugar, and boile them a little : then strew the powder of double refined Sugar upon them, and turne them, and let them boile a little longer, taking the dish from the Fire : then strew more powdered Sugar on the contrary side of the flowers. These will dry of themselves in two or three houres in a hot sunny day, though they lie not in the Sunne.—*The Queen's Closet Opened*, by W. M., Cook to Queen Henrietta Maria, 1655.

CONSERVE OF BORAGE FLOWERS AFTER THE ITALIAN MANNER.—Take of fresh Borage flowers four ounces, fine Sugar twelve ounces, beat them well together in a stone Mortar, and keep them in a vessel well glazed.—*Ibid*.

BRAMBLE

" Then said all the trees unto the bramble, Come thou and reign over us ! And the bramble said unto the trees, if in truth ye anoint me King over you, then come and put your trust in my shadow ; and if not let fire come out of the bramble, and devour the Cedars of Lebanon."—Judges ix. 14.

According to tradition, the bramble was the burning bush in which Jehovah appeared to Moses. A good many curious superstitions cling to the bramble, and one still hears of cases of the survival of the old custom of passing sickly children nine times over and under a blackberry stem, rooted at both ends, and this must always be done with the sun, i.e. from east to west. Throughout the British Isles there is a widespread belief amongst the old peasantry that on

Michaelmas day the Devil curses all the blackberry bushes, and that is why the fruit is so unwholesome in the late autumn. In Cornwall bramble leaves moistened with spring water are still used for burns, and when the leaves are applied this charm is said :

" There came three Angels out of the East,
One brought fire and two brought frost ;
Out fire and in frost ;
In the name of the Father, Son, and Holy Ghost."

The bramble has always been the friend of poor folk. The wool it collects from sheep used to be collected by the old countrywomen and made into " mops " which they sold for a few pence. The cottager used the long strong stems to bind the thatch to his roof, and when he died it was the bramble which held in place the green turves over his grave.

BLACKBERRY WINE.—Bruise the berries, and to every gallon of fruit add a quart of boiling water. Let the mixture stand for twenty-four hours, stirring it occasionally ; then strain off the liquid, adding to every gallon a couple of pounds of refined sugar, and keep it in a cask tightly corked until the following October, when it will be ripe and rich.—Dr. Fernie, *Herbal Simples*, 1897.

BROOM

" If you sweep the house with blossomed broom in May
You are sure to sweep the head of the house away."
Old Sussex Proverb.

Broom has always been the emblem of humility. On his wedding day, St. Louis of France established

the order of knighthood called l'Ordre du Genest.
The knights of this order wore a chain of golden
broom flowers and white enamelled fleur-de-lis placed
alternately, and from this chain hung a cross on which
was inscribed, " Deus exaltat humiles." Only one
hundred knights belonged to it at a time ; they formed
the King's bodyguard, and in later days it was an order
Richard II was proud to wear.

Broom—the " gen " of the Celts—has from time
immemorial been the badge of Brittany, but it is more
popularly associated with the Plantagenets of Anjou.
It is said that Fulk, the founder of the house, went on
a pilgrimage to Jerusalem to atone for having murdered
his brother, and after having been scourged with
broom he took the plant for his crest and surname.
It was first used officially on the Great Seal of Richard I.
According to the old herbalists broom cured many disorders, and Gerard tells us : " That worthy Prince of
famous memory, Henry VIII of England, was wont to
drink the distilled water of Broom-flowers against sur-
feits and diseases thereof arising." Pickled broom-
buds were an ordinary ingredient in salads in Tudor
and Stewart days.

To Pickle Broom-buds and Pods.—Make a strong
pickle of White Wine, Vinegar and Salt able to bear an
Egg. Stir very well till the Salt be quite dissolved,
clearing off the Dregs and Scum. The next day pour
it from the Bottom, and having rubbed the Buds dry,
pot them up in a Pickle Glass, which should be frequently shaken till they sink under it, and keep it well
stopt and covered. Thus may you pickle any other
Buds.—John Evelyn, *Acetaria*, 1699.

BUGLOSS

The old herbalists apply the name bugloss with the utmost impartiality to borage and anchusa. It is interesting to remember that probably the most ancient of all the paints for the face was made from the root of anchusa, and in Pliny's day it was commonly used for dyeing. In the fifteenth century anchusa leaves were used as pot-herbs.

SYRUP OF THE JUYCE OF ANCHUSA.—In sixe pound of the juyce of buglosse, boyle a pound of the flowers then strain them and clarifie them ; boyle with the decoction four pound of sugar, and the Syrup commeth to twopence the ounce.—*The Charitable Physitian*, by Philbert Guibert, Physitian, Regent in Paris, 1639.

BURNET

" L'Insalata non é buon ne bella ove non é la pimpinella."
Italian Proverb.

In Hungary burnet is called " Chabairje " (Chaba's Salve) because the virtues of this plant were first discovered by King Chaba after the terrible battle he fought with his brother. He is said to have cured the wounds of 15,000 of his soldiers with the juice of burnet. In Iroe Grego's book, which professes to be a translation of a book written by King Solomon, magicians are advised to anoint their swords with the blood of a mole and the juice of burnet leaves. Burnet has a pleasant cucumber-like flavour, and recently a gardening paper advocated that it should be revived as a salad herb. It does not take kindly to cultivation, for it loves a very poor soil and chalky uplands. But in districts where it grows plentifully there is no reason why it should not be again used both in salads and as a pot-herb. Only the young tops and leaves should be picked.

BURNET is a perennial, putting out new pennate leaves every year. Sow the seeds in shallow drills a foot apart. It is best to sow them as soon as ripe in the autumn, or propagate by division of the roots in the spring. Choose a dry, sunny position for the bed, and if the soil is deficient in lime, fork in a little before sowing. The leaves should be cut when four inches long, as a fresh crop will follow. Burnet will flourish for years in the same spot.

CAMOMILE

" Have a mind thou maythen,
    What thou mentionedst
    What thou accomplishedst
    At Alderford.
    That never for flying ill
    Fatally fell man
    Since we to him maythen
    For medicine mixed up.
              Saxon MS. Herbal (Harleian), 1585.

" To comfort the braine smel to camomill, eate sage . . . wash measurably, sleep reasonably, delight to heare melody and singing."
Ram's Little Dodoen, 1606.

" All parts of this excellent plant are full of virtue."—
Sir John Hill, 1772.

It is a pity we have so entirely given up the beautiful old Saxon name " Maythen," or " maegthe," for " camomile " (which is derived from a Greek word meaning " earth-apples "). The Spaniards call it manzilla (little apple), and this is also the name of one of their light wines which is flavoured with camomile. One now rarely sees the old-fashioned camomile of which Falstaff said, " the more it is trodden on the faster it grows," but formerly the seats in the herbers and those hollowed out of the bank round the herb garden were frequently covered with camomile, and paths were made of it instead of turf in order to enjoy the pleasant refreshing scent when one walked on it. Evelyn tells us that " in October it will now be good to Beat Roll and Mow carpet walks and camomile, for now the ground is supple and it will even all inequalities." Modern scientific gardeners weed out camomile ruthlessly because it takes so much goodness out of the ground ; but old-fashioned gardeners say it is the best of all " plant doctors," and that it will revive any sickly plant near which it is planted. One of the best known French tissanes is made of dried camomile flowers, and perhaps when our herbal knowledge equals that on the other side of the Channel, we shall rate camomile at its proper value.

To Make Oyle of Camomile.—Take oyle a pint and a halfe, and three ounces of camomile flowers dryed one day after they be gathered. Then put the oyle and the flowers in a glasse and stop the mouth close and set it into the Sun by the space of forty days. —*The Good Housewife's Handbook*, 1588.

CAMOMILE TEA.—Pour half a pint of boiling water on five or six of the dried flowers. When it has stood for ten minutes strain and sweeten with sugar or honey.

CARAWAY

" Come, cousin Silence ! we will eat a pippin of last year's graffing with a dish of carraways and then to bed ! "—*Henry IV*.

Caraway is not a native of our islands, but it is frequently found growing in waste places in the south of England. Formerly bread, cheese and soup were frequently flavoured with the seeds ; and the young roots, which are excellent, were eaten like parsnips. Canon Ellacombe says that little saucerfuls of caraway seeds were still served in his day with roast apples at some of the London livery dinners.

CARAWAY is a hardy biennial, and is best sown in the early autumn, though it may also be sown in March or April.

CELERY

Celery is a famous old remedy for rheumatism, etc., but treated as it so often is now—i.e. soaked in water in order to make it " curl "—is fatal to the remedial properties of the plant, for prolonged soaking in cold water extracts the valuable salts. It should be quickly washed.

CELERY SEED TEA.—One ounce of celery seed boiled in one pint of water until reduced to half a pint. Strain and bottle. Take one teaspoonful every day. A great many people who have used this old-fashioned cure for rheumatism, neuritis, etc., tell me that the effect of this simple remedy is miraculous.

CHERVIL

" Sweet Chervil or Sweet Cis is so like in taste unto Anis seede that it much delighteth the taste among other herbs in a sallet."
JOHN PARKINSON, *Paradisus*, 1629.

The Romans taught us to use this herb, so it is a very old inhabitant of the herb garden ; and a fifteenth-century MS. of Cookery recipes lists it as one of the necessary plants to grow for use in the kitchen. For some unknown reason it has almost disappeared from English gardens, though it is common enough in France. Sweet Chervil or Sweet Cicely is a native of this country. Evelyn in his *Acetaria* says chervil should " never be wanting in sallets as long as they may be had, being exceedingly wholesome and cheering the spirits." He adds that " the roots boiled and eaten cold are much commended for aged persons." Chervil was also largely used for flavouring sauces and tarts, and also for garnishing. The bulbous-rooted chervil is rarely seen on English tables, but it is extensively used on the Continent. The roots should be carefully washed but never scraped, and they take a long time cooking. Parboiled roots of chervil fried in butter are excellent ; formerly they were always eaten during a time of plague.

Parkinson says, " Common chervil is much used of the French and Dutch people to bee boiled or stewed in a pipkin either by itself or with other herbs, whereof they make a Loblolly and so eate it. Sweete chervil gathered while it is young and put among other herbs for a sallet addeth a marvellous good relish to all the rest."

CHERVIL likes a light, well-drained soil, and plenty of chalk. Sow the seeds from February to August for succession in drills eight inches apart, and thin the seedlings to six inches apart. The leaves are ready to be used when a few inches high.

To MAKE CHERVIL POTTAGE THE DUTCH WAY (usually eat in the Months of March and April).—Take a Knuckle of Veal all chopped in little Pieces, except the Marrow-bone ; season the Flesh with a little Salt, Nutmeg, pounded Biscuit, and Yolks of Eggs, and make little Force-meat Balls, the Bigness of a Pigeon's Egg ; which, being boiled in a Broth-pot, for the Space of a full Hour ; take three or four Handfuls of Chervil picked clean, two or three Leeks, and a good Handful of Beet-leaves ; mince them together, and add two or three Spoonfuls of Flour well mixt with two or three Spoonfuls of Broth, that it may not be lumpy, and do it over the Stove, as you would do Milk-pottage. This Pottage must appear green. On Fish-days cut some Eels in Pieces, with which make the Broth, and you may put in a Handful of Sorrel among the other Herbs.—From *The Receipt Book of Vincent La Chapelle*, Chief Cook to the Prince of Orange, 1744.

ANOTHER SORT OF CHERVIL BROTH.—Instead of boiling your Chervil, pound it, and take about a glass of its Juice, mix it with your Broth, whilst it is hot, but not boiling, lest the Juice lose its Taste and Quality. This Broth is very cooling, though it does not look pleasing to the Eye, by reason of its Greenness; but it has more Vertue in the Spring, to sweeten and purify the Blood, than in any other Season.—*Ibid.*

CHICKWEED

This herb grows wild in all the habitable parts of the world. Formerly it was an esteemed pot-herb, and as it is particularly rich in salts of potash, we might with advantage use it again as an ingredient in vege-table soups. Linnæus had a " dial " made of herbs, and flowers which opened at the successive hours. Ingram in his *Flora Symbolica* gives a list of plants to make this sort of dial, and the list begins with Goat's Beard (opening at three a.m.) and ends with Chick-weed which only opens at 9.15 a.m.

CHICKWEED TEA.—One quart of boiling water poured on to two large handfuls of the plant.

CLARY

A few cooks now put young Clary tops in soups, but it is astonishing how much the young leaves and tops were used formerly as a pot-herb. Evelyn tells us that when tender it is a good addition to salads, the flowers being strewn on salads, the leaves (chopped) used in Omelets ; and the tender leaves, " made up with cream," were fried in butter and then eaten with sugar flavoured with Orange or Lemon juice. It was an ingredient in perfumes, in ale and beer and nearly all the home-made wines and metheglins, and Clary wine was famed for its narcotic properties. Hogg in his *Vegetable Kingdom and its Products* says it was used in Austria in fruit jellies, to which it gave a flavour of pineapple.

Clary does well on any soil provided it is not too moist. It is a biennial. Propagate by sowing the seed in spring, and when the seedlings are large enough to handle transplant.

CLARY WINE.—Ten gallons of water, thirteen pounds of sugar to the gallon, and the whites of sixteen eggs well beat. Boil it slowly one hour and skim it well. Then put it into a tub till it is almost cold. Take a pint of Clary flowers with the small leaves and stalks, put them into a barrel with a pint of ale yeast, then put in your liquor and stir it twice a day till it has done working. Make it up close and keep it four months, and then bottle it off.—John Murrell, *A*

Delightful Daily Exercise for Ladies and Gentlemen,
1621.

To MAKE CLARY WINE.—Take twelve pounds of
Malaga Raisins, after they have been pick'd small and
chop'd, put them into a Vessel, a quart of Water to
each pound. Let them stand to steep for ten or twelve
Days, being kept close covered all the while, stirring
them twice every Day; afterwards strain it off, and
put it up in a Cask, adding a quarter of a Peck of the
Tops of Clary, when it is in Blossom; then stop it up
close for six weeks, and afterwards you may bottle it
off, and it will be fit to drink in two or three Months.
It will have a great Settlement, therefore it should be
tap'd pretty high, or drawn off by Plugs.—From *The
Receipt Book of Charles Carter*, Cook to the Duke of
Argyll, 1732.

CLARY FRITTERS.—Make a good stiff batter with half
a pint of new milk, four eggs, and flour; grate in a
little lemon-peel and some nutmeg, put in two ounces
of powder sugar, and a small glass of brandy; then
take a dozen Clary leaves, cut away the stalks, put
them into batter, taking care that they have plenty of
it on both sides; have a pan of boiling hog's-lard,
put them in one by one, and fry them quick on both
sides of a light brown; then take them out, lay them
on a sieve to drain a moment, put them in a dish,
strew powder sugar over them, and glaze them with a
hot iron.—Note. You may dress Comfrey or Mulberry leaves the same way.—From *The Receipt Book
of Richard Briggs*, many years Cook at the Globe

Tavern, Fleet Street, the White Hart Tavern, Holborn, and at the Temple Coffee House, 1788.

COLTSFOOT

" Black heaths are patched with coltsfoot-gold bizarre."

W. DOWSING.

Herbalists are never weary of telling us that when Nature gives any herb in abundance it is a sure sign that it is possessed of great virtue.   Nettles, Yarrow, Plantain, Dandelion, Coltsfoot, and a hundred other so-called " weeds " all testify to the truth of this. Even in the heart of London it would be difficult to find any waste land without Coltsfoot growing on it. From the days of Hippocrates a decoction of Coltsfoot has been held a sovereign remedy for all chest troubles, and in olden days the apothecaries in Paris used to paint a coltsfoot flower on their door-posts, a silent testimony to their opinion of the value of the plant. Sir John Hill, after dilating on the value of coltsfoot tea for colds and coughs says, " the patient should also have some of the leaves dried and cut small and smoke them as tobacco. This is an old practice, and experience shows it right and excellent " ; then he adds, " Here let us stop a moment and adore the goodness of Divine Providence which makes the best things the most common. The Segroms which can do only mischief are found in but a few places : this so full of excellence grows at our doors, and we tread it everywhere under our feet."

Formerly the Bavarian peasants made garlands of

Coltsfoot flowers on Easter Day and threw it into the fire, but the origin of this is unknown. In the Highlands there are still women who stuff their pillows with the silky Coltsfoot down, and it makes the softest pillows imaginable. In other parts of Scotland there is a curious belief that where Coltsfoot grows abundantly it indicates the presence of coal, and they also say that when Coltsfoot down flies away when there is no wind it is a sure sign of coming rain.

SYRUP OF COLTSFOOT.—Make three infusions, one after another, of colts-foot, each time halfe a pound in a quart of water ; the last infusion being strained, clarifie it and put it into a pound and a halfe of good Sugar, and boil it to the height of a Syrup : the which Syrup amounteth to penny half-penny the ounce.— *The Charitable Physitian*, by Philbert Guibert, Physitian Regent in Paris, 1639.

COLTSFOOT TEA.—Pour a quart of boiling water on two handfuls of the leaves.

CORIANDER

" And the house of Israel called the name thereof Manna : and it was like Coriander seed, white ; and the taste of it was like wafers made with honey."—Exodus xvi. 31.
" Coriander taken out of season doth trouble a mann's witt with great jeopardy of madness."—WILLIAM TURNER, *A Newe Herball*, 1551.

Coriander, Mallows, Chervil and Dill love to grow near each other, is told us by nearly all the old herbalists, and as they flower about the same time, they look very well together. Coriander was one of the bitter herbs ordained to be eaten at the Passover ; and in Egypt, where it was largely cultivated, the seeds were bruised to mix with bread. All Eastern nations esteem it highly, but apart from drugs, we only use it now in liqueurs and for the little sugar balls beloved by children ; but formerly it was commonly grown in herb gardens, and is one of the plants described in the oldest original English treatise on gardening.—*The Feate of Gardening*, by Mayster Jon Gardener, 1440. Coriander seed has the delightful quality of becoming more fragrant the longer it is kept. The foliage of the plant has an almost offensively strong odour.

CORIANDER is a hardy annual. Sow the seeds in April. They are slow in germinating.

CORIANDER WATER.—Take a handful of Coriander seeds, break them and put them into about a quart of water, and so let it stand, put in a quarter of a pound of sugar, and when your sugar is melted and the water well taken the taste of the seeds, then strain it out through a cloath and drink it at your pleasure. You may do the same with aniseeds.—*A Perfect School of Instruction for the Officers of the Month*, by Giles Rose, one of the Master Cooks to Charles II, 1682.

COSTMARY

" Fresh costmarie and healthfull camomile."—*Muiopot*.

The chief use of Costmary or Alecost was a
stewing herb. It was also an ingredient in sweet
washing waters, and it was dried like lavender and
put, so Parkinson tells us " to lye upon the toppes of
beds, presses, etc., for the sweet sent and savour it
casteth."

COWSLIP

" As blake (yellow) as a paigle (cowslip)."—*East Anglian Proverb*.

" Where the bee sucks, there suck I ;
In the cowslips bell I lie :
There I crouch when owls do cry."
The Tempest, Act V, Scene 1.

" Cowslips wan that hang the pensive head."—*Lycidas*, Canto 139

What endless uses our ancestors made of cowslips !
They used the young leaves and flowers in salads and
for pot-herbs, and made cowslip creams, puddings,
tarts and wines. They candied and pickled the flowers,
made cowslip tea and syrup, and one of the most
famous complexion washes was made of cowslips and
cucumbers.[1]

COWSLIP CREAM.—Take the Cowslips when they
are green and in Blossom, and bruise them in mortar,

[1] See under Cucumber.

and to a good handful or two so done put a quart of Cream and boil it up gently with them. Put in a blade of Mace, season with fine sugar and Orange-Flower water. Strain it and draw it up with the Yolks of two or three Eggs, and clip off the tops of a handful of the Flowers and draw up with it and dish as you please.— From *The Receipt Book of Joseph Cooper*, Cook to Charles I, 1654.

ANOTHER WAY.—Take two ounces of Syrup of Cowslips and boil up in your Cream and season it as before. Thicken, it with the Yolks of three or four Eggs, and put in two ounces of candy'd Cowslips when you draw it up. Dish it in Basons and Glasses, and strew over some candy'd cowslips.—*Ibid.*

TO KEEP COWSLIPS FOR SALATES.—Take a quart of White Wine Vinegar, and halfe a quarter of a pound of fine beaten Sugar, and mix them together, then take your Cowslips, pull them out of the podds, and cut off the green Knobs at the lower end, put them into the pot or glasse wherein you mind to keep them, and well shaking the Vinegar and Sugar together in the glasse wherein they were before, powre it upon the Cowslips, and so stirring them morning and evening to make them settle for three weeks, keep them for your use.—*A Book of Fruits and Flowers*, 1653.

TO CONSERVE COWSLIPS.—Gather your flowers in the midst of the day when all the dew is off, then cut off all the white, leaving none but the yellow blossome so picked and cut, before they wither, weigh out ten

Distilling in a Herb Garden

ounces, taking to every ten ounces of them, or greater proportion, if you please, eight ounces of the best refined Sugar, in fine powder, put the Sugar into a pan, and candy it, with as little water as you can, then taking it off the fire, put in your Flowers by little and little, never ceasing to stir them till they be dry, and enough ; then put them into glasses, or gallypots, and keep them dry for your use. These are rather Candied then Conserved Cowslips.—*Ibid.*

SYRUPE OF COWSLIPS.—Instead of running water you must take distilled water of Cowslips, put thereto your Cowslip flowers clean picked, and the green knobs in the bottome cut off, and therewith boyle up a Syrupe. It is good against the Frensie, comforting and staying the head in all hot Agues, etc. It is good against the Palsie, and procures a Sick Patient to sleep ; it must be taken in Almond-milk, or some other warm thing.—*Ibid.*

PICKLED COWSLIPS.—Pickt very clean ; to each Pound of Flowers allow about one pound of Loaf Sugar and one pint of White Wine Vinegar, which boil to a Syrup, and cover it scalding hot.—John Evelyn, *Acetaria*, 1699.

TO CANDY COWSLIPS OR ANY FLOWERS OR GREENS IN BUNCHES.—Steep your gum arabic in Water, wet the flowers with it and shake them in a cloth that they may be dry ; then dip them in fine sifted Sugar, and hang them on a String tied across a chimney that has a Fire in it ; they must hang two or three days till the

Flowers are quite dry.—From *The Receipt Book of Mrs. Mary Eales*, Confectioner to Queen Anne, 1719.

To make a Cowslip Tart.—Take the Blossoms of a Gallon of Cowslips, mince them exceeding small, and beat them in a Mortar ; put to them a Handful or two of grated Naples Bisket, and about a Pint and a half of Cream, boil them a little over the Fire, then take them off, and beat them in eight Eggs with a little Cream ; if it does not thicken, put it over again till it does ; take heed that it do not curdle. Season it with Sugar, Rose-water, and a little Salt ; bake it in a Dish or little open Tartest. It is best to let your Cream be cold before you stir in the Eggs.—From *The Receipt Book of Patrick Lamb*, Head Cook successively to Charles II, James II, William and Mary, and Anne, 1716.

Cowslip Wine.—Nine pints of water, two pounds of Sugar. Boil and skim well. Pour it hot on one quart of picked cowslips. Next day strain and add two spoonfuls of yeast. Let it stand in an earthen pan a fortnight to work, covered close and stirred three times a day for the first three days. Then drain into bottles and stop it tight. It will keep for a year.— E. G. Hayden, *Travels round our Village*.

Cowslip Pudding.—Half a peck of cowslips, pick off the flowers and chop fine with ¼ lb. Naples Bisket grated, 1½ pints new milk or cream. Boil them all together, then take them off the fire. Beat up the yolks of eight and the whites of four eggs in a little cream and a spoonful of rose-water. Sweeten to taste. Stir over a slow fire till it is thick, and then set it away to cool. Lay a puff paste round the edge of the dish, pour in the pudding, and bake it half an hour. When ready sprinkle fine powdered sugar and serve hot.—*Ibid.*

COWSLIP SYRUP.—Three pounds of the fresh blossoms infused in five pints of boiling water, and then simmered with sugar to a syrup.—Dr. Fernie, *Herbal Simples*, 1897.

CUCUMBER

Cucumber was the basis of one of the most famous complexion lotions of olden days and was usually made with quince blossoms. Rose petals or cowslips were sometimes used instead, but quince blossoms were preferred as they have a very whitening effect on the skin.

CUCUMBER LOTION.—Half a peck of quince blossoms put in a pan, covered with cold water and simmered gently for an hour. Cut two large cucumbers into very thin slices and then chop finely. Put into the saucepan with the quince blossom water and boil for five minutes. Strain through muslin, and when quite cold pour into bottles and tie down. To use, smear the lotion on the face and leave on for at least ten minutes before washing.

CUMIN

" The fitches are beaten out with a staff and the cummin with a
rod."—Isaiah xxviii. 27.

In Biblical times cumin seeds, which were " beaten
out with a rod," were used both as spice and medicine.
In mediæval times it was accounted the best of the
condiments, but it is seldom grown in this country
nowadays. Our supplies come chiefly from the Medi-
terranean, and in France the seed is still used for
flavouring soups. Cumin is a native of Egypt, but in
warm summers it will ripen its seed in this country.

Sow in moderate heat, harden off in a cold frame
and transplant to a sunny position. When transplanting avoid root disturbance as far as possible.

DAISY

" Shut not so soon ; the dull-eyed night
　　Has not as yet begunne
To make a seisure on the light,
　　Or to seale up the Sun."—HERRICK.

In mediæval flower symbolism the daisy always
stands for the innocence of the Holy Child. The
Gaelic poet, Ossian, tells us how daisies were first
sown. When Malvina was weeping beside Fingal's
tomb for her infant son, the maids of Morven com-
forted her by telling her they had seen the baby boy
showering many beautiful flowers from heaven on to
the earth, and amongst them the daisy. Sir John Hill

says, " the daisy has great but neglected virtues worthy of a serious attention. Their taste is that of Coltsfoot, but more mucilaginous and without its bitterness. The infusion should be made like coltsfoot, and once boiled. Drink it with an equal quantity of milk. Asses milk has ten times the effect if this be taken with it." Daisy roots are still eaten by the Italian and Spanish peasants, and formerly the young leaves were an ordinary ingredient in our salads. Many herbalists refer to the curious old belief that if daisy roots are boiled in milk and given to puppies it will stunt their growth ; and there is the old fairy story of the wicked fairy Milkah who fed her royal foster-child on this food to make him a pigmy. One herbalist says that to put daisy roots under your pillow is to ensure pleasant dreams of those you love most.

DANDELION

" The French country people eat the roots, and 'twas with this homely sallet the good wife Hecate entertained Theseus."
JOHN EVELYN, *Acetaria*, 1699.

Dandelion was formerly used not only as a pot-herb in broths, but also much more than they are now in salads. Folkard gives a curious account of a Donegal simpler who treated her patient with " heart fever " thus. " She measures the sufferer three times round the waist with a ribbon, to the outer edge of which is fastened a green thread. If the patient be mistaken in supposing herself affected with heart fever, this green thread will remain in its place, but should he really have the disorder, it is found that the green thread has left the edge of the ribbon and lies curled up in the centre. At the third measuring the simpler prays for a blessing. She next hands the patient nine leaves of heart-fever grass, or dandelion, gathered by herself, directing him to cut three leaves on three successive mornings."

DANDELION TEA.—One pint of boiling water on two handfuls of the pips and left till lukewarm.

DANDELION WINE.—Four pints of dandelion bloom (in calyx), 4 lbs. Demarara sugar, 2 (or 3) lemons, gallon of water.

Boil bloom in water for 20 minutes. Strain boiling liquor on to the sugar. Halve lemons, peel and pip them : put remainder into liquor. Put $\frac{1}{2}$ oz., or less, of yeast on a small piece of toast and lay it on the liquor when it has partly cooled, is warm but not hot. When it has fermented, probably at the end of two days, skim off yeast and toast and bottle, adding the lemon peel.

If you are putting the wine into sufficiently large vessels it is unnecessary to peel the lemons : after being pipped they can go in in halves or quarters with the peel on.

DANDELION WINE.—To make nine gallons of wine. Boil twenty-seven quarts of pips in nine gallons of water for an hour. Strain and boil again with $13\frac{1}{2}$ lbs. best Demerara sugar, 1 oz. of hops, $\frac{1}{2}$ lb. brown ginger, and sufficient orange and lemon peel to taste. Slice eighteen Seville oranges and twelve lemons, and put to them 13½ lbs. sugar as above. Pour over them, and boiling beyond when blood warm, add a little brewer's yeast. Strain again before putting into a barrel. The wine should be allowed to work three or four days before being bunged tight. Bottle in six months. Like a sharp liqueur.—E. G. Hayden, *Travels round our Village*.

DILL

" I am always pleased with that particular time of the year which is proper for the pickling of dill and cucumbers."

ADDISON in *The Spectator*.

For hundreds of years Dill was always grown in herb gardens and used as a pot-herb. Both in appearance and taste dill is very like fennel, but the taste is more pungent. The name dill is supposed to be derived from the Saxon *dillan*—to lull, because a decoction was made from the seeds to soothe babies to sleep. It is one of the herbs used by magicians in their spells, and also in charms against witchcraft. Formerly the young leaves were used in salads and for flavouring. Dill grows wild in the cornfields of Spain but not in those of northern Europe.

DILL seed can be sown any time in March or April or in the autumn. Sow in drills six inches apart.

To PICKLE CUCUMBERS IN DILL.—Gather the tops of the ripest Dill, and cover the bottome of the vessel, and lay a layer of Cucumbers, and another of Dill, till you have filled the vessel within a handful of the top, then take as much water as you think will fill the vessel, and mix it with Salt, and a Quarter of a Pound of allom to a gallon of water, and poure it on them, and presse them down with a stone on them, and keep them covered close.

For that use I think the water will be best boyl'd and cold, which will keep longer sweet, or if you like not this pickle doe it with Water Salt and White Wine Vinegar, or (if you please) pour the Water and Salt on them scalding hot, which will make them ready to use the sooner.—From *The Receipt Book of Joseph Cooper*, Cook to Charles I, 1640.

DILL AND COLLY-FLOWER PICKLE.—Boil the Colly-flowers till they fall in Pieces ; then with some of the Stalk and worst of the Flower, boil it in a part of the Liquor till pretty strong. Then being taken off, strain it ; and when settled, clean it from the Bottom. Then with Dill, gross pepper, a pretty quantity of Salt, when cold add as much vinegar as will make it sharp, and pour all upon the Colly-flower.—John Evelyn, *Acetaria*, 1699.

ELDER

" The common people formerly gathered the Leaves of Elder upon the last day of Aprill, which to disappoint the charmes of Witches they had affixed to their Doores and Windowes. I doe not desire any to pin their Faiths upon these reports, but only let them know there are such which they may believe as they please."
—WILLIAM COLES, *The Art of Simpling*, 1656.

However tiny the herb garden, there should be at least one elder in it, for all herbs are under the protection of the spirit of the Elder. She is the Elder Mother, or elder woman, who never fails to avenge any injury done to the tree, and when elder is picked or cut, she must first be asked to give her permission. " Lady Elder, give me some of thy wood, and then will I also give thee some of mine when it grows in the forest." The Elder plays a conspicuous part in all the mythology and folklore of the Scandinavian nations, and every child loves Hans Andersen's beautiful story of Mother Elder. The Russian peasants say that the spirit of the elder is full of compassion for human beings, and drives away all evil spirits from them, and gives long life also. The Danes believe it is the height of ill-luck to have furniture made of elder, or to board the floors with its wood, and if a cradle is made of the wood, the Elder Mother will come and pull the child out of it. The pith of the tree has wonderful powers, for, if cut in round, flat shapes, and dipped in oil, lighted, and then put to float in a glass of water, its light on Christmas Eve will reveal to the owner all the witches and sorcerers in the neighbourhood. In the Tyrol they trim an elder bush into the form of a cross, and plant it on a newly made grave. If it blooms this is a sign that the dead person's soul is in Paradise. Our English peasantry had formerly a great veneration for elder, and many still testify to its wonderful healing properties. If you plant an elder in your herb garden, you must be sure to stand under it at midnight on Midsummer Eve, and then you will see the King of the Elves and all his train go by.

To take away the Freckles in the Face.—Wash your face, in the wane of the Moone, with a sponge, morning and evening, with the distilled water of Elder-leaves, letting the same dry into the skinne. Your water must be distilled in May. This from a Traveller, who hath cured himselfe thereby.—Sir Hugh Platt, *Delights for Ladies*, 1659.

To TAKE AWAY FRECKLES IN THE FACE.—Take one Pint of White Wine Vinegar and put it into a glass with Six Oaken Apples and a few elder leaves Set in the Sun and wash your Face therewith.—*MS. Book of Receipts* by Thomas Newington, 1719.

THE LADY THORNBURGH'S SYRUP OF ELDERS.—Take Elderberries when they are red, bruise them in a stone Mortar, strain the juyce, and boyl it to a Consumption of almost half, skum it very clear, take it off the fire whilest it is hot, put in Sugar to the thickness of a Syrup ; put it no more on the fire, when it is cold put it into glasses, not filling them to the top, for it will work like Beer.—*The Queen's Closet Opened*, by W. M., Cook to Queen Henrietta Maria, 1655.

To PICKLE ELDER BUDS.—Put the Buds into Vinegar, season'd with Salt, whole pepper, large mace, lemon-peel cut small, let them have two or three walms over the Fire ; then take them out and let the Buds and Pickle both cool, then put the Buds into your Pot and cover them with the Pickle.—From *The Receipt Book of John Nott*, Cook to the Duke of Bolton, 1723.

To PICKLE ELDER TOPS.—Break the tops of young Sprouts of Elder, about the middle of April, six inches long, let them have half a dozen walms in boiling Water, then drain them ; make a pickle of wine water, salt, and bruised pepper, put them into the Pickle, and stop them up close.—*Ibid.*

ELDER VINEGAR.—Put dryed Elder flowers into Stone or double Glass Bottles, fill them up with good Wine Vinegar, and set them up in the Sun or by the Fire till their Virtue is extracted.—*Ibid.*

ELDER FLOWER FRITTERS.—Gather your Bunches of Elder Flowers, just as they are beginning to open, for that is the time of their Perfection, they have just then a very fine Smell and a spirited Taste, but afterwards they grow dead and faint ; we complain of these flowers having a sickly Smell, but this is only when they are decaying, when fresh and just open they have the same Flavour, but it is spirited and just the contrary of what it is afterwards. The Elder Flowers being thus chosen, break each Bunch into four regular Parts, lay these carefully in a Soup Dish ; break in a Stick of Cinnamon, pour to them a Wine Glass of Brandy ; and when this has stood a Minute or two, add half a Pint of Sack, stir the Flowers about in the Liquor, cover them up, and let them Soak about an Hour, in covering and stirring them about at Times, to see how they are kept moist ; put a Handful of the finest Flour into a Stew-pan, add the Yolks of four Eggs beaten, and afterwards their Whites beat up quite to a Foam ; add some White Wine and a little Salt, and put in the Whites of the Eggs last : Let all this be very perfectly and thoroughly mixed ; when the Batter is thus made, set on a Quantity of Hog's

Lard in a Stew-pan, when it is very hot, fry the Fritters, the Method is this : The Elder Flowers are to be taken out of their Liquor, and put into the Batter, and the Quantity for each Fritter is one of the Bunches of Elder, with as much Batter as agreeably covers it, and hangs well about it. While they are frying, heat the Dish they are to be sent up in, rub a Lemon upon it, not cut, and lay in the Fritters as they come out of the Pan, strew a little of the finest Orange-flower Water over them, and serve them up.—*Ibid*.

ELDER WINE.—To every Gallon of Water a peck of berries. To every Gallon of Juice three pounds of Sugar, half of Ground Ginger, six cloves, and one pound of raisins. A quarter of a pint of brandy to every gallon of wine, and three or four tablespoons of brewer's yeast to every nine gallons of wine.

Pour boiling water on the berries and let them stand covered for twenty-four hours. Then strain the whole through a bag or sieve, breaking the berries to extract the juice. Measure the liquid, and to every gallon allow three pounds of sugar. Boil the juice with the sugar and other ingredients for one hour, skimming the whole time. Let it strain until lukewarm. Then pour into a clean dry cask with the proportion of yeast as above. Let it ferment for a fortnight, add the brandy. Bung up the cask, and let the wine remain thus six months before bottling.—E. G. Hayden, *Travels round our Village*.

ELDER WINE.—Pick the elderberries at midday on a hot sunny day. To half a bushel of berries allow

6 gallons of water, 6 pounds best Demerara Sugar, 2 pounds Valencia rasins, 1 oz. finely ground ginger, 8 cloves. Pick the berries free of stalks and pour on them the boiling water and leave for 24 hours. Strain through muslin, breaking the berries to extract all the juice. Add the other ingredients and boil, removing the scum. Remove from the fire and leave the pot to stand until the contents are blood-heat. Strain through muslin into a cask and allow 4 tablespoons fresh brewer's yeast to each 9 gallons of wine. Leave to ferment a fortnight. Then to every gallon of wine allow quarter pint of old Cognac. Bung up tightly and leave for three or four months before bottling.

The above is an old farm-house recipe and a great point is made of gathering the berries ' hot in the sun.'

ELDER LEAF TEA.—Simmer six or eight leaves of elder which have been torn in shreds for ten minutes in half a pint of water, and take a cup every morning fasting.

ELDER ROB.—Put a quart of elderberries into a saucepan with just a tablespoon water to prevent the berries burning. Simmer slowly, crushing the berries till all the juice is extracted. Strain, and to every pint of juice allow one pound of sugar. Boil for twenty minutes. Bottle when cold.

The real old-fashioned elder rob should be of a thick syrupy consistency. For colds, coughs, etc., allow one tablespoon or two tablespoons of elder rob to half a pint of boiling water.

ELDER CREAM.—Two pounds of the best fresh lard. Melt this in a lined saucepan and then add as many handfuls of elder flowers as the melted fat will cover. Simmer gently for three-quarters of an hour to an hour. Strain through clean muslin into small pots and when quite cold cover in the same way as jam. In picking the elder flowers and stalking them care must be taken to shake off as little of the pollen as possible. To make the cream stronger add a fresh quantity of flowers to the fat when the first lot have been strained off.

I have some pots of this cream made three years ago and the cream is as good as when first made. This is the famous old-fashioned cream for whitening and softening the skin.

ELDER BLOSSOM AND PEPPERMINT TEA.—Pour one and a half pints of boiling water on two handfuls of the Elder-blossom and peppermint.

ELECAMPANE

" Excellent herbs had our fathers of old—
　Excellent herbs to ease our pain—
　Alexander and Marigold,
　Eyebright, Orris and Elecampane,
　Basil, Rocket, Valerian, Rue,
　(Almost singing themselves they run),
　Vervain, Dittany, Call-me-to-you—
　Cowslip, Melilot, Rose of the Sun.
　　Anything green that grew out of the mould
　　Was an excellent herb to our fathers of old.
　　　　　　　　　　RUDYARD KIPLING.

When Paris carried off Helen of Troy she is supposed to have had her hands full of this herb, and according to another tradition, it sprang from her tears. Whatever may be its origin, the plant which takes its name from her has been renowned for its virtues since the earliest days. They were grown in the oldest herb gardens of which we have any record, and throughout the Middle Ages our ancestors used it, and it is only we foolish moderns who do not include this stately golden-flowered plant amongst our herbs. Sir John Hill says of elecampane : " It is famous for all diseases of the chest, and strengthens the digestion. 'Twere vain to expect these virtues in the dried Root sold at drug-gists, which has been baked, ground in a mill, and tho' cheap enough in itself, yet mixed with flour to make it cheaper. In that state it has little either of taste, smell, or virtue. The garden must supply it fresh to those who would know its real value. There as it rises freely from Nature it is full of these excellent qualities. The taste and smell compared with the dry will abundantly show this before we feel its good effects. The root which is long and large contains the virtues of the Plant, and few have greater. It is a native of our meadow grounds, and from its virtues is become common in our gardens. It is a robust, stately plant, a perennial with a firm and handsome appearance." It may be propagated either by sowing the seed, or by division of the roots after flowering. It will flourish any-where.

CONSERVE OF ELECAMPANE ROOT.—Cleanse and scrape the root. Cut them into thin round slices, letting them soke in water over the hot embers for a long space, and boil them till all the liquor be wasted. Beat them in a stone mortar, very fine. Boyle the whole with a like weighte of honey or sugar two or three times over.

All other roots may in like manner be candied and made into Conserve, but far pleasanter in the eating if to the confection a quantity of cinnamon be added. Candy the roots in October.—Thomas Hill, *The Gardener's Labyrinth*, 1577.

To make Paste of Elecampane Roots, an Excellent Remedy against the Cough of the Lungs.—Take the youngest Elecampane roots and boyl them reasonably tender ; then pith them and peel them, and so beat it in a mortar, then take twice as much sugar as the pulp doth weigh, and so boyl it to a candy height with as much Rose-water as will melt it ; then put the pulp into the sugar, with the pap of a roasted Apple, then let it boyle till it be thick, then drop it on a Pye plate, and so dry it in an Oven till it be dry.—*The Queen's Closet Opened*, by W. M., Cook to Queen Henrietta Maria, 1655.

Elecampane Tonic.—Slice the fresh root thin, and to a quarter of a pound of it pour three pints of boiling water. After standing all night, boil it a few minutes, and when cold, strain the liquor off. To a pint of this add a quarter of a pint of mountain wine, and let a full wineglass of this be drank four times a day.—Sir John Hill, *The British Herbal*, 1772.

ENDIVE

In appearance, at least, there seems little connection between our common garden Endive and the Succory of the fields. Is there any flower quite so ethereal a blue as the latter ? If the Roumanian legend is true, the wild Succory was once a beautiful woman whom the Sun wished to marry, but she refused. So he transformed her into Succory, and condemned her for ever to gaze on him from the moment he rose till he set. There is a curious trace of this legend in the widespread old belief that Succory must never be uprooted save with gold or a stag's horn (emblems of the Sun's rays). Succory ensures constancy in love, and it was a frequent ingredient in the old love philtres. Its leaves were used as a pot-herb, and the flowers as cordials.

A SALLET OF WILD, GREEN SUCCORY.—Take the Leaves of this Herb, cut them small, and put them into fair water, and so let them lye two hours, change your water three or four times, then swing it out very well, and Dish it up on a Plate, and garnish it with anything, either white or red. You may do the same with the white, or wilde Succory, only garnish it with either red or green, or both if you please.—*A Perfect School of Instructions for the Officers of the Month*, by Giles Rose, one of the Master Cooks to Charles II, 1682.

EGGS WITH SUCCORY.—Blanch someSuccory, squeeze it well, give it three or four Cuts with a Knife, put it

into a Stew-pan, moisten it with a little Fish-broth,
season it with Pepper, Salt, a Bunch of Savory Herbs,
let it simmer half an hour, and then thicken it with
a Fish-Cullis, lay it handsomely in the Dish, and
having poached your Eggs in Butter, and cut them
round, lay them upon the Succory, and serve them in
Plates or little Dishes, or for Hors-d'œuvres.—*Ibid.*

EYEBRIGHT

Eyebright—*Euphrasia officinalis*—is one of the
loveliest of minute herbs. The ancient Greeks named
it after the linnet, who first revealed its virtues to man-
kind. It has always had the reputation of restoring lost
vision, and Culpepper tells us that if only we knew how
to use it properly, spectacle makers would soon lose
their trade. Many herbalists also recommend eyebright tea.

Eyebright Tea.—One pint of boiling water poured
on to an ounce of the whole herb.

FENNEL

" He who sees fennel and gathers it not, is not a man but a
devil."—*The Book of Iago ab Dewi.*

> " Fennel in potage and in mete
> Is good to done whane yu schalt ete.
> All grene looke it be corwyn (carved) small
> In what mete you usyn schall."
>
> *Fourteenth Century MS.*

" Then went I forth on my right hond
  Downe by a little path I fond
    Of mintes full and fennell greene."
                                CHAUCER.

" Above the lowly plants it towers,
    The fennel, with its yellow flowers,
    And in an earlier age than ours
    Was gifted with the wondrous powers,
        Lost vision to restore.
    It gave new strength and fearless mood ;
    And gladiators, fierce and rude,
    Mingled it in their daily food ;
    And he who battled and subdued,
        A wreath of fennel wore."
                    LONGFELLOW, *The Goblet of Life.*

We only use fennel in fennel sauce, and that far
too seldom, for it is a most wholesome herb.   In the
Middle Ages the poor folk used it not only to relieve
the pangs of hunger, but also to make unsavoury food
palatable.   It was also used in large quantities in the
households of the rich, and Lady Cecil points out
that from the Wardrobe Accounts of Edward I's
household, it may be seen that eight and a half pounds
of fennel were brought for one month's supply.   Fin-
nochio is a popular Italian dish, and this sweet fennel
is now becoming more common in English gardens.
Fennel has always been renowned for its power of
restoring the eyesight since Pliny's days, and one herbalist tells us, " A serpent doth so hate the ashtree that
she will not come nigh the shadow of it, but she delights
in fennel very much, which she eates to cleare her eyesight."   Formerly, the seeds used to be coated with
sugar and eaten like Coriander seeds.   The young
stalks were peeled and used like celery, and the tender
tufts and leaves were an ingredient in Salads.

FENNEL can be raised either by sowing the seed in
the spring, or by dividing the roots at any time excepting when the plant is in flower. Sweet Fennel (*fin-
nochio*) requires a richer soil than our common fennel.

FOR TO MAKE ONE SLENDER.—Take fennel and seethe
it in water, a very good quantity, and wring out the
juice thereof when it is sod, and drink it first and last,
and it shall swage either him or her.—T. Dawson, *The
Good Housewife's Jewell*, 1585.

A SALLET OF FENNEL.—Take young Fennel about
a span long, in the spring, tye it up in bunches as you
do Sparragrass ; when your Skillet boyls, put in enough
to make a dish ; when it is boyled and drained, dish
it up as you do Sparragrass, pour on Butter and Vinegar
and send it up.—William Rabisha, *The Whole Body of
Cookery Dissected*, 1675.

TO MAKE WHITE FENNEL.—Take the branches of
fennel, make them very clean, and lay them a drying,
and when they are dry take the white of an Egg and
a little orange-flower water, beat this well together,
and dip your Fennel into it and let it steep a little, then
sprinkle fine sugar in powder over it, and lay it to dry
before the fire upon a sheet of paper.—*A Perfect School
of Instructions for the Officers of the Month*, by Giles
Rose, one of the Master Cooks to Charles II, 1682.

FENNEL AND GOOSEBERRY SAUCE.—Brown some
Butter in a saucepan with a pinch of flour, then put
in a few cives shred small, add a little Irish broth to

moisten it, season with salt and pepper ; make these boil, then put in two or three sprigs of Fennel and some Gooseberries. Let all simmer together till the Gooseberries are soft and then put in some Cullis.—From *The Receipt Book of Henry Howard*, Free Cook of London, 1710 ; and Cook to the Duke of Ormond.

To Pickle Fennel.—Make water boil, tie your Fennel up in bunches and put them into the water ; give them half a dozen Walms ; drain them, put them into a Pot, and let your Pickle be Vinegar.—From *The Receipt Book of John Nott*, Cook to the Duke of Bolton, 1723.

Fennel Tea.—Half a pint of boiling water poured on a teaspoonful of bruised fennel seeds.

FEVERFEW

" In the worst headaches this Herb exceeds whatever else is known."—Sir John Hill, *The British Herbal*, 1772.

Feverfew is still used by country people in England to cure headaches. Sir John Hill quotes many instances of cures effected by it, and amongst them the following : " A lady of greate worth and virtue, the mother of the late Sir William Bowyer, told me that having in the younger part of her life a very terrible and almost constant Headache, fixed in one small spot, and raging at all times almost to distraction, she was at length cured by a maid-servant with this Herb."

FEVERFEW TEA.—Pour a quart of boiling water on two handfuls of the flowers and leaves.

GILLYFLOWERS

" As they are in beauty and sweetness so are they in virtue and wholesomeness."—W. LAWSON, *The Country Housewife's Garden*.

" The conserve of the Carnation Gillyflower is exceeding Cordiall eaten now and then."—TRYON.

There has always been much learned discussion as to exactly what the old gillyflowers was, but any child looking at the old illustrations would identify it with the pink or carnation, and this is near enough for all practical purposes. The good old English name of Gillyflower is such a much prettier name than Carnation that it is a pity we do not use it. There are numerous illustrations of the cultivated gillyflowers in Parkinson's *Paradisus*, and some of them have enchanting names : " Master Tuggie's Princesse," " Lustie Gallant," " Fair Maid of Kent," " Master Bradshawe his daintie Ladie," " John Wilke his great tawny gillowflower," " Speckled Tawny," " Master Tuggie his Rose gillowflower." Another common name for gillyflowers was " Sops in Wine," because wine was flavoured with them when they were in flower.

Many of the old writers give curious directions of how to improve or alter the colour and scent of gillyflowers which seem to have held a place in our affection only second to roses throughout the Middle Ages. Hyll says, " These gilliflowers you may make of any colours you please in such sort as is shewed you for

the colouring of lillyes, and if you please to have them
of mixt colours you may also by Grafting of contrary
colours one with another, and you may with as great
ease graft the gilliflowers as any fruit whatsoever by
the joynings of the knots one unto another and then
wrapping them about with a little soft silke and covering the place close with soft, red waxe, well tempered.
And you shall understand that the grafting of gilliflowers maketh them exceeding great double and most
orient of colour. Now if you will have your gilliflowers of divers smels or odours, you may also with
great ease, as thus for example : if you will take two or
three great Cloves, steepe them for four and twenty
hours in Damaske Rose-water. Then take them out
and bruise them and put them into a fine Cambrick
ragge and so binde them about the heart roote of the
gilliflower near to the setting on of the Stalk, and so
plant it in a fine, soft and fertile mould, and the flower
which springeth from the same will have so delicate
a mixt smell of the clove and the Rose-water that it
will breed both delight and wonder. If in the same
manner you take a stocke of cinnamon and steepe it in
Rose-water, and then bruise it and bind it, as aforesaid,
all the flowers will smell strongly of cinnamon, if you
take two grains of fat muske or mix it with two drops
of Damaske Rose-water, and bind it, as aforesaid, the
flowers will smell strongly of muske, yet not too hot
nor offensive, by reason of the connection of the Rose-
water, and in this sort you may doe either with Amber-
greece storac, Benjamin, or any other sweet drugge
whatsoever, and if in any of these confections before
named you steep the seedes of your gilliflowers foure
and twenty houres before you sowe them, they will

take the same smels in which you steept them, onely
they will not be so large or double, as those which are
replanted or grafted."

To Make Syrup of Clove Gillyflowers.—Take
a quart of water, half a bushel of Flowers, cut off the
whites, and with a Sive sift away the seeds, bruise
them a little ; let your water be boyled and a little
cold again, then put in your Flowers, and let them stand
close covered twenty-four hours ; you may put in
but half the Flowers at a time, the strength will come
out the better ; to that liquor put in three pounds of
Sugar, let it lye in all night, next day boyl it in a Gallypot, set it in a pot of water, and there let it boyl till all
the Sugar be melted, and the Syrup be pretty thick,
then take it out and let it stand in that till it be thorough
cold, then glass it.—*The Queen's Closet Opened*, by
W. M., Cook to Queen Henrietta Maria, 1655.

To Make Gillyflower Wine.—Take two ounces of
dryed Gillyflowers, and put them into a bottle of Sack,
and beat three ounces of Sugar candy, or fine Sugar,
and grinde some Ambergreese, and put it in the bottle
and shake it oft, then run it through a gelly bag, and
give it for a great Cordiall after a week's standing or
more. You make Lavender Wine as you doe this.
—*Ibid*.

Conserve of Gillyflowers.—Pickle up stratum
super stratum, a lay of flowers, and then strawed over
with fine, dry and powdered Sugar, and so lay, after
lay strawed over untill the pot be full you meane

to keepe them in, and after filled up or covered over with Vinegar.—John Parkinson, *Paradisus*, 1629.

GILLYFLOWER VINEGAR.—Gillyflowers infused in Vinegar and set in the Sun for certaine dayes, as we do for Rose Vinegar do make a very pleasant and comfortable vinegar, good to be used in time of contagious sickness, and very profitable at all times for such as have feeble spirits.—John Evelyn, *Acetaria*, 1699.

To CANDY GILLYFLOWERS.—Take the weight of your Flowers in refin'd Sugar or sugar candy, sift it, put to it some rose-water, and set it over a gentle Charcoal fire, put in your Flowers, and stir them till the Sugar be of a candied Height; then keep them in a dry Place for Use.—From *The Receipt Book of John Nott*, Cook to the Duke of Bolton, 1723.

To PICKLE GILLYFLOWERS.—Take the Flowers just blown, take them out of the Husks, clip the white Bottoms, and put them in fair water; boil up White Wine Vinegar and scum it till no more scum will rise; let it stand by to cool; then squeeze the water out of the Gillyflowers, and put them into the Vinegar; put in some broken Cinnamon, a few Blades of Mace, melt some double refin'd Sugar in Rose Water, and put to the Pickle, and stop them up close.

When you use them mince them small, put a little Vinegar to them, and strew over them a little fine Sugar. They are a very good sauce for Lamb or Mutton. —*Ibid*.

GILLYFLOWER SYRUP.—The flowers are used. Make a Syrup of five pints of boiling water poured on three pounds of the flowers picked from the husks, and with the white heels cut off. After they have stood twelve hours, strain off the clear liquor without pressing, and dissolving in it two pounds of the purest sugar to every pint. This makes the most beautiful and pleasant of all Syrups.—From *The Receipt Book of Henry Howard*, Free Cook of London, 1710 ; and Cook to the Duke of Ormond.

TO MAKE CLOVE-GILLYFLOWER WINE.—Take six Gallons and a half of Spring Water, and twelve Pounds of Sugar, and when it boils skim it, putting in the White of eight Eggs, and a Pint of Cold Water, to make the Scum rise ; let it boil for an Hour and a half, skimming it well ; then pour it into an Earthen Vessel, with three Spoonfuls of Baum ; then put in a Bushel of Clove-Gillyflowers clip'd and beat, stir them well together, and the next Day put six Ounces of Syrup of Citron into it, the third Day put in three Lemons sliced, Peel and all, the fourth Day tun it up, stop it close for ten Days, then bottle it, and put a Piece of Sugar in each Bottle.—Sarah Harrison, *The House-keeper's Pocket Book*, 1739.

GROUND IVY

There are few herbs with a greater variety of names than this humble, attractive little plant, which has such a surprisingly strong aromatic scent :

Gill-go-by-the-ground, Lizzy-run-up-the-hedge, Cat's foot, Devil's Candlesticks, Alehoof, are only a few of its local names. The ordinary name, Ground Ivy, is very misleading, as it is not an ivy at all. Our Saxon ancestors used Ground Ivy in their beer, and hence the places where this beer was sold were called Gill houses. Ground Ivy tea is a tonic much recommended by many herbalists, and the herb used to be sold in the London streets.

GROUND IVY TEA.—One quart of boiling water poured on to two handfuls of the plant when it is in flower (May and June).

HERB ROBERT

The wild cranesbill—herb Robert—was the " geranium " of the Middle Ages, and it is one of the plants described in Mayster Jon Gardener's book, *The Feate of Gardening*—the earliest original English treatise on gardening—the MS. of which is in the library of Trinity College, Cambridge. Herb Robert was one of the plants used for edging before the ugly box edgings superseded the charming old borders of hyssop, thyme and other herbs.

HOREHOUND

" Syrup made from the greene fresh leaves of horehound and sugar is a most singular remedy against the cough and wheezing of the lungs."—T. TRYON, *A Treatise of Cleanness in Meats*, 1692.

The botanical name of white horehound—*marrubium* —is of Hebrew derivation, from *marrob*, a bitter juice.

Many cottagers still grow horehound in order to make horehound tea and syrup themselves. Black horehound has a very disagreeable smell, and it was formerly supposed to be an antidote against the bite of a mad dog. Water horehound used to be called " gipsywort," " because the rogues and runagates which name themselves Egyptians do colour themselves black with this herbe."

Horehound is a hardy herbaceous perennial. It likes a little shade and dry, chalky soil. Sow the seeds in March or increase by dividing the roots. If increased by cuttings they should be inserted in a shady border.

HOREHOUND TEA.—On one ounce of the fresh leaves pour one pint of boiling water and sweeten with honey.

CANDIED HONEY.—Boil some horehound till the juice is extracted. Boil up some sugar to a feather height, add your juice to the sugar, and let it boil till it is again the same height. Stir it till it begins to grow thick, then pour it on to a dish and dust it with sugar and when fairly cool cut into squares. Excellent sweetmeat for colds and coughs.—R. Thornton, *The Family Herbal*, 1810.

HYSSOP

Our hyssop is probably not the hyssop mentioned in the Bible, and the identity of that plant has never yet been settled. The old mazes were frequently " sette with isope." The young tops and flowers were used in pottages and strewn on salads, and hyssop tea and syrup were famous cordials. Tusser includes hyssop in his list of herbs to be strewn in chambers.

Hyssop is a hardy evergreen. It likes a light sandy soil and not too much sun. It should be cut back after flowering. Sow the seeds in March or April, or increase by dividing the roots in spring or autumn. Cuttings should be taken in April or May.

HYSSOP TEA.—Pour one pint of boiling water on one dram of the green tops.

A WATER TO CAUSE AN EXCELLENT COLOUR AND COMPLEXION.—Drink six spoonfuls of the juice of Hyssop in warm Ale in a Morning and fasting.—From *The Receipt Book of John Nott*, Cook to the Duke of Bolton, 1723.

TO MAKE SYRUP OF HYSOP FOR COLDS.—Take an handful of Hysop, of Figs, Raysins, Dates, of each an ounce, French Barley one ounce, boyl therein three pintes of fair water to a quart, strain it and clarifie it with two Whites of Eggs, then put in two pound of fine Sugar and boyl it to a Syrup.—*The Queen's Closet Opened*, by W. M., Cook to Queen Henrietta Maria, 1655.

LAVENDER

> " Here's your sweet lavender,
>   Sixteen sprigs a penny,
> Which you will find, my ladies,
>   Will smell as sweet as any."
>
> *Old London Street Cry.*

" I judge that the flowers of Lavender quilted in a cap and dayly worne are good for all diseases of the head that come of a cold cause and that they comfort the braine very well."—WILLIAM TURNER, *A Newe Herball,* 1551.

Lavender is an old inhabitant of our English herb gardens, and with the different kinds a garden of lavender alone could be made. The white lavender, which is less hardy than the purple, has a very delicate scent, and it was evidently a favourite with Queen Henrietta Maria, for in the Survey of the Garden at Wimbledon, which belonged to her, there were " very great and large borders of Rosemary, Rue, white Lavender and great variety of excellent herbs and some choice flowers—which borders, herbs, flowers . . . we value to be worth £3." Gerard calls French lavender Sticadove. This is *L. Stæchas,* which formerly grew in such abundance on the islands near Hyères that they were named after the plant, the Stœchades. The Spaniards now made lavender oil from this *L. Stæchas* by putting it in a bottle of olive oil and leaving the bottle tightly closed in the sun. Parkinson says that " lavender in Spain grows so abundantly in many places, so wilde and little regarded that many have gone and abiden there to dystill the oyle thereof whereof great quantities now commeth over from thence unto us and also from Languedoc and Provence in France." In England they had formerly the charmingly dainty custom of serving any small dessert fruits or sweets on lavender sticks.

CONSERVE OF THE FLOWERS OF LAVENDER.—Take the flowers being new so many as you please, and beat them with three times their weight of White Sugar, after the same manner as Rosemary flowers ; they will keep one year.—*The Queen's Closet Opened*, by W. M., Cook to Queen Henrietta Maria, 1655.

LAVENDER WATER.—Put two pounds of lavender pipps in two quarts of water, put them into a cold still, and make a slow fire under it ; distill it off very slowly into a pot till you have distilled all your water ; then clean your still well out, put your lavender water into it, and distill it off slowly again ; put it into bottles and cork it well.—*The New Art of Cookery*, by Richard Briggs, many years Cook at the Globe Tavern, Fleet Street, the White Hart Tavern, Holborn, and the Temple Coffee House, 1788.

LAVENDER WATER WITHOUT DISTILLATION.—Mix one pint rectified spirits, four ounces distilled water, three drams oil of lavender, three drams orange-flower water, five minims each of oil of cloves and oil of cinnamon and four minims otto of roses. Allow this mixture to stand for a fortnight, then filter through carbonate of Magnesia and bottle. Keep for three months before using.—*The Still Room by* Mrs. Charles Roundell.

LAVENDER TEA.—One pint of boiling water poured on half an ounce of the young leaves.

LAVENDER WINE. See under GILLIFLOWERS.

LOVAGE

" This herbe for hys sweete savoure is used in bathe."—THOMAS HYLL, *The Gardener's Labyrinth*, 1577.

Lovage was one of the herbs introduced by the Romans, and until the middle of the last century it was always grown in English herb gardens. It has such a quaint, old-fashioned name that one regrets its exclusion from the modern herb garden. One old writer tells us, it " joyeth to growe by wayes and under the eaves of a house, it prospers in shadowy places and loves running water." Lovage grows wild on the sea-coasts in parts of Scotland and Northumberland. Parkinson says of it : " The whole plant and every part of it smelleth strongly and aromatically and of a hot, sharpe, biting taste. The Germans and other Nations in times past used both the roote and seede instead of Pepper to season their meates and brothes and found them as comfortable and warming."

Lovage seed should be sown in late summer in any good garden soil. Transplant in spring or autumn. Increase by root division in spring.

MADONNA LILY

"Lyllies and Roses planted together will both smell the pleasanter."—WILLIAM LANGHAM, *The Garden of Health*, 1579.

The Madonna Lily is one of our oldest " herbs."
It is said to be a native of the Levant and to have
been introduced into this country by the Romans.
Bartholomaeus Anglicus, the great mediæval scholar
wrote this beautiful description of it : " The Lily is
an herbe with a white flower : and though the leaves
of the floure be white yet within shineth the likenesse
of golde. The Lily is next to the Rose in worthiness
and nobleness. . . . Nothing is more gracious than
the Lily in fairness of colour, in sweetnesse of smell
and in effect of working and vertue." The lily has
always been the symbol of purity, and Chaucer, it
will be remembered, gives this charming derivation of
Saint Cecilia's name—" Heaven's lily."

> " First wol I you the name of Sainte Cecilie
> Expoune as men may in hire storie see :
> It is to sayn in English, Hevens lilie,
> For pure chasteness of virginitee,
> Or for the whitnesse had of honestee,
> And grene of conscience, and of good fame
> The swote savour, lilie was her name."

Its chief use formerly, as now, was for healing
wounds. The roots and leaves were also used for
various ills. William Langham says : " The flowers
are the best part, then the roots and then the leaves."
The roots roasted and mixed with oil of roses was used
to take out wrinkles on the face. To whiten the

skin the roots were boiled in water until the water was reduced to a third and then the water was used nine successive nights.

MALLOW

" For want and famine they were solitary, fleeing into the wilderness . . . who cut up mallows by the bushes and juniper roots for their meat."—Job xxx. 3, 4.

" If thou wilt seem all inflamed or set on fire take white great mallows or hollyhocks, and anoint your body, then with alum, and then brimstone, and when the fire is enflamed it hurteth not, and yf thou make it upon the palme of thy hande, thou shalt be able to holde ye fire without hurte."—*The Boke of Secrets of Albertus Magnus of the vertues of Herbes, Stones and certaine beastes*, 1525.

" If that of health you have any special care
Use French Mallowes that to the body wholesome are."
JOHN GERARD, *The Herball*, 1597.

The Ancient Romans greatly esteemed mallows, and they are still eaten by the Egyptians, Syrians and Chinese. From the earliest times they have been celebrated for their soothing, healing properties, and they were one of the commonest pot and salad herbs throughout the Middle Ages. It is a tradition that when the ordeal of holding a red-hot iron was inflicted the suspected person covered his hands with a paste made of marsh-mallows and white of egg, and could with impunity hold a red-hot iron for a moment.

Mallow was held to be a herb of sovereign virtue against witchcraft. There is a curious old legend that Mahomet, being pleased with a robe made of the fibre of mallow stalks, transformed the plant into a pelargonium. Parkinson says of the Venice mallow : " These flowers are so quickly faded and gone that you shall hardly see any of them blowne open unlesse it be betimes in the morning before the sun doth grow warme upon them. For as soon as it feeleth the sunnes warme heat it closeth up and never openeth againe so that you shall very seldom see a flower blowne open in the day time after nine o'clock in the morning." Gerard tells us of the beautiful hedges of tree-mallows, " wherewith the people of Narbonne in France doe make hedges to sever or divide their gardens and vineyards." Hollyhocks are of the mallow tribe, and their leaves were also used as a pot-herb, but, as Evelyn says, " they are only commended by some."

Mallow seeds should be sown in March ; the plants may be increased by dividing the roots in spring and autumn.

A SALLET OF MALLOWES.—Strip off the leaves from the tender stalkes, saving the toppes : let they lye in water and seethe them tender and put them in a Dish over coales, with Butter and Vinegar : let them stand a while : then put in grated Bread and Sugar betweene every lay.—*A Booke of Cookerie*, by Edward Allde, 1588.

SYRUP OF MARSH MALLOWS.—A Decoction is made with the Roots, hearbs, fruits and seeds, in sufficient quantity of water, boyled to foure pints, in the which is clarified and boyled to the height three pound of Sugar ; and the Syrup commeth to three half pence

the ounce.—*The Charitable Physitian*, by Philbert
Guibert, Physitian Regent in Paris, 1639.

SUCKET OF MALLOW STALKS.—To candy or preserve
the tender stalks of Mallows, do thus : Take them in
the spring, when they are very young and tender ; and
peel off the strings that are round about the outside,
as you do French-beans, and boil them till they are
very tender. In the meantime prepare a high Syrup
of pure Sugar, and put the boiled Stalks into it, whiles
it is boiling hot, but taken from the fire. Let them
lie soaking there till the next morning. Then take out
the Stalks, and heat the Syrup again, scalding hot, and
return the Stalks into it, letting them lie there till next
morning ; (Note, that the Stalks must never boil in
the Syrup). Repeat this six, or eight, or nine times,
that is to say till they are sufficiently Imbibed with the
Syrup. When they are at this pass, you may either
keep them as a wet Sucket in Syrup, or dry them in
a Stove upon Papers, turning them continually, in
such sort as dried sweet-meats are to be made. I like
them best dry, but soft and moist within. In Italy
these tender Stalks of Mallows are called Mazzocchi,
and they eat them (boiled tender) in Salletts, either
hot or cold, with Vinegar and Oyl, or Butter and
Vinegar, or juyce of Oranges.—*The Closet of Sir
Kenelm Digby Opened*, 1669.

TO MAKE MALLOW STALKS PASS FOR GREEN PEAS.—
Peel the Stalks and cut them in the Form of Peas, boil
them in a Skillet with Pepper tied up in a Rag, boil
them with a quick fire, drain them in a cullender, and

dress them like Peas with Butter, Pepper and Salt. They taste so much like green Peas that they are call'd March Peas and some at eating them have taken them for such.—From *The Receipt Book of John Nott*, Cook to the Duke of Bolton, 1723.

To Pickle the Stalks of Marsh Mallows.— Gather them about the latter end of March. Peel off the outward Peel, put them into boiling water, seasoned with Salt. Let them have half a dozen Walms, take them up, drain them, let them stand to cool, make a pickle of Vinegar, Salt and Gross Pepper and put them into it.—*Ibid*.

MARIGOLD

" Golde is bitter in savour,
    Fayre and zelu is his flower ;
Ye golde flour is good to seene."
            Fourteenth Century Medical MS.

" Then with these marygolds I'll make,
My garland somewhat swelling."
            Michael Drayton.

" Here's flowers for you :—
Hot Lavender, mints, savour marjoram :
The marigold that goes to bed wi' the Sun,
And with him rises weeping."
            Winter's Tale, IV. iv.

" No marigolds yet closéd are
    No shadows great appeare—"
            Herrick.

" Open afresh your round of starry folds,
 Ye ardent marigolds !
Dry up the moisture of your golden lids,
 For great Apollo bids.
That in these days your praises should be sung
 On many harps which he has lately strung ;
And when again your dewiness he kisses,
 Tell him I have you in my world of blisses !
So haply when I rove in some far vale,
 His mighty voice may come upon the gale."

KEATS.

Marigolds were frequently called " golds " in olden
days and in Provence " gauchefer," because the flowers
with their golden discs were suggestive of shields which
were worn on the left arm—they were the emblems of
jealousy, and Chaucer speaks of " Jealousy that werede
of yelwe guldes a garland." It owes its botanical name,
Calendula, to its reputation of blossoming on the first
days of every month in the year. In the *Boke of the
Secrets of Albertus Magnus* we are told " the vertue of
this herbe is mervelous : for if it be gathered the sunne
beynge in the sane Leo, in August, and be wrapped in
the leafe of a Laurell, a baye tree and a wolves tothe
be added thereto, no man shall be able to have a word
to speake agaynst the bearer thereof, but wordes of
peace. And yf any thing be stolne, yf the bearer of
the thynges namen, laye them under hys head in the
night he shall se the thefe and all his condiciouns."
Marguerite of Valois, grandmother of Henry IV, had
a marigold turning towards the Sun for her device,
with the motto " Je ne veux suivre que lui seul." In
the Tudor days a bunch of marigolds and heartsease
signified " happiness stored in recollections." " Others

Gardener working in a Sixteenth Century Herb Garden

name it the sunnes bride and sunnes hearbe, in that
the flowers of the same follow the sunne, as from the
rising by the south unto the west, and bye a notable
turning obeying to the sunne in such manner that what
part of heaven he possesseth, they into the same turned,
behold and that in a cloudie and thicke ayre like
directed, as they should be revived, quickened, and
moved, with the spirit of him.   Such is ye love of it
knowen to be toward that royall starre."   Marygolds
steeped in vinegar and rubbed well on the teeth and
gums were " a soveraigne remedie for the assuaging of
the grevious paine of the Teeth."   Large quantities of
the flowers were dried every year to flavour broths and
pottages throughout the winter.   They figured commonly in salads and conserves, and syrups were made
from them as from other flowers.   Turner says, " some
use to make their heyre yelow wyth the floure of this
herbe not beyinge content wyth the natural colour
which God hath gyven them."   Parkinson says that
the single kind grow wild in Spain, " from whence I
received seed gathered by Guillaume Boel in his time
a very curious and cunning searcher of simples."

MARIGOLD PUDDING.—Take a pretty quantity of
marygold flowers very well shred, mingle with a pint
of Cream or New milk and almost a Pound of Beef
Suet chopt very small, the gratings of a Twopenny
loaf and stirring all together put it into a Bag flower'd
and tie it fast.   It will be boil'd within an hour—or
bake in a pan.—John Evelyn, *Acetaria*, 1699.

TO PICKLE MARIGOLD FLOWERS.—Strip the flower-
leaves off, when you have gather'd the flowers, at noon,

or in the Heat of the Day, and boil some salt and water ; and when that is cold, put your marygold-flower leaves in a gallypot, and pour the salt and water upon them ; then shut them up till you use them, and they will be of a fine colour and much fitter for Porridge than those that are dry'd.—*The Country Housewife and Lady's Director*, 1732.

MARYGOLD WINE.—To every gallon of water put two pounds of sugar, let it boil for an Hour, then set it by to cool ; make a good brown Toast, spread it well on both sides with yeast ; but before you put it in, put in an ounce and half of Syrup of Citron to each gallon of Liquor, and beat it well in, then put in the Toast while it is of a proper warmth for working, and let it work which it will do for two Days ; during which time put in your marygold flowers a little bruised, but not much stamp'd, a Peck to each gallon, and two Lemons slic'd with the Rinds to each gallon ; add a pint of White or Rhenish Wine to each gallon, and let it stand two Days, then tun it up in a sweet Cask.— From *The Receipt Book of Charles Carter*, Cook to the Duke of Argyll, 1732.

MARJORAM

" *Clown.* Indeed, Sir, she was the sweet marjoram of the Salad, or rather the herb of grace."—*All's Well that Ends Well*, IV, v.

Venus is supposed to have been the first to raise sweet marjoram. Wild marjoram, according to tradition, was once a youth in the service of King Cinyras

of Cyprus. One day he was carrying a vase of perfumes which he dropped, and in his terror he lost
consciousness and finally became metamorphosed into
this sweet herb. The botanical name, origanum, means
" Joy of the Mountain," and one cannot imagine a
more appropriate name for this fragrant plant. One
old herbalist tells us that to smell wild marjoram frequently keeps a person in good health. The ancient
Greeks believed that if marjoram grew on a tomb the
dead person was happy ; " may many flowers grow on
this tomb, violets, and marjoram and the narcissus
growing in water, and around Thee may all Roses
grow," was an old prayer.

Marjoram was one of the strewing herbs, and it was
always put into the sweet-bags for the linen.

Marjorams love sun, and they cannot have too much
of it. They like a light, dry soil. Sow seeds of marjoram in March or April, and increase by dividing the
roots or taking slips any time during the spring or
autumn. Sweet marjoram can only be grown from
seed, as it is an annual.

A CONSERVE OF MARJORAM.—Take the tops and
tenderest parts of Sweet Marjoram, bruise it well in a
wooden Mortar or Bowl ; take double the weight of
Fine Sugar, boil it with Marjoram Water till it is as
thick as Syrup, then put in your beaten marjoram.—
From *The Receipts of John Nott*, Cook to the Duke of
Bolton, 1723.

WILD MARJORAM TEA.—One pint of boiling water
poured on a good handful of the young leaves and

flowering tops of wild marjoram. The wild marjoram has a pungent taste, warmer than that of sweet or pot marjoram.

MEADOWSWEET

" Queen Elizabeth of famous memory did more desire it than any other sweet herbe to strew her chambers withal."—JOHN PARKINSON, *The Theatre of Plants*, 1640.

Bridewort was one of the old names of this beautiful flower, and it was formerly one of the wedding herbs. " Queen of the meadow " is another of its appropriate names, and children nearly always call it this. Gerard tells us that " the leaves and flowers of meadowsweet excel all other strong herbes for to deck up houses, to strew in chambers, halls, and banqueting houses, in the summer time ; for the smell thereof makes the heart merrie and delighteth the senses." Incidentally in connection with strewing herbs, what a pity it is that the old office of the King's Herb-strewer has fallen into disuse. It has never been formally abolished. At George IV's coronation several customs that had long been obsolete were revived, amongst them that of the herb strewing. The King's Herb-strewer (Miss Fellowes) wore the old costume, a white gown and a scarlet mantle with gold lace ; on her head a wreath of laurel and oak leaves and round her neck her badge of office. She was attended by six maidens, attired in white adorned with flowers and greenery, and each pair carried between them a two-handled basket from which they strewed the herbs.

A little meadowsweet gives an excellent flavour to soup, and there are still numbers of country folk in England who dry a quantity of it every year to make an infusion of it for colds.

MEADOWSWEET TEA.—A quart of boiling water poured on an ounce of the dried leaves and flowering tops.

MINT

" Eat Betoyne and Mynts prepared in honey, use herbs grace in thy Wine."—April, *Ram's Little Dodoen*, 1606.

Mint takes its name from Minthé, who was loved by Pluto. This nymph was metamorphosed by Pluto's wife, Proserpine, with the herb called after her. Thomas Hyll, in *The Gardener's Labyrinth*, gives some curious advice to the gardener who cannot procure the garden mint. " Let him plant the seed of the wild mint, setting the sharper ends of the seeds downwards, whereby to tame and put away the wildness of them." In France mint was called " Menthe de Notre Dame," and in Italy " Erbe Santa Maria." The cultivated herb is said to have been introduced into England by the Romans. All the different varieties have the quality of preventing milk from curdling, and for this reason herbalists recommend them to people who are put on to a milk diet. Formerly they were one of the herbs strewn in churches, and they were also used in baths. Culpepper records the curious old belief that if a wounded man eats mint he will never recover, and it is a superstition which has not quite died out that mint must never be cut with an instrument of iron.

All the mints except Corn-mint like moisture. Catmint will grow anywhere. To have early mint make a small hotbed in January with two feet of manure with six inches of good earth on top. Plant the roots closely. They will be up in about a fortnight. If only a small quantity is required plant a few roots in pots and give bottom heat. Forced roots decay rapidly and are useless after the leaves have been taken.

" Mintes put into milk, it neyther suffereth the same to crude, nor to become thick, insomuch that layed in curded milke, this would bring the same thinne againe." —*The Good Housewife's Handmaid*, 1588.

To MAKE SYRUP OF MINT.—Take a quart of the Syrup of Quinces before they are full ripe, juice of mint two quarts, an ounce of Red Roses, steep them twenty-four hours in the juices, then boil it till it is half wasted, strain out the remainder and make it into a syrup with double refined sugar.—From *The Receipt Book of John Nott*, Cook to the Duke of Bolton, 1723.

MINT WATER.—Take a good quantity of mint, pennyroyal and balm. Steep them in canary or the lees of it for twenty-four hours. Stop them up close and stir them now and then. Distil them in an alembick with a quick fire, sweetening it with sugar in your receiver.—*Ibid*.

PEPPERMINT WATER.—Take Peppermint six handfuls, cut it a little, and infuse it two Days in six quarts of clean Spirit ; then draw it off in a cold Still, marking every Bottle, as it fills, with a number, for the first Bottle will be far the strongest, the second less strong, and the third weaker than the second ; and so as we draw off more, they will be still weaker till at last it becomes almost insipid, and somewhat sourish, but take none of that ; then cover the mouth of your Bottles with Papers prick'd full of Holes, and let them stand a Day or two ; then pour your first Bottle into a large earthen glaz'd Pan ; and to that the second, and then the third, and the fourth, and so on, till by mixing they all become of a sufficient strength ; then put them in Bottles with a knob or two of double refin'd Loaf-Sugar, and cork them close. This is an incomparable pleasant Dram, tasting like Ice, or Snow in the mouth, but creates a fine warmth in the stomach, and yields a most refreshing flavour.

This sort of Mint is hard to be met with ; but is lately cultivated in some Physick Gardens at Mitcham ; it must be kept well weeded, and the Top of the bed where it grows must, when we cut it, be pricked up a little, with a small Fork, or the earth made fine with a Trowel, because the Runners of this sort of Mint shoot along the surface of the ground, and so at the joints strike root, which is contrary to other sorts of Mint, which shoot their Runners under ground.—R. Bradley, *The Country Housewife's and Lady's Director*, 1732.

PEPPERMINT TEA.—Half a pint of boiling water poured on a large handful of the leaves. An old remedy for colds and indigestion.

MINT BUTTER.—A handful of mint leaves and a handful of parsley. Boil slowly for 5 minutes in as small a quantity of water as possible. Drain and rub the pulp through a sieve. Work it into 4 ozs. of butter until smooth. Add pepper or cayenne pepper.

MINT PASTY.—Equal quantities of brown sugar, currants and chopped mint. Use as a filling in a turnover instead of apple. This old-fashioned pasty is still very popular in Yorkshire.

MUGWORT

" Eldest of worts
    Thou hast might for three
    And against thirty.
    For venom availest
    For flying vile things,
    Mighty gainst loathed ones
    That through the land rove."

Saxon MS. Herbal (Harleian), 1585.

" If they would drink nettles in March
    And eat mugwort in May,
So many fine maidens
    Wouldn't go to the clay."

Old Proverb.

" Yf this herbe be within a house there shall no wycked spyryte abyde."—*The Grete Herball,* 1539.

" If a Footman take mugwort and put it into his shoes in the morning, he may goe forty miles before Noon and not be weary."—WILLIAM COLES, *The Art of Simpling,* 1656.

In Italy the peasants still use mugwort to know if a
sick person will recover. They put it under his pillow
without telling him, and if he goes to sleep it means he
will recover. If he lies awake it is a sure sign he will
die. Nearly everywhere on the Continent mugwort is
called the herb of St. John the Baptist. Lupton, in
his *Notable Things*, relates this superstition. " It is
commonly affirmed that on midsummer eve, there is
found under the root of mugwort a cold which keeps
safe from the Plague, carbuncle, lightning, and the
quartan ague, them that bear the same about them,
and Mizaldus, the writer hereof, saith that it is to be
found the same day under the root of Plaintain, which
I know for a truth, for I have found them the same day
under the root of Plaintain, which is especially and
chiefly to be found at noon." The following is an old
Russian legend about mugwort : In the district of
Starodubsk, on the day of the exaltation of the Cross,
a young girl was searching for mushrooms in a forest,
when she saw a number of serpents curled up. She
endeavoured to retrace her steps, but fell into a deep
pit, which was the abode of the serpents. The pit
was dark, but at the bottom she found a luminous
stone ; the serpents were hungry ; the queen of the
golden-horned serpents guided them to the luminous
stone, and the serpents licked it, and satisfied their
hunger ; the young girl did the same, and remained
in the pit till the Spring. On the arrival of Spring,
the serpents interlaced themselves in such a manner
as to form a ladder on which the young girl ascended
to the mouth of the pit. But in taking her leave of
the queen of the serpents, she received, as a parting
gift, the power of understanding the language of plants,

and of knowing their medicinal properties, on the condition that she should never name the Mugwort, or Tchornobil (that which was black) ; if she pronounced that word, she would forget all that she had come to know. The damsel soon understood all that the plants talked about ; but one day, a man suddenly asked her, " What is the plant which grows in the fields by the side of the little footpaths ? " Taken by surprise, the girl replied, " Tchornobil " ; and at the same moment all her knowledge forsook her. From that time, it is said, the Mugwort obtained the additional name of Zabytko, or the Herb of Forgetfulness. Sir John Hill says of this herb : " The leaves and tops of the young shoots and flowers in this plant are all full of virtue, they are aromatic to the taste with a little sharpness. The herb has been famous from the earliest time, and Providence has placed it everywhere about our doors so that reason, and authority, as well as the notice of our senses, point it out for use, but chemistry has banished natural medicines."

Mugwort Tea.—One pint of boiling water poured on to an ounce of the flowering tops.

MULLEIN

" It is a plant whereof is made a manner of lynke (torch) if it be tallowed."—Gerard, *The Grete Herball*, 1597.

Even when fading mulleins are picturesque, with the " torches " still alight at the tip, the seeds ripening at the base and the flannel-like leaves fretted and tattered by the mullein moth caterpillars, which have just left them to turn to pupæ in the soil.

In the Irish papers one frequently sees advertisements for the mullein leaves, in whose healing properties, especially for chest complaint, the peasants have the utmost faith, but in England it is a much neglected herb. Gerard tells us the old story of Circe using mullein in her incantations, and formerly the plant was often called " Hag-taper."

The Romans used to dip the stalks in suet and burn them as torches, and it is said this was also done in England. The Romans valued mullein highly for chest troubles, and they are supposed to have taught the English the use of it.

MULLEIN MILK.—Boil a handful of the leaves in a pint of milk for ten minutes, then strain and drink hot.

MUSTARD

" Our ancient forefathers, even the better sort, were not sparing in the use thereof . . . but nowadays it is seldom used by the successors, being accounted the clownes sauce, and therefore not fit for their tables."—JOHN PARKINSON, *Theatrum Botanicum*, 1640.

It was formerly the custom to make up mustard into balls with honey or vinegar, and in Italy powdered dried lemon or orange peel was added. It was a Mrs. Clements of Durham who, in the eighteenth century, invented the modern way of making up mustard flour like wheat flour—and thereby made a fortune

NASTURTIUM

One does not think of nasturtiums as a herb, but they are included in old gardening lists as such. Some people make use of the young leaves in salad, but for some unknown reason we have abandoned the custom of adding the flowers to our salads. They taste very much like the leaves, only a little more delicate, and there is always a little drop of honey in them. Pickled in vinegar the seeds make a good substitute for capers.

To pickle Nerstusan Seeds and Flowers gather the buds whilst they are greene with the Stalkes an Inch long.

Take a quart of Clarret and a quart of white wine Vinegar and Som cloves and mace if you please a prity deale of Salt and make it boyle and then take it of and let it Stand till it be cold and put the flowers and the buds into an Earthen pott and Power the pickle upon them and Stop it with a cork and cover it with a lether and keep them for your use.—*MS. Book of Receipts* by Thomas Newington, 1719.

To Pickle Nasturtium Seeds.—Gather your little knobs quickly after your blossoms are off ; put them in cold water and salt for three days, shifting them once a day ; then make a pickle (but do not boil it at all) of some white wine, exchallot, horse-radish, pepper, salt, cloves, and mace whole and nutmeg quartered ; then put in your seeds and stop them close ; they are to be eaten as capers.—E. Smith, *The Complete House-wife*, 1736.

NETTLES

" He that holdeth this herbe in hys hand with an herbe called
Mylfoyle, or noseblede, is sure from all feare and fantasye or vysion
and yf it be put with the juyce of houselyke, and the bearers hande
be anoynted with it, and the residue be put in water if he enter in
ye water where fyshes be, they will gather together to hys handes.
And yf hys hande be drawen forth they will leape agayne to theyr
owne places where they were before."—*The Boke of the Secrets of
Albertus Magnus.*

" The flower of the dead nettle is like a weasell's face."—
W. COLES, *The Art of Simpling.*

One of the varieties of nettle (*urtica pilulifera*) is said
to have been introduced into England by the Roman
soldiers who brought the seed of it with them. The
tradition is that they were told the climate of England
was so terrible that it was scarcely endurable, so they
sowed these seeds in order to have a plentiful supply
of nettles wherewith to rub their bodies and so to keep
them warm. In mediæval flower symbolism the nettle
stands for envy. In Scandinavian mythology nettles
are sacred to Thor, and to this day in the Tyrol
peasants throw nettles on to the fire during a thunder-
storm to prevent the house being struck by lightning.
Nettles afford nourishment to a large number of in-
sects. It is the only food of the caterpillars of three
of our most beautiful butterflies—the Atalanta, Paphia
and Urticæ, and the principal food of a fourth, Iö.
Whipping with nettles was formerly strongly recommended for rheumatism. The bags of " poison "
which set up irritation can be seen with the naked eye
at the bottom of the prickles on the stalk of a full-
grown nettle. Nettles are one of the most valuable of
our neglected herbs, for they contain such health-

giving salts. Boiled as spinach they afford excellent green food during the early spring when green vegetables are scarce in the garden. Their value as a green food is well known to poultry fanciers. One of the best-known exhibitors in England has such a high opinion of the value of nettles that for the prize stock large quantities of nettles are dried in order that the birds may be supplied with them during the winter months. To make it palatable to the fowls the boiling water is poured on to the nettles, and meal is added to make it into a mash. Nettles are good for poultry at any time, but they are only good for human consumption during the early spring months. They should never be eaten when they have gone to seed.

NETTLE TEA.—One quart of boiling water poured on to five large handfuls of the young tops and left to infuse for several hours.

NETTLE SPINACH.—Boil the young nettle tops in as little water as possible, and when sufficiently cooked rub through a sieve. Add butter, salt and pepper.

PARSLEY

" If you will have the leaves of the parcelye grow crisped, then before the sowing of them stuffe a tennis ball with the sedes and beat the same well against the ground whereby the seedes may be a little bruised or when the parcelye is well come up go over the bed with a waighty roller whereby it may so presse the leaves down or else tread the same downe under thy feet."—*The Grete Herball*, 1539.

Hercules is said to have selected parsley to form the first garlands he wore. The Greeks had a great venera-

tion for parsley, and of it the victor's crown was made
at the Isthmian games ; and Grecian gardens were
often bordered with parsley, and rue, and sprigs of
this herb were strewn on the dead. Canon Ellacombe
says that parsley has the curious botanic history that
no one can tell what is its native country. " Probably
the plant has been so altered by cultivation as to have
lost all likeness to its original self." It is said that
Charlemagne having once tasted a cheese flavoured
with parsley seeds, ordered two cases of these cheeses
to be sent to him yearly.

Thomas Hyll gives the amateur gardener this advice :
" To make the seedes appear more quickly steep them
in vinegar and strew the bed with the ashes of bean-
water with the best *aqua vitæ*, and then cover the beds
with a piece of woolen cloth, and the plants will begin
to appear in an hour." Then he adds : " he must
take off the cloth so that they may shoot up the higher
to the wonder of all beholders ! "

In the southern states of America the negroes consider it unlucky to transplant parsley from the old
home to the new, and in England old-fashioned gardeners will often tell you they never transplant parsley,
as it would bring misfortune on every one in the house.
It is said that parsley seed goes seven times to the Devil
and back before it germinates, and that is why it is so
slow in coming up !

Formerly parsley roots were much eaten, and the
young roots are still recommended by modern herbalists.

A Sauce for a rosted Rabbit used to King
Henry the Eight.—Take a handfull of washed

Percely, mince it small, boyle it with butter and verjuice upon a chafing-dish, season it with suger and a little pepper grosse beaten ; when it is ready put in a fewe crummes of white bread amongst the other : let it boyle againe till it be thicke, then laye it in a platter, like the breadth of three fingers, laye of each side one rosted conny and so serve them.—*The Treasurie of Hidden Secrets and Commodious Conceits*, by John Partridge, 1586.

PLANTAIN

" And thou waybroad (plantain)
  Mother of worts
  Open from eastward
    Mighty within ;
Over thee carts creaked
    Over thee queens rode
    Over thee brides bridalled
    Over thee bulls breathed.
All these thou withstoodst
And with stound stayedst
As thou withstoodst
    Venom and vile things
And all the loathly ones
    That through the land rove."

Saxon MS. Herbal.

The plantain is said to have been once a maiden who, after constantly watching the roadway for her lover, was changed into this plant which still clings to the roadside. It has frequently been pointed out that wherever the English flag is carried the plantain in an incredibly short time makes its appearance, so it merits a place in the herb garden quite apart from its virtues. From the days of our Saxon ancestors, who called it "way broade" (a much more appropriate name than plantain), it has always been highly valued. A tea made from its leaves is excellent, and both Chaucer and Shakespeare refer to its use for healing wounds. The young leaves were formerly used in salad, and the seeds, being very mucilaginous, are a good substitute for linseed. Canaries are very fond of plantain seed.

PLANTAIN TEA.—One quart of boiling water poured on to two large handfuls of the young leaves and left to infuse several hours.

TO REMEDY THE FEETE THAT ARE SORE WITH TRAVELLING.—Take Plantaine and stampe it well, and anoynt your feete with the juice thereof and the greefe will swage.—*The Good Housewife's Handmaid*, 1588.

PURSLANE

"Lord, I confess too when I dine
The pulse is thine—
And all those other bits that be
There placed by Thee.
The worts, the purselain, and the mess
Of Water Cress."
HERRICK.

Purslane, which we so seldom use now even in salads, was formerly recommended for a vast number of diseases, including teeth set on edge, " flashings by lightening or planets, and for burning of gunpowder ! "

Purslanes like a light, rich soil, and as they are tender annuals, they must be sown either on a hot-bed or in the open ground in May. They should not be transplanted. The leaves are generally ready to be gathered six weeks after planting the seeds. Green purslane is hardier than golden purslane.

PRESERVED PURSLANE.—This for a dainty dish, with many served first at the table in the winter time, preserved after this manner, the greatest stemmes and leaves of the Purslane without rootes were gathered and these wyth water thoroughly cleansed from the fyne sands, hanging on and the filthe and corrupt leaves, if any such were, clean purged away, and these so long they dryed until they were somewhat withered. Then were they infused in verjuice made of soure grapes strewed thicke over wyth green fennell bestowed in an earthen pot glasd within or for the lacke of it in a sweete vessel of woode, after this the whole sprinkled well over wyth salte, laying green fennell again over the salte, and sundry courses of Purslane, with salt and fennell bestowed to the filling up of the pot and over the upper bed of the Purslane againe a thicke course of greene fennell strewed, whiche settled the whole mixture downe into the pot. This being done, the verjuice was poured upon in such order so full that the same reached uppe to the brimme or lippe of the vessell. The same pickle or sauce close covered with a lid was set up again in a dry place to be preserved far from the beames of the Sun coming ; when they served it at the table they cleansed it with sweet wine, pouring sweet oyle on the purslane. They set it as a first dish on the table to procure an appetite afore the guests sette downe to meate.—Thomas Hyll, *The Gardener's Labyrinth*, 1577.

PICKLED PURSLANE.—Lay the stalks in an earthen pan ; then cover them with Beer Vinegar and water, keeping them down with a competent weight to imbibe three days. Being taken out put them into a pot with as much white-wine vinegar as will cover them again and close the Lid with paste (made with flour and water) to keep in the steam ; then set them on the Fire for three or four hours, often shaking and stirring them. Then open the Cover and turn, and remove those stalks which be at the Bottom to the Top and boil them as before till they are all of a colour. When all is cold pot them with fresh white-wine vinegar, and so you may preserve them the whole year round.— John Evelyn, *Acetaria*, 1699.

To PICKLE PURSLANE.—Put your Purslane stalks into as much wine as water, with a little salt. Then boil it, put it into a Pot, and pour in as much white-wine vinegar as will cover it ; if you please you may add sugar to your white wine.—From *The Receipt Book of John Nott*, Cook to the Duke of Bolton, 1723.

To MAKE SALLET OF PURSLANE.—Take it when it is young, and pick it very well, and wash it, and swing it, and then lay it upon a Plate garnished with the slices of Lemon, or with all sorts of herbs at your own discretion.—*Ibid.*

A SALLET OF LETTICE AND PURSLAN.—Take of the newest Purslan, pick and wash it very well, swing it out, and lay it in the round of the Plate, and Lettice round about it, garnish the brims with Charvile and Flowers hashed together of divers colours, very small. —*A Perfect School of Instructions for the Officers of the Month*, by Giles Rose, one of the Master Cooks to Charles II, 1682.

A PURSLANE SOUP.—When your Purslane is young, you need only cut the spriggs off, but keep their whole length, boil them in a small kettle, with some Pease-soup and Onion Juice, both of the same quantity, when your Purselane is boiled enough, soak some crusts in some Broth ; when soaked, dish it, garnish it with the said Purslane, let the Broth be relishing, pour it over, and serve it up hot.—*The Modern Cook*, by Vincent La Chapelle, Cook to the Prince of Orange, 1744.

RAMPION

John Evelyn recommends the tender roots of rampion, eaten in spring, as being more nourishing than radishes ; and Parkinson says that the roots may be eaten " either raw or boyled and stewed with butter and oyle and some black or long pepper cast on them." Major Kenny Herbert recommends rampion leaves prepared like spinach. Unfortunately if one wishes to eat the roots, the plants must not be allowed to flower, and it is so beautiful that this seems a foolish sacrifice. Distilled water of rampion was highly esteemed as a complexion beautifier.

If the roots are wanted, rampion should not be sown before the end of May. They like a light soil and a shady border, and they do not bear transplanting unless very carefully done. The roots are fit for use in November.

ROCKET

" Whosoever taketh the seed of Rocket before he be whipt, shall be so hardened that he shall easily endure the paines."—JOHN GERARD, *The Herball*, 1597.

Galen forbade the eating of lettuce without purslane, or lettuce without rocket, or rocket without purslane or lettuce. Formerly one of the rockets was in common use as a salad herb, but few of the old herbalists have much to say in its favour. Turner recommends the seed as being efficacious " against the bitings of the shrew-mouse and other venemous beasts." Folkard tells us that the London Rocket first appeared in the metropolis in the spring succeeding the Great Fire of London, when young rockets were seen everywhere among the ruins, where they increased so marvellously that in the summer the enormous crop crowding over the surface of London " created the greatest astonishment and wonder."

ROSE

"Let us crown ourselves with Roses before they be withered."
—*Wisdom*, II. i.

"Dry roses put to the nose to smell do comfort the brayne and the herte and quickeneth the spyryte."—R. BANCKES, *A little Herball*, 1525.

"Of their sweet death are sweetest odours made."—SHAKESPEARE.

"Rose ! Thou art the fondest child
Of dimpled spring the wood nymph wild."

THOMAS MOORE.

Our ancestors prized the rose above all for its sweet scent, and in spite of the magnificence of our modern roses, the old-fashioned housewife would have had none of them in her garden. For rose-water she needed the cabbage and damask roses, and these, with musk and Provence roses and sweet-briar, are the only roses for a herb garden. England's association with the rose is of very ancient date, for did not Pliny doubt whether the country was called Albion from the white cliffs, or the white roses which grew here in such glorious abundance ? Like gillyflowers, another favourite with our ancestors of the Middle Ages, roses were often accepted as quit rent. In 1576 the Bishop of Ely granted to Sir Christopher Hatton the greater portion of Ely House, Holborn, on condition that the latter paid yearly a red rose, and the Bishop had also the right of free access to the garden with the privilege of gathering twenty bushels of roses every year. The *Baillée des Roses* existed in France till the end of the sixteenth century. It consisted of a tribute of roses

which had to be given by the peers of France to the
Parlement. Each Peer in turn had to see that the
rooms of the palace were strewed with roses, flowers
and sweet herbs. As he went through the rooms a
large silver bowl was carried before him, and in it were
crowns of roses for every member of the Parlement.
Parkinson says that the double yellow rose was " first
procured to be brought into England by Master
Nicholas Lete, a worthy merchant of London and a
great lover of flowers, from Constantinople, which
(as we heare) was first brought thither from Syria ;
but perished quickly both with him and with all other
to whom it imparted it ; yet afterwards it was sent to
Master John de Franqueille, a Merchant also of
London, and a great lover of all rare plants, as well as
flowers, from which is sprung the greatest store that is
now flourishing in this kingdom." Sir John Hill tells
us that nothing equals the sweetness of the true
Provence rose, which were " so esteemed in the Indies
that sometimes they will sell for their weight in gold."
He speaks also of the honey of roses made by boiling
honey and the fresh juice of Provence roses together.
In our great-grandmothers' time they used to put
fragrant damask rose-petals into a cherry pie before
putting on the crust, and in the earlier days rose-water
was used to flavour cakes. I have given one receipt
for a cake so flavoured. See " To bake a cake after
the way of the Royal Princess, the Lady Elizabeth,
daughter to King Charles the First."

To make Sirop of Roses or Violets.—Take of
violets or roses a pounde, steepe them in three pints
of warme water, put it in an earthen pot with a narrow

mouth the space of seven houres or more, after, straine it, and warme the water againe, and put in againe so many Roses or Violets, and likewise let them lye in steepe eight houres, and thus do at the least five times, the oftener the better, in especiall the roses, and after take to every pint a pounde of sugar and steepe them together, till the sugar be molten, then seethe them together with a soft sweet fire to the height of a Sirrup : if you have more Roses or Violets, or fewer, and let so much be the proportion of the water, according to the proportion before.—*The Good Housewife's Handmaid*, 1585.

DAMASK ROSE SYRUP.—Pour boiling water on a quantity of Damask roses just enough to cover them. Let them stand four-and-twenty hours. Then press off the liquor and add to it twice the quantity of sugar. Melt this, and the syrup is completed.—T. Tryon, *A Treatise of Cleanness in Meates*, 1692.

HONEY OF ROSES.—Cut the white heels from Red Roses, take half a pound of them and put them into a stone jar, and pour on them three pints of boiling water. Stir well and let them stand twelve hours. Then press off the liquor, and when it has settled add to it five pounds of honey. Boil it well, and when it is of the consistence of a thick syrup it is ready to put away.—*Ibid.*

TO MAKE VINEGAR OF ROSES.—In summer time when roses blowe, gather them, ere they be full spred or blowne out, and in drie weather, pluck the leaves, let

them lie half a day upon a faire borde, then have a
vessel with vinegar of one or two gallons (if you will
make so much Roset), put therein a great quantitie of
ye said leaves, stop the vessell close after you have
styrred them wel together, let it stand a day and a night,
then divide your Vinegar and Rose leaves together in
two parts, put them in two great glasses, set them upon
a shelfe under a wall side, on the south side without
your house, where the sunne maye come to them the
most part of the day, let them stand there all the
whole summer long ; and then strain the Vinegar
from the Roses and keep the Vinegar. If you do
once in ten days take and straine out the rose leaves
and put in new leaves of half a dayes gathering the
Vinegar will have the more favour and odour of
the Rose.

You may use in steade of Vinegar wine that it may
wax egre and receive the virtue of the Roses, both at
once.   Moreover you make your Vinegar of wine,
white, red or claret.   This is Vinegar Roset.—John
Partridge, *The Treasurie of Hidden Secrets and Commodious Conceits*, 1586.

To make Conserve of Roses or other Flowers.—
Take the buds of Red Roses, somewhat before they
be ready to spread ; cut the red part of the leaves from
the white, then take the red leaves and beat and grind
them in a stone morter, with a pestle of wood, and to
every ounce of roses put in three ounces of sugar in
the grinding after the leaves are well beaten, and grind
them together till they be perfectly incorporated, then
put in a glass made for the nonce, or of purpose ; or
else into an Earthen pot, stop it close and so keep it.

Thus yee may make conserves of all kinde of flowers used thereunto.—*Ibid.*

To MAKE OYLE OF ROSES.—Take of oyle eighteen ounces, the buds of Roses (the white ends of them cut away) three ounces, lay the Roses abroad in the shadow four and twenty houres, then put them in a glass to the oyle, and stop the glass close ; and set it in the sunne at least forty dayes.—*Ibid.*

To MAKE OYNTMENT OF ROSES.—Take oyle of Roses four ounces, white wax one ounce, melt them together over seething water, then chafe them together with Rose-water and a little white vinegar.—*Ibid.*

ROSES AND GILLYFLOWERS KEPT LONG.—Cover a Rose that is fresh, and in the bud, and gathered in a faire day after the dew is ascended, with the whites of eggs well beaten, and presently strew thereon the fine powder of searced sugar, and put them up in luted pots, setting the pots in a coole place in sand or gravell : with a fillip at any time you may shake off this inclosure. —Sir Hugh Platt, *Delights for Ladies*, 1594.

HOW TO DRY ROSE LEAVES, OR ANY OTHER SINGLE FLOWERS WITHOUT WRINKLING.—If you would performe the same wel in rose leaves, you must in rose time make choice of such roses as are neither in the bud, nor full blowne (for these have the smoothest leaves of all other), which you must especially cull and chuse from the rest ; then take sand, wash it in some change of waters, and drie it thoroughly well, either in

an oven, or in the sunne; and having shallow, square
or long boxes of four, five or six inches deepe, make
first an even lay of sand in the bottom, upon which lay
your rose leaves, one by one (so as none of them
touch other) till you have covered all the sand, then
strowe sand upon those leaves, till you have thinly
covered them all, and then make another laie of leaves
as before, and so lay upon lay, etc. Set this box in
some warme place in a hot, sunny day (and commonly
in two hot sunny dayes they will bee thorow dry), then
take them out carefully with your hand without breaking. Keepe these leaves in Jarre glasses, bound about,
with paper, neere a chimney, or stove, for feare of
relenting. I finde the red Rose leafe best to be kept
in this manner; also take away the stalkes of pansies,
stock gillyflowers, or other single flowers; pricke them
one by one in sand, pressing downe theire leaves smooth
with more sand laid evenly upon them. And thus
you may have Rose leaves, and other flowers to lay
about your basons, windows, etc., all the winter
long. Also this secret is very requisite for a good
simplifier, because hee may dry the leaf of any herb
in this manner; and lay it, being dry, in his herbal
with the simple which it representeth, whereby he
may easily learne to know the names of all simples
which he desireth.—*Ibid.*

How to dry Rose Leaves in a most excellent
manner.—When you have newly taken out your bread,
then put in your Roses in a sieve, first clipping away
the whites that they may be all of one colour, lay them
about one inch in thickness in the sieve; and when
they have stood halfe an houre, or thereabout, they

will grow whitish on the top : let them yet remaine
without stirring, till the uppermost of them bee fully
dried : then stirre them together, and leave them
about one other halfe houre : and if you finde them
dry in the top, stirre them together againe, and so
continue this worke, until they bee thorowly dried :
then put them hot as they are into an earthen pot
having a narrow mouth, and being well leaded within
(the Refiners of gold and silver call these pots Hookers) :
stop it with corke and wet parchment, or with wax and
rosin mixed together ; and hang your pot in a chimney,
or near a continuall fire, and so they will keepe exceeding faire in colour, and most delicate in sent. And
if you feare their relenting, take the Rose leaves
about Candelmas, and put them once againe into
a sieve, stirring them up and downe often till
they be dry: and then put them againe hot into
your pot.—*Ibid.*

A SINGULAR MANNER OF MAKING THE SIRUP OF ROSES.
—Fill a silver Bason three-quarters full of rain-water
or Rose-water, put therein a convenient proportion of
Rose leaves ; cover the bason, and set it upon a pot
of hot water (as we usually bake a custard) : in three-
quarters of an houre, or one whole houre at the most,
you shall purchase the whole strength and tincture of
the Rose : then take out those leaves, wringing out all
their liquor gently, and steepe more fresh leaves in
the same water : continue this iteration seven times,
and then make it up in a sirup : and this sirup worketh
more kindely than that which is made meerly of the
juice of the Rose. You may make sundry other sirups
in this manner.—*Ibid.*

ANOTHER WAY FOR THE DRYING OF ROSE LEAVES.—
Dry them in the heat of a hott sunny day upon a Lead,
turning them up and downe till they be dry (as they
do hay) : then put them up into glasses well stopt
and luted, keeping your glasses in warme places ; and
thus you may keepe all flowers : but herbs, after they
are dried in this manner, are best kept in paper bags,
placing the bags in close cupboards.—*Ibid.*

HOW TO PRESERVE WHOLE ROSES, GILLYFLOWERS,
MARIGOLDS, ETC.—Dip a Rose that is neither in the
bud, nor overblowne, in a sirup, consisting of sugar,
double refined, and Rose-water boyled to his full
height, then open the leaves one by one with a fine
smooth bodkin either of bone or wood ; and presently
if it be a hot sunny day, and whilest the sunne is in some
good height, lay them on papers in the sunne, or else
dry them with some gentle heat in a close roome,
heating the room before you set them in or in an oven
upon papers, in pewter dishes, and then put them up
in glasses ; and keepe them in dry cupboards neere
the fire : you must take out the seeds, if you meene
to eat them. You may proove this preserving with
sugar-candy instead of sugar if you please.—*Ibid.*

ROSE-WATER AND ROSE-VINEGAR OF THE COLOUR OF
THE ROSE, AND OF THE COWSLIP, AND VIOLET VINEGAR.
—If you would make your Rose-water and Rose-
vinegar, of a Rubie colour, then make choyce of the
crimson-velvet coloured leaves, clipping away the
whites with a paire of sheers : and being thorow dryed,
put a good large handfull of them into a pint of Damask

or red Rose-water : stop your glasse well, and set it
in the sunne, till you see that the leaves have lost their
colour : or, for more expedition you may performe
this worke *in balneo* in a few hours ; and when you take
out the old leaves you may put in fresh, till you finde
the colour to please you. Keepe this Rose-water in
the glasses very well stopt ; the fuller the better.
What I have said of Rose-water, the same may also
be intended of Rose-vinegar, violet, marigold and
cowslip vinegar : but the whiter vinegar you chuse for
this purpose, the colour thereof will bee the brighter :
and therefore distilled vinegar is best for this purpose.—
Ibid.

To make Sugar of Roses.—Take the deepest-
coloured red Roses, pick them, cut off the white buttons
and dry your red leaves in an oven, till they be as dry
as possible, then beat them to powder, and searse
them, then take a halfe pound of sugar beaten fine,
put it into your pan with as much fair water as will
wet it, then set it in a chafing dish of coals and let it
boyle till it be sugar again ; then put as much powder
of the Roses as will make it look very red, stir them
well together, and when it is almost cold, put it into
pales, and when it is thoroughly cold, take them off,
and put them in boxes.—*Ibid.*

To make Lozinges of red Roses.—Boyle your sugar
to sugar again, then put in your red Roses, being finely
beaten and made moist with the juyce of a Lemon ;
let it not boyle after the Roses are in, but pour it upon
a Pye plate and cut it in what form you please.—*Ibid.*

OF SUNDRY HERBS

To MAKE A TART OF HIPS.—Take hips, cut t
take out the seeds very clean, then wash tl
season them with sugar, cinnamon and ging
the tart, bake it, scrape on sugar and serve it in.—*The
Art and Mystery of Cookery Approved by the Fifty-five
Years' Experience and Industry of Robert May*, 1671.

To CANDY ROSE LEAVES AS NATURAL AS IF THEY GROW
ON TREES.—Take of your fairest Rose leaves, Red or
Damask, and on a sunshine day sprinkle them with
Rose-water, lay them on one by one on a fair paper,
then take some double refined sugar beaten very fine,
put it in a fine lawne searse when you have laid abroad
all the rose leaves in the hottest of the sun, searse sugar
thinly all over them and anon the sun will candie the
sugar ; then turn the leaves and searse sugar on the
other side, and turn them often in the sun, sometimes
sprinkling Rose-water and sometimes searsing sugar
on them, until they be enough, and come to your liking,
and, being thus done, you may keep them.—William
Rabisha, *The Whole Body of Cookery Dissected*, 1675.

MUSK ROSE-WATER.—Take two handfuls of your
Musk Rose-leaves, put them into about a quart of
fair water and a quarter of a pound of sugar and finish
this as you did your Jeseme water. (See Jasmine water
in Chapter X).—*Ibid.*

CONSERVE OF RED ROSES.—Doctor Glisson makes
his conserve of red roses thus : Boil gently a pound of
red Rose-leaves in about a pint and a halfe (or a little
more, as by discretion you shall find fit, after having

done it once; *The Doctor's Apothecary* takes two
pints) of Spring water; till the water have drawn out
all the Tincture of the Roses into it self and that the
leaves be very tender, and looke pale like Linnen;
which may be in good half hour, or an hour, keeping
the pot covered while it boileth. Then pour the
tincted Liquor from the pale leaves, strain it out,
pressing it gently, so that you may have Liquor enough
to dissolve your sugar, and set it upon the fire by it self
to boil, putting into it a pound of pure double-refined
sugar in small powder; which as soon as it is dissolved
put in a second pound; then a third, lastly a fourth,
so that you have four pounds of sugar to every pound
of Rose leaves (the Apothecary useth to put all the
four pounds into the Liquor together at once). Boil
these four pounds of sugar with the tincted Liquor,
till it be a high syrup, very near a candy height (as
high as it can be, not to flake or candy). Then put the
pale rose-leaves into this high syrup as it yet standeth
upon the fire, or immediately upon the taking it off
the fire. But presently take it from the fire, and stir
them exceeding well together to mix them uniformly;
then let them stand till they be cold, then pot them
up. If you put up your Conserve into pots, while
it is yet thoroughly warm, and leave them uncovered
some days, putting them in the hot sun or stove,
there will grow a fine candy upon the top which will
preserve the conserve with paper upon it, from
moulding till you break the candied crust, to take out
some of the conserve.

The colour both of the Rose leaves and the syrup
about them, will be exceeding beautiful and red, and
the taste excellent; and the whole very tender and

smoothing, and easie to digest in the stomack without clogging it, as doth the ordinary rough conserve made of raw Roses beaten with sugar, which is very rough in the throat.—*The Closet of Sir Kenelm Digby Opened*, 1669.

To MAKE WAFERS.—Put the yolks of four eggs, and three Spoonfuls of Rose-water, to a quart of flour ; mingle them well, make them into a Batter with cream and double-refined sugar, pour it on very thin, and bake it on Irons.—From *The Receipt Book of John Nott*, Cook to the Duke of Bolton, 1723.

To MAKE CONSERVE OF RED ROSES.—Let your Roses be gather'd before they are quite blown, pound them in a stone-mortar, and add to them twice their weight in double-refined sugar, and put them into a glass close stopt up, but do not fill it full. Let them stand three months before you use them, remembring to stir them once a Day.—*Ibid.*

To DRY OR KEEP ROSES.—Take the Buds of Damask Roses before they are fully blown, pull the leaves and lay them on Boards, in a Room where the Heat of the Sun may not come at them ; when they are pretty dry, let a large Still be made warm, and lay them on the Top of it till they are crisp ; but let them not lie so long as to change their Colour. Then spread them thin ; and when they are thoroughly dry'd, press them down into a Earthen Pan, and keep close cover'd.—*Ibid.*

To MAKE CONSERVE OF ROSE HIPS.—Gather the hips before they grow soft, cut off the heads and stalks, slit them in halves, and take out all the seeds and white that is in them very clean ; then put in an earthern pan, and stir them every day else they will grow mouldy ; let them stand till they are soft enough to rub through a coarse hair sieve ; as the pulp comes take it off the sieve ; they are a dry berry, and will require pains to rub it through ; then add its weight in sugar, and mix it well together without boiling ; keeping it in deep gallipots for use.—E. Smith, *The Complete Housewife*, 1736.

To MAKE ROSE-DROPS.—The roses and sugar must be beat separately into a very fine powder, and both sifted ; to a pound of sugar an ounce of red roses, they must be mixed together, and then wet with as much juice of Lemon as will make it into a stiff paste ; set it on a slow fire in a silver porringer, and stir it well, and when it is scalding hot quite through take it off and drop in small portions on a paper ; set them near the fire, the next day they will come off.—*Ibid*.

To MAKE ROSSOLY THE ITALIAN WAY.—Gather fresh Damask Roses, Orange Flowers, Jessamy Flowers, Cloves and Gillyflowers ; pick them clean, set on some Water to boil, when it has boiled well let it stand to cool a little ; put these clean Flowers into a China Bason, pour the Water upon them when it is not hotter than to bear the finger in it ; then cover it up, and let it stand Three Hours, gently pour all into a fine Linen Bag, and let the Water run off without squeezing the

Flowers ; to a Pint of this Water, add a Quart of fine Melasses Spirit, and half a Pint of strong cinnamon water : add three teaspoons of Essence of Amber-grease, and stir all well together. This is the true Rossoly.—From *The Receipt Book of Elizabeth Cleland*, 1759.

SAUCE EGLANTINE (from Briar Rose) served frequently at Balmoral in Queen Victoria's time.

Made from the hips, the seeds being first removed and a sweet *purée* made of the red berries in pulp with a little Lemon-juice added.

MARMALADE FROM ROSE-HIPS.—To every pound of hips allow half a pint of water ; boil till the fruit is tender, then pass the pulp through a sieve which will keep back the seeds. To each pound of pulp add one pound of preserving sugar and boil until it Jellies.— E. G. Hayden, *Travels Round our Village*.

TO MAKE A CAKE WITH ROSE-WATER THE WAY OF THE ROYAL PRINCESS, THE LADY ELIZABETH, DAUGHTER TO KING CHARLES THE FIRST.—Take half a peck of Flowre, half a pinte of Rose-water, a pint of Ale yeast, a pint of Cream, boyl it, a pound and a half of Butter, six Eggs (leave out the whites), four pound of Currants, one half pound of sugar, one Nutmeg, and a little salt, work it very well and let it stand half an hour by the fire, and then work it again, and then make it up, and let it stand an hour and a halfe in the Oven ; let not your Oven be too hot.

ROSEMARY

" For the sickly take this wort rosemary, pound it with oil, smear the sickly one, wonderfully thou healest him."—*Saxon MS. Herbal.*

" The rosemary has all the virtues of the stone called Jet."—*The Physicians of Myddvai.*

" Make thee a box of the wood of rosemary and smell to it and it shall preserve thy youth."—BANCKES, *Herball*, 1525.

" As for rosemary I lette it runne all over my garden walls, not onlie because my bees love it, but because it is the herb sacred to remembrance and to friendship, whence a sprig of it hath a dumb language."—SIR THOMAS MOORE.

Of all fragrant herbs rosemary and lavender hold perhaps the foremost place, but of the former how little real use is made ! How many people know the taste of rosemary wine or rosemary cordial ? In the French language of flowers rosemary represents the power of rekindling lost energy, and in olden days it was held in the highest repute for its invigorating effects both as a scent and a cordial. The name rosemary means " dew of the sea," and the plant which grows naturally near the sea always has the smell of it. What is more beautiful in winter than its glistening grey-green foliage and delicious fragrance ? One rarely sees a large bunch of its graceful long stems as a decoration in a room, but what a joy it is when one does ! Formerly the aromatic scent of the plant was highly valued for its protective power against infection. It was carried at funerals, burnt in sick rooms, used in spells to ward off black magic, and for festival days in churches ; and

banqueting halls and ordinary living-rooms were
lavishly decorated with long boughs of it. An old
French name for rosemary is *incensier*, because it was
so often used instead of incense when the latter was
too costly. In the British Museum there is an interesting old MS. on the virtues of rosemary, which was
sent by the Countess of Hainault to her daughter,
Queen Philippa of England. In it one reads of rosemary, " it mighteth the boones and causeth goode and
gladeth and lighteth alle men that use it. The leves
layde under the heade whanne a man slepes, it doth
away evell spirites and suffereth not to dreeme fowle
dremes ne to be afeade. But he must be out of deedely
synne for it is an holy tree. Lavender and Rosemary
is as woman to man and White Roose to Reede. It is
an holy tree and with ffolke that been just and Right-
fulle gladlye it groweth and thryveth." In this MS.
there is recorded an old tradition I have never seen
elsewhere : that rosemary " passeth not commonly
in highte the highte of Criste whill he was man in
Erthe," and that when the plant attains thirty-three
years in age it will increase in breadth, but not in height.
Perhaps there was no time when rosemary was more
loved than in Tudor times. At every wedding branches
of gilded rosemary were given by the bridesmaids to
the bridegroom. A bunch of it was a pretty New Year
gift ; and sprigs were thrown " for remembrance "
into the grave by the dead persons' friends and rela-
tives. Hentzner mentions in his *Travels* (1598) that
in English gardens the walls were frequently covered
with rosemary, and at Hampton Court he says : " it
was so planted and nailed to the walls as to cover them
entirely." Gerard tells us " wild rosemary groweth

in Lancashire in divers places, especially in the fielde called Little Reede amongst the Hurtleberries near unto a small village called Mandslay, there found by a learned gentleman often remembered in our History (and that worthily), Master Thomas Hesketh." The double-flowered rosemary is mentioned by Parkinson in his *Paradisus*, but he adds that it is " more rare than all the other because few have heard thereof, much less seene it, and myself am not acquainted with it but am bold to deliver it upon credit. It hath stronger stalks, not so easie to breake, fairer, bigger, and larger leaves of a faire greene colour and the flowers as double as the Larkes heele or spurre. This I have only by relation which I pray you accept untill I may by sight better enforme you." He describes the wood of rosemary being used to make lutes " or such like instruments," and also carpenters' rules. Rosemary flowers are, as every one knows, one of the most exquisite shades of blue imaginable, and the Spaniards say that the flowers were white originally, but that ever since the Virgin Mary threw her robe over them they have preserved the memory of her having thus honoured them by turning the colour she wore. According to another tradition rosemary was one of the bushes near which she sheltered during the flight into Egypt, and the Spanish name of the plant *romero* (the pilgrim's flower) preserves this legend. Throughout Spain it is valued for its supposed power against magic, and Borrow in the *Bible in Spain* described an incident showing the widespread belief of the Spanish peasants in its protective power against the evil eye. It would be possible to fill a book with all the old herbalists have to say about rosemary, but I give only what one enthusiastic lover of this beautiful herb tells us of how it should be used.

" Take the flowers thereof and boyle them in fayre water and drinke that water for it is much worthe against all manner of evils in the body.

" Take the flowers thereof and make powder thereof and binde it to thy right arme in a linnen cloath and it shale make thee lighte and merrie.

" Take the flowers and put them in thy chest among thy clothes or among thy Bookes and Mothes shall not destroy them.

" Boyle the leaves in white wine and washe thy face therewith and thy browes and thou shalt have a faire face.

" Also put the leaves under thy bedde and thou shalt be delivered of all evill dreames.

" Take the leaves and put them into wine and it shall keepe the Wine from all sourness and evill savours and if thou wilt sell thy wine thou shalt have goode speede.

" Also if thou be feeble boyle the leaves in cleane water and washe thy self and thou shalt wax shiny.

" Also if thou have lost appetite of eating boyle well these leaves in cleane water and when the water is colde put thereunto as much of white wine and then makes sops, eat them thereof wel and thou shalt restore thy appetite againe.

" If thy legges be blowen with gowte boyle the leaves in water and binde them in a linnen cloath and winde it about thy legges and it shall do thee much good.

" If thou have a cough drink the water of the leaves boyled in white wine and ye shall be whole.

" Take the Timber thereof and turn it to Coales and make powder thereof and rubbe thy teeth thereof, and it shall keep thy teeth from all evils. Smell it oft and it shall keep thee youngly.

" Also if a man have lost his smelling of the ayre that he may not draw his breath, make a fire of the wood and bake his bread therewith, eate it and it shall keepe him well."

TO MAKE ROSEMARY WATER.—Take the rosemary and the flowers in the middest of May, before sunne arise, and strippe the leaves and the flowers from the stalke, take four of five elecampane roots and a handful or two of sage, then beate the rosemary, the sage and the rootes together, till they be very small, and take three ounces of cloves, three ounces of mace, one and a half pounds of aniseed and beat these spices every one by itself. Then take all the hearbes and spices and put therein foure or five gallons of good white wine, then put in all these hearbes and spices and wine into an earthen pot, and put the same pot in the ground the space of sixteen days, then take it up and still in a Still with a very soft fire.—*The Good Housewife's Jewell*, 1585.

HOW TO CANDY ROSEMARY-FLOWERS, ROSE-LEAVES, ROSES, MARIGOLDS, ETC., WITH PRESERVATION OF COLOUR.—Dissolve refined or double-refined sugar, or sugar candy itselfe, in a little Rose-water ; boile it to a reasonable height : put in your roots or flowers when your sirup is eyther fully cold, or almost cold : let them rest therein till the sirup have pierced them sufficiently : then take out your flowers with a skimmer, suffering the loose sirup to runne from them so long as it will : boile that sirup a little more, and put in more flowers, as before ; divide them also : then boile all the sirup which remaineth, and is not drunke up in the flowers, putting in more sugar if you see cause, but no more Rose-water, put your flowers therein when your sirup is cold, or almost cold and let them stand till they candy.—Sir Hugh Platt, *Delights for Ladies*, 1594.

To make Conserve of Rosemary Flowers.—Take two Pound of Rosemary-flowers, the same weight of fine Sugar, pownd them well in a Stone-Mortar ; then put the Conserve into well-glaz'd Gallipots. It will keep a Year or Two.—*Ibid.*

To make Rosemary Water.—Take a quarter of a Pound of Rosemary when it is at its Prime, Flowers and Leaves, a quarter of a Pound of Elecampane-root, half a handful of Red Sage, six Ounces of Anniseeds, and one Ounce and a half of Cloves ; beat the Herbs together, and the Spices each by themselves, put them to a gallon of White Wine ; and let them stand a Week to infuse, then distill them.—*Ibid.*

Hungary-Water.[1] From Mrs. Du Pont, of Lyons ; which is the same, which has been famous,

[1] In what was formerly the Imperial Library at Vienna there is still preserved the receipt for the famous " Hungary Water," which was invented for Queen Elizabeth of Hungary, who suffered from paralysis, and who is said to have been cured by being rubbed every day with it. Tradition says that a hermit gave the Queen this receipt.

ABOUT MONTPELIER.—Take to every gallon of Brandy, or clean Spirits, one handful of Rosemary, one handful of Lavender. I suppose the handfuls to be about a Foot long a-piece ; and these Herbs must be cut in Pieces about an Inch long. Put these to infuse in the Spirits, and with them, about one handful of Myrtle, cut as before. When this has stood three Days, distil it, and you will have the finest Hungary-Water that can be. It has been said the Rosemary-flowers are better than the Stalks ; but they give a faintness to the Water, and should not be used, because they have a quite different smell from the Rosemary, nor should the Flowers of Myrtle be used in lieu of the Myrtle, for they have a scent ungrateful, and not at all like the Myrtle.—R. Bradley, *The Country Housewife and Lady's Director*, 1732.

SPIRIT OF ROSEMARY.—Gather a Pound and a half of the fresh Tops of Rosemary, cut them into a Gallon of clean and fine Melasses Spirit, and let them stand all Night ; next Day distill off five pints with a gentle Heat : this is of the nature of Hungary-Water, but not being so strong as that is usually made, it is better for taking inwardly : A Spoonful is a dose, and it is good against all nervous Complaints.—From *The Receipt Book of Elizabeth Cleland*, 1759.

TO MAKE SNOW.—Take a quart of thick Creame, and five or six whites of Eggs, a saucer full of Sugar finely beaten and as much Rose-water, beat them all together and always as it riseth take it out with a spoon, then take a loaf of Bread, cut away the crust, set it in a platter, and a great Rosemary bush in the middest of it, then lay your Snow with a Spoon upon the Rosemary, and so serve it.—*A Book of Fruits and Flowers*, 1653.

Rosemary Tea.—One pint of boiling water poured on an ounce of the young tips.

Rosemary Wine.—Infuse a bunch of rosemary tips (about six inches long) in sound white wine for a few days, when the wine will be fit to use.

Rosemary Flowers made up into plates with Double Refine Sugar after the manner of Sugar Rossets and eaten Comfort the heart and make it Merry. Quicken the Spirits and make them more lively.—*MS. Book of Receipts* by Thomas Newington, 1719.

RUE

"There's rue for you and here's some for me ;
We may call it herb grace o' Sundays."
Hamlet, IV. v.

"It is set downe by divers of the Ancients that Rew doth prosper much and becometh stronger if it be set by a Fig tree : which (we conceive) is caused not by reason of Frendship but by extraction of a contrary juyce, the one drawing juyce fit to result sweet, the other bitter."—Bacon, *Sylva Sylvarum*.

"The Weasell when she is to encounter the serpent arms herselfe with eating of Rue."—W. Coles, *The Art of Simpling*, 1656.

"Buy rue, buy sage, buy Mint
Buy rue, sage, Mint, a farthing a bunch."
Old London Street Cry.

The antidote which Mercury gave to Ulysses against the beverage of the Enchantress Circe has always been supposed to be rue, and from the earliest times rue has had a wonderful reputation. Galen, we are told, ate coriander and rue raw, with oil and salt, against infection, and Dioscorides recommends the juice as a counter-poison. Rue was the chief constituent in the famous counter-poison of Mithridates, King of Persia, and in later days in the noted " Vinegar of the four thieves." According to tradition this vinegar enabled four thieves, during the great plague of Marseilles, to enter all the stricken houses with impunity and carry off all they chose. When gunpowder was first used in Europe, it was a popular belief that if the gun-flint were boiled in rue and vervain the shot could not miss. The Italian peasants still believe in rue as a protection from the evil eye, and many of them wear it concealed on their persons. The name " Herb of grace " is by many believed to be due to the fact that holy water was scattered with an aspergillum made of rue, but Britten says there is no ground for this supposition. To the first Duke of Saxony, Frederick Barbarossa in 1181 gave the right to bear a chaplet of rue on his arms, and six centuries later (1807) the first King of Saxony created the Order of the Crown of Rue. This order was conferred on King George when he was Prince of Wales in 1902.

Rue likes a poor, clayey loam mixed with calcareous rubbish. Sow the seeds in March or April, or increase cowslips any time during spring. Rue must never be allowed to run to seed.

A PREVENTIVE AGAINST THE PLAGUE.—A handful each of rue, sage, sweet-briar and elder. Bruise and strain with a quart of white wine, and put thereto a little ginger and a spoonful of the best treacle, and drink thereof morning and evening.—*The Good Housewife's Jewell*, 1585.

The sting of a Bee or Waspe. Take Rue a handfull and stampe the Juyce of the leaves and aply to any part hurt by the Sting of a bee or a waspe. A present Remedy. *M.S. Book of Receipts* by Thomas Newington. 1719.

SAFFRON

" Thy plants are an orchard of Pomegranates, with pleasant fruits ; Camphire, with Spikenard, Spikenard and Saffron ; Calamus and Cinnamon, with all trees of Frankincense ; Myrrh and Aloes, with all the chief spices."—*Song of Solomon*, IV. 13, 14.

> " Pare saffron plot
> Forget it not
> His dwelling made trim
> Look shortly for him
> When harvest is gone,
> Then saffron comes on ;
> A little of ground
> Brings saffron a pound."

TUSSER, *Five Hundred Points of Good Husbandry*, 1580.

" For those at death's doore and almost past breathing saffron bringeth breath again."—JOHN GERARD, *The Herball*, 1597.

The saffron used in cookery for flavouring comes from the *crocus sativus*, and from meadow saffron is obtained the drug which is still much prescribed. Of the latter Turner says, " It is sterke poyson and will strongell a man and kill him in the space of one day ! " The saffron used in cookery was formerly much more popular than it is now, and presumably our ancestors liked strong flavours. Nowadays it is only in Cornwall that it is used to any extent, and very few people unless

born and bred to it like saffron cakes. Hakluyt tells
us that saffron was brought to this country by a pilgrim
who concealed a head of it in his staff, and " so he
brought the root into this realm with venture of his
life, for if he had been taken, by the law of the countrey
from whence it came he had died for the fact." Saffron
is the only herb with a town named after it—Saffron
Walden, in Essex, where it was grown in enormous
quantities for over two hundred years. Several of
our kings were presented with saffron in a silver bowl
when they visited the town. Bacon had a very high
opinion of this herb, and said that " what made the
English people sprightly was the liberal use of saffron
in their broths and sweetmeats." Samuel Trowell, in
his *New Treatise of Husbandry Gardening and other
Curious Matters* (1739), says of saffron that the common
method of drying it in a kiln made of clay with charcoal
is not to be commended, as it dries all the virtue out of
the plant. He recommends picking an ounce or two,
putting it in a bladder, and carrying it about till dry
(they were leisurely folk in those days !), " which small
quantitie so dried hath been kept two years or more."
Saffron used to be made into balls with honey, and when
thoroughly dried these balls were powdered.

Saffron likes a sandy soil. It may be grown from
seed or increased by offsets from the bulb in the early
summer.

To MAKE SYRUP OF SAFFRON.—Take a pint of the
best canary, as much balm-water, and two ounces of
English saffron ; open and pull the saffron very well,
and put it into the liquor to infuse, let it stand close
cover'd (so as to be hot but not boil) twelve hours ;

then strain it out as hot as you can, and add to it two pounds of double refined sugar ; boil it till it is well incorporated, and when it is cold bottle it, and take one spoonful in a little sack or small cordial, as occasion serves.—E. Smith, *The Compleat Housewife*, 1736.

SAGE

" How can a man die who has sage in his garden ? "—*Arabian Proverb*.

" He who would live for aye
Must eat sage in May."

Old English Proverb.

" Also take sage and marjoram
Hit schall the kepe in savetee
Sounde and clene for to bee
Quyken the vaynes and the mynde
And all thy vertues kepe in kynde
Comfort the herte and kepe the sight
No man of erthe can telle his myghte."

Fifteenth Century MS. Herbal.

" This herb yf left to putrify with the blood of a serpent or a bird like a oysell, if it be touched on ye brest of a man he shall lose his sence or felynge the space of fifteen dayes or more. And yf the foresaid serpent be burned and the ashes of it put in ye fyre, anone shall there be a rayne bowe with an horible thunder. And yf ye aforesaide ashes be put in a lampe, and be kindled, it shal appeare that all the house is full of serpints and this hath been proved of men of late tyme."—*The Boke of the Secrets of Albertus Magnus*, 1560.

" 'Tis a plant, indeed, with so many and wonderful properties as that the assiduous use of it is said to render men immortal."—JOHN EVELYN, *Acetaria*, 1699.

From time immemorial sage has been renowned for its wonderful health-giving properties. The very

name of the plant, *Salvia*, means health, and the
Arabians have a proverb which was old in the days of
Charlemagne : " How can a man die who has Sage in
his garden ? " The Chinese valued this herb so highly
that the Dutch in old days carried on a profitable
trade by exchanging sage for tea, and for one pound of
dried sage leaves the Chinese gave three pounds of
tea. The proper time of year to eat sage or to drink
sage tea is in spring, and formerly country folk used
to eat quantities of it with bread and butter or bread
and cheese. There is an old belief that where sage
prospers in a garden the woman rules, and another
that the plant flourishes or withers according to the
prosperity of the master of the house. Sage used to
be held in such repute that both bread and cheese were
flavoured with it in the making, and one herbal doctor
even advocated its use instead of tobacco. Red sage
is rarely seen, but what a handsome plant it is when
well grown ! There are few leaves more beautiful
than its deep maroon-coloured ones, especially in
early spring when they contrast so well with the tender
green of the young shoots. Old-fashioned country folk
say that red sage never does well unless the original
slip were planted by some one with a " lucky hand."

Sir John Hill tells us he knew an old man who had
some special secret in preparing sage. " This," Sir
John Hill says, " remained upon my mind, and it
brought into my thoughts the mighty praises that had
been written of sage, and the little that we see of it in
comparison with these wonders. The Greek physicians
had the highest opinion of sage, and they called it the
sacred herb. Wherever sage is found we read in early
and late times equally its praises." He goes on to say

he remembered " a woman of the little town of Stan-
ground, near Peterborough, so old that for that reason
only she was called a witch. About five yards square
of ground, enclosed with a mud wall, before the door
of her little habitation was planted with sage, and 'twas
not only her account but that of all the place that she
lived upon it. Her exact age could not be known, for
she was older than the register, but the people in
general remembered their fathers calling her the old
woman. In the cathedral church of Peterborough, on
the left hand as one enters the great isle, is a picture
and monumental inscription of a man who was once
sexton of the place—I think the name is Scarlet—who
lived so long in that office as to bury, so says the inscription, all the inhabitants of the place twice over.
The full date of his age is not mentioned, but he was
considered by more than one generation as a living
miracle. There is great reason to attribute this also
to sage, for I remember to have seen at that place when
I was a boy a spot of ground near the churchyard where
there was at that time left against an old south wall of
stone the remainder of a broad, oak bench, which they
then used to call this old man's bed ; on this 'tis said
he slept away almost the whole day, during the latter
years of his life. By it there were then, and perhaps
are still, some antient tufts of sage and rue planted
alternately, which mixed together he used to make his
drink. People there remember still an old Latin line
which he learned, I suppose, from some clergy of the
place and which he was continually repeating." The
leaves and seeds of sage, Sir John Hill says, possess
the greatest powers. " I have been engaged at times
some years in this my garden at Bayswater (I thank

God, the King and my great Patron gives me ample
opportunity). The common red sage has the greatest
virtue, and also that which Dioscorides says grows in
barren, dry and rugged places. The leaves are at their
best before the flower stalks rise : this is in May.
They were therefore right who told our ancestors to
eat them at that season. Those who would use them
constantly should dry them at that time for the rest
of the year. The roots are slightly flavoured and of
little value ; of the nature of the leaves but inferior
by many degrees. The seeds are warm amd cordial
beyond the leaves, carminative and friendly to the
nerves, but still in no way adequate or indeed approach-
ing to the powers attributed to the plant. Fewer
disappointments have stopped many an inquiry, but
the faith I placed in the old writers, a faith founded on
experience in many other instances, lead me still to
prosecute this subject. I have long observed that there
are certain juices contained in or secreted from particular
parts of plants at certain seasons which do not exist
in the same plant at other seasons or in any other part.
(He gives other instances, and amongst them the very
familiar one of the fragrant resin present in the cup of
the moss rose, the liquid balsam being present only
during flowering time.) " I examined the cups of
sage, and found there what I had sought before in
every other part of the plant so much in vain. Just
when the flowers of sage begin to open there is in their
cups a fragrant resin of this kind, highly flavoured,
bamy, delicate, and to the taste, one of the most
delicious cordials that can be thought, warm and
aromatic. I no longer doubted anything that had been
said of sage ; the smell, the taste, the flavour here

promised all. Lord Bacon," he continues, "laments justly that physicians have applied themselves solely to the cure of diseases, neglecting the prolongation of human life. Sage, properly prepared, will retard that rapid progress of decay that treads upon our heels so fast in the latter years of life, will preserve the faculties and memory, more valuable to the rational mind than life itself without them ; and will relieve under that faintness, strengthen under that weakness and prevent absolutely that sad depression of spirits, which age often feels and always fears, which will long prevent the hands from trembling and the eyes from dimness and make the lamp of life, so long as nature lets it burn, burn brightly."

SAGE CREAM.—Boil a quart of cream, pound red sage in a mortar, put into the cream a quarter of a pint of canary, and a quarter of a pint of Rose-water with half a pound of sugar. After the same manner you may do by any sort of good herbs.—From *The Receipt Book of Joseph Cooper*, Cook to Charles I, 1654.

SAGE WATER.—Take sage flowers, sprinkle them with white wine, or water. Let them stand awhile. Then distil them.—*Ibid.*

CONSERVE OF SAGE.—Take new flowers of Sage one pound, Sugar one pound ; so beat them together very small in a Marble Mortar, put them in a vessel well glased and steeped, set them in the Sun, stir them dayly; it will last one year.—*The Queen's Closet Opened*, by W. N., Cook to Queen Henrietta Maria, 1655.

SAGE TEA.—Take a little sage, a little Balm, put it into a pan, slice a Lemon, peel and all, a few knobs of sugar, one glass of white wine ; pour on these two or three quarts of boiling water ; cover it, and drink when thirsty. When you think it strong enough of the herbs take them out otherwise it will make it bitter.—*The New Art of Cookery*, by Richards Briggs, many years Cook at the Globe Tavern, Fleet Street, the White Hart Tavern, Holborn, and at the Temple Coffee House, 1788.

SAGE TEA.—On an ounce of the leaves (use the young tips) pour one pint of boiling water. Half a pint to be taken at a time.

For a Sore Throat : Pour half a pint of boiling vinegar on to small handful of sage leaves and then inhale ; or,

For a Sore Throat or Cough : Pour a pint of boiling water on a handful of sage leaves, and when moderately cool add a little vinegar and honey. Take a teaspoonful at a time ; use also as a gargle.

To MAKE SAGE WINE.—Take three gallons of water and Six pound of Lose Sugar boyle the water and Sugar together and as the Scum rises take it of and when it is well boyled put it into a Clean Tubb have ready in the Tubb one gallon of Sage leaves free from Stalks. So let it then Stand till it be allmost cold then Put to it the Juice of 6 Lemmons beat them with a litle Ale yes† brew it well together cover it very close that no Aire come in let it Stand 48 houers then Streyne it through a fine Sieve put it into a Small Runlet that it

Scene in a Sixteenth Century Herb Garden

may be just full and when it hath don working Stop it very close and let it Stand three weeks or a month before you bottle it. Putting into each bottle A litle lump of lose Sugar this wine is best kept a quarter of a year or longer before it is Drankt.—*M.S. Book of Receipts*, by Thomas Newington, 1719.

SAGE WINE.—Take thirty pounds of Malaga raisins picked clean and shred small, and one bushel of green sage shred small; then boil five gallons of water and let it stand till it is lukewarm. Put into a tub the water, sage and raisins, let it stand five or six days, stirring it two or three times a day. Then strain and press the liquor from the ingredients, put it in a cask and let it stand six months, then draw it clean off into another vessel. Bottle it in two days, and in a month or six weeks it will be fit to drink; but it is best when a year old.

SAMPHIRE

" You cannot provide too much of this excellent ingredient in all crude sallads."—JOHN EVELYN, *Acetaria*, 1699.

What would John Evelyn have said of our modern herb gardens where no samphire is ever to be seen ? It used to be called St. Peter's herb, perhaps because it grows on rocks. Samphire no longer grows on the cliffs which Shakespeare describes in *King Lear*, but it is found in Cornwall, growing, as it is traditionally supposed to grow, just out of reach of the waves, but where the spray falls on it. In Tudor days it was a favourite salad herb and was grown in every garden. Gerard says of it : " Samphire is the pleasantest sauce most familiar and best agreeing with man's body." The young shoots may be eaten either fresh or pickled.

To PICKLE SAMPHIRE.—Take samphire that is green and has a sweet smell, gathered in the month of May, pick it well, lay it to soak in water and salt for two days, afterwards put it into an earthen pot, and pour to it as much white-wine vinegar as will cover it. Put it into a saucepan, sit it over a gentle fire, cover it close, and let it stand till it is green and crisp, but do not let it stand till it is soft and tender. Then put it into the pan again and tye it down close for use.—John Evelyn, *Acetaria*, 1699.

SAMPHIRE PICKLE.—Let it be gathered about Michaelmas or the Spring and put two or three hours into a Brine of Water and Salt ; then into a clean pot in three parts of strong white-wine Vinegar and one part of water and salt as much as will cover the Samphire keeping the vapour from issuing out by pasting up the Pot lid and so hang it over the Fire for half an hour only. Being taken off let it remain cover'd till it be cold, and then put up into small Barrels or Jars with the Liquor and some fresh Vinegar, Water and Salt ; and thus it will keep very green. If you be near the Sea that water will supply the Brine. This is the Dover Receit.—John Evelyn, *Acetaria*, 1699.

SAVORY

"Here's flowers for you,
Hot Lavender, Mints, Savory, Marjoram."
Winter's Tale, IV. iv.

There are about fourteen species of this highly aromatic herb, but as a rule only two are grown in England—summer savory which is a hardy annual and winter savory which is a hardy perennial. Both are used for flavouring. According to Culpepper, " Mercury claims the dominion over this herb. Keep it dry by you all the year, if you love yourself and your ease, and it is a hundred pounds to a penny if you do not." Savory leaves were formerly used to cure bee and wasp stings.

Both the summer savory and the winter savory can be propagated from seed sown in April. Winter savory can be increased by cuttings of the young shoots taken with a " heel."

SCURVY GRASS

This is a true herb of the sea, for however far it grows away from the coast it always has a salt taste. It is supposed to be the much-praised " Herba Brittanica " of the old herbalists, and all our great navigators bore testimony to its wonderful virtues.

SCURVY TEA.—Pour one quart of boiling water on two ounces of the whole plant including the roots.

Mix with the juice of Seville orange, and take every day for six weeks in spring.

SALLET OF SCURVY GRASS.—Being finely picked short, well soaked in clean water and swung dry, dish it round in a fine clean dish with capers and currans about it, carved lemon and orange round that and eggs upon the center not boiled too hard, and parted in halfs, then oyl and vinegar ; over all scraping sugar and trim the brim of the dish.—From *The Receipt Book of Elizabeth Cleland*, 1759.

TO MAKE SCURVY-GRASS WINE.—Take fresh Scurvy-grass six Handfuls, powned it well in a Mortar, pour upon it three quarts of Rhenish Wine, set it in a cool place for three or four days ; then strain it, and let it settle, then draw it off from the Dregs.—*Ibid.*

SKIRRET

" Skirret roots boiled in milk are excellent restorative to people who have suffered through long illness."—T. TRYON, *The Good Housewife*, 1692.

Skirrets are only just beginning to find their way back into our gardens, but our ancestors valued them highly. According to Gerard they were seldom eaten raw, but they were boiled, stewed, roasted under the embers, baked in pies—whole, sliced or in pulp. He solemnly adds : " 'Tis reported they were heretofore something bitter ; see what culture and education effects." Evelyn tells us that the Emperor

Tiberius liked them so much that he accepted them for tribute.

Sow Skirret early in April in drills twelve inches apart. Thin the plants to a foot apart. The roots are fit for use in Autumn. Old roots throw off offsets in the Spring, and the plants may be increased by taking these and planting them. Skirrets like a light, rich, loamy soil.

SKIRRET PIE.—Take your skirrets and boil them, skin them, then cut them to lengths about two or three inches. Wash them with yolks of eggs and season with salt, ginger, cinnamon, nutmeg. Put to them some chestnuts boiled and blanched and some yolks of hard-boiled eggs split, and lay over some sliced lemon. Put over butter and close it in a raised coffin.—From *The Receipt Book of Joseph Cooper*, Cook to Charles I, 1654.

FRIED SKIRRETS.—Boyle your skirrets and peel them : this done roul them in Batter made with eggs, ginger, cinnamon, flower of wheat and salt. If you will have them green put in your juice of spinage and fry them in Butter very carefully, for they are apt to stick together and burn ; if you fry them brown, for the sauce after take Butter, sugar and the juice of an orange and dish them. If green take Butter, sugar, and sliced Nutmeg, the yolks of two or three eggs with the juice of spinach, beat up thick together and serve it up with this sauce ; garnish it with some pretty cuts of puff-paste or other with sugar scraped in it.—*Ibid.*

SKIRRET MILK.—Is made by boiling the Roots
tender and the pulp strained out, put into Cream or
Milk new boiled with Ham or four yolks of eggs,
sugar, large mace and other spice, etc.   And thus is
composed any other root milk.—John Evelyn, *Acetaria*,
1699.

SKIRRET PYE.—Boil your biggest skirrets and blanch
and season them with cinnamon, nutmeg, and a very
little ginger and sugar.   Your pye being ready lay in
your skirrets ; season also the marrow of three or four
bones with cinnamon, sugar, a little salt and grated
bread.   Lay the marrow in your pye and the yolks
of hard eggs, a handful of chestnuts boiled and blanched,
and some candied Orange-peel in slices.   Lay butter
on the top and lid your pye.   Let your caudle be white
wine and sugar, thicken it with the yolks of eggs,
and when the pye is baked pour it in and serve it hot.
Scrape sugar on it.—E. Smith, *The Compleat Housewife*, 1736.

SKIRRET FRITTERS.—Boil some skirret-roots till they
are very tender, take off the outside, and beat a pint
of the pulp very fine, rub it through a sieve, and mix it
with a large spoonful of flour and four eggs beat well,
sweeten it with powdered sugar, and put in a little
grated nutmeg and ginger, and mix it into a thick
batter (if a large spoonful of flour is not sufficient put
in more) ; have a pan of hogs-lard boiling hot, drop
them in with a spoon, and fry them quick and brown ;
put them on a sieve before the fire to drain a minute,
put them in a dish, and garnish with Seville oranges
cut into quarters, or dried sweetmeats.—*The New Art*

of Cookery, by Richard Briggs, many years Cook at
the Globe Tavern, Fleet Street, the White Hart
Tavern, Holborn, and at the Temple Coffee House,
1788.

SMALLAGE

Smallage has little but its old-fashioned name to
recommend it, for it has a very disagreeable taste. It
is wild celery, and as Hyll says, " It joyeth in the
shadow and cometh well in any ground. Leave only
a stem or two and it will endure for ever without any
weeding whatever." The old herbalists claim for it
the same virtues as parsley, and it was formerly used
in salads and in pottages.

SMALLAGE GRUEL.—In a Marble Mortar beat great
Oatmeal to meal (which requireth long beating) then
boil it three or four hours in Spring water. To a posset
full of two or three quarts of water put about half a
Porrenger full of Oatmeal, before it is beaten ; for
after beating it appeareth more. To this quantity put
as much Smallage as you buy for a penny, which
maketh it strong of the Herb and very green. Chop
the smallage exceeding small and put it in a good half
hour before you are to take your posset from the
fire : You are to season your Gruel with a little salt,
at the due time ; and you may put in a little Nutmeg,
and Mace to it. When you have taken it from the fire,
put into it a good proportion of butter, which stir well,
to incorporate with the Gruel, when it is melted.—
The Closet of Sir Kenelm Digby Opened, 1669.

SORREL

Both garden sorrel and French sorrel are good " pot-
herbs," but the French sorrel is not so bitter. Formerly
sorrel was eaten like spinach, and it was commonly put
in soups also. Mrs. Bardswell tells us that " when
no apples are forthcoming for apple sauce sorrel leaves
are a good substitute."

Sorrel seeds should be sown in March. French sorrel
likes a dry soil, and garden sorrel plenty of moisture.
Both can be increased by division of roots in spring
or autumn.

" Sorrel plays a very important part in Belgian cookery, and consequently the presence of the Belgians
in England created a demand for it ; and during the
autumn of 1916 it could be bought very cheaply in
London, 1d or 2d. a pound. It is an excellent substitute
for spinach. One of the best recipes is to wash it in
many waters as if it were spinach. Then put it in a
stew-pan with a large lump of butter. When it is
fairly dry add a little fine oatmeal, salt, pepper and
a very little diluted meat extract. Very carefully add
two well-beaten eggs, and serve it with meat or with
grilled fish. The famous sorrel soup can be made with
milk, but is better and cheaper with potatoes. The
sorrel is fried for a few minutes in butter, and then
put in boiling water with the potatoes cut up in small
pieces. Salt and pepper are added, and the whole
gently cooked and served without straining. A very
old French cookery book, published in 1796, ' with the
approbation and privilege of the king,' says, that
without any doubt at the end of September all good

managers will preserve sorrel for winter use, as when properly done it remains as good as fresh. The method is very simple. The sorrel with plenty of salt is cooked over a slow fire with a large piece of butter until all the water drawn from it is evaporated. When it is half cold it is well packed into pots and pressed down with a spoon. When quite cold, tepid dissolved butter is poured over it, and the pots are covered and kept in a dry place. The sorrel will keep until Easter, but once opened not more than three weeks. It is not only healthy for winter use, but extensively useful, as it need only be put into hot stock to make good soup, or be heated in butter and thickened with beaten eggs and a little milk to form a delicious vegetable garnish."—From an article in *Truth*, November, 1916.

To take Staines out of ones Hands presently.— You may do this with the iuyce, of Sorrell, washing the stained parts therein.

Eggs with the Juice of Sorrel.—Poach your Eggs in Boiling Water ; and having pounded some Sorrel, put the Juice of it in a Dish with some Butter, two or three raw Eggs, Salt and Nutmeg : make all this into a Sauce, and pour it on your poach'd Eggs ; so serve them.—From *The Receipt Book of Patrick Lamb*, Master Cook to Charles II, James II, William and Mary, and Queen Anne, 1716.

A Tart of the Juice of Sorrel.—Beat sorrel in

a Mortar and strain out the juice put it into a Dish with three makaroons, a piece of fresh Butter, the yolks of three raw eggs, green citron grated, orange flowers, and sugar and cinnamon, stir all this together over a fire and make a Cream of it and put it into a Pan sheeted very thin with fine paste and when it is baked serve it away with sugar over it.—*A Perfect School of Instruction of the Officers of the Month*, by Giles Rose, one of the Master Cooks to Charles II 1682.

To DRESS SORREL WITH EGGS.—Put two handfuls of Sorrel clean pick'd and washed into a saucepan, with a Bit of Butter, a Pinch of Flower, a little Salt, Pepper and Nutmeg, stew it, and a quarter of an Hour before you use it, pour in two or three spoonfuls of drawn Butter. Garnish it with hard eggs, cut in quarters, laying one End on the Sorrel, and the other on the Side of the Plate, with the Yolks uppermost, and serve it up, either for a course at Dinner, or else for a Supper. —From *The Receipt Book of John Middleton*, Cook to the Duke of Bolton, 1734.

To MAKE A SORREL OMELET.—Pick, wash and blanch your Sorrel; then having cut it, fry it in Sweet Butter, with a little Parsley and Chibbol; when it is fry'd, pour in some Cream, season them, and let them boil over a gentle Fire. In the meantime make an Omelet of Eggs and Cream, seasoned at Discretion. When it is enough, dress it on a Dish, thicken your sorrel with the Yolks of a couple of Eggs, and turn it on the Omelet, and serve it up hot.—*Ibid.*

A Ragoo of Sorrel.—Having pick'd your Sorrel clean from the Stalkes, set a sauce-pan over the Fire half full of Water, make it boil; then put in your Sorrel, giving it a Scald; then take it out, squeezing it as hard as you do Spinage, and drain it. Put it into a Sauce-pan and some thin Cullis of Veal and Ham; Season it with Salt and Pepper, and set it a simmering over the Fire: When it has simmered enough, put to it some Essence of Ham. This may be us'd in all those dishes in which you use Sorrel.—*Ibid.*

SOUTHERNWOOD

Southernwood, or Lad's Love, is nearly always to be found in old-fashioned gardens, but not often in modern ones. It has a most invigorating scent, and French people use it to keep moths out of clothes; hence one of its French names, " Garde-robe." Sir John Hill says of Field Southernwood that " It wants but to be more common and more known to be very highly valued."

Southernwood Tea.—Clip four ounces of the leaves fine and beat them in a mortar with six ounces of loaf sugar till the whole is like a paste. Three times a day take the bignesse of a nutmeg of this. It is pleasant and one thing in it is particular, it is a composer and always disposes persons to sleep.—Sir John Hill, *The British Herbalist*, 1772.

SPEEDWELL

About two centuries ago " the opinion was so prevalent that this plant cured gout that speedwell was in a manner destroyed for many miles about London." But we moderns seem to have lost our faith in the virtues of this lovely wild herb, and only very old-fashioned cottagers make speedwell tea nowadays.

SPEEDWELL TEA.—One pint of boiling water poured on to one ounce of the plant.

STRAWBERRY

> " Then unto London I dyd me hye
>   Of all the land it beareth the pryse
> ' Hot pescodes ' one began to crye
>   ' Strabery rype ' and ' cherryes in the ryse.' "
>
> LYDGATE, *London Lyckpeny.*

> " Wife unto thy garden and set me a plot
>   With strawbery rootes of the best to be got,
>   Such growing abroade, among thornes in the wood,
>   Wel chosen and picked proove excellent good."
> TUSSER, *Five Hundred Points of Good Husbandry,* 1580.

> " Rare ripe strawberries and
>   Haut boys sixpence a pottle
>   Full to the bottom haut boys.
>   Strawberries and cream are charming and sweet,
>   Mix them and try how delightful they eat."
>
> *Old London Street Cry.*

Until the nineteenth century our present garden strawberry was unknown in England. Till then wild strawberries were cultivated and improved in size and flavour ; " The strawberry requires small labour but by diligence of the gardener becometh so great that he same yeeldeth faire and big Berries as Berries of the Bramble in the hedge. The Berries in Summer time eaten with creame and sugar is accounted a great refreshing to men, but more commended being eaten with wine and sugar." Thomas Hyll says, " Certaine skilful men by diligence and care procure the berries to alter from the proper red coloure into faire white, delectable to the eye." He also points out " the marvellous innocency of this herb, though divers venemous things creep over the herbes yet are they in no manner infected with any venemous contagion, which is a note that the herbe (of propertie) hath no affinite with poyson." In mediæval flower symbolism the wild strawberry signifies the fruits of righteousness. Formerly an excellent tea was made from wild strawberry leaves, also from equal quantities of strawberry leaves and woodruff. Strawberry leaves were commonly added to cooling drinks, the leaves were also strongly recommended to be used in baths for those who suffered from " grievious aches and paynes of the hyppes," and the juice of wild strawberries was used as a complexion wash. Strawberry wine was a favourite with Sir Walter Raleigh.

Coles in *The Art of Simpling* (1656) gives this advice : " Among strawberries sow here and there some Borage seed and you shall finde the strawberries under those leaves farre more larger than their fellowes."

FOR A FACE WASH.—Take a quart of wild strawberries, wild tansy, three pintes of new Milke. Still all these together and wash your face therein.—*The Good Housewife's Handmaid*, 1585.

Strawberry and Almond Tansy.—Take four quarts of new milk and half a pound of the sweet almond flour, two ounces of lemon juice and half a pint of strawberry juice. Put to these two pounds of fine sugar and a quart of Canary. Stir them together and beat them till they froth, and become of a pleasant colour.—*Ibid*.

Strawberry Leaf Tea.—On two large handfuls of the young leaves pour a quart of boiling water.

Strawberry and Woodruff Tea.—On equal quantities of young strawberry leaves and woodruff pour one quart of boiling water.

A Cordial Water of Sir Walter Raleigh.—Take a gallon of Strawberries, and put them into a pinte of *aqua vitæ*, let them stand so four or five days, strain them gently out, and sweeten the water as you please, with fine Sugar, or else with perfume.

Strawberry Water.—To a quart of water you must have a pound of strawberries which squeeze in the same water, then put in four or five ounces of sugar with some lemon juice ; if the lemons are large and juicy one lemon is enough to two quarts of water. All being well mixed put it through a straining bag, put it in a cool place and give it to drink.—From *The Receipt Book of Vincent la Chapelle*, Chief Cook to the Prince of Orange, 1744.

TANSY

" I have heard that if maids will take wild Tansy and lay it to soake in Buttermilk for the space of nine days and wash their faces therewith, it will make them look very faire."—*The Virtuose Boke of Distyllacion*, by MASTER JHEROM BRUNSWYKE, 1527.

Our garden tansy was originally the wild tansy, but all the old herbalists say that the latter has far more virtue both in its leaves and flowers. The name tansy is derived from Athanasia (immortality), and the plant is dedicated to St. Athanasius. A tansy was a favourite dish in the eighteenth century, and was as inseparable from a bill of fare for Easter as roast goose at Michaelmas, or a gooseberry tart at Whitsun. Before mint became recognised as the proper accompaniment to roast lamb, tansy was used in the same way. Tansy puddings and tansy cakes were commonly eaten during spring, and tansy tea was a recognised cure for colds and rheumatism.

TANSY TEA.—Dry bunches of tansy (leaves and flowers) in the summer. On one ounce of the dried tansy pour a pint of boiling water.

HOW TO MAKE A TANSY IN LENT.—Take all maner of hearbes and the spawn of a Pike or of any other fish

and blanched almond and a few crums of bread and
a little faire water and a pinte of Rose-water and
mingle altogether and make it not too thin and frie
it in oyl and so serve it in.—*The Good Housewife's
Handmaid*, 1588.

HOW TO MAKE A TANSY.—Take a little tansy, feather-
few, parsley and violets, and stampe them altogether
and straine them with the yolkes of eight or tenne
eggs, and three or foure whites, and some vinegar and
put thereto sugar or salt and frie it.—*Ibid*.

TANSY PUDDING.—Blanch and pound a quarter of
a pound of Jordan almonds, put them into a stew
pan, add a gill of a syrup of Roses, the crumb of a
French roll, some grated nutmeg, half a glass of brandy,
two tablespoonfuls of tansy juice, three ounces of
fresh butter and some slices of citron. Pour over it
a pint and a half of boiling cream or milk ; sweeten
and when cold mix it, add the juice of a lemon and eight
eggs beaten. It may be either boyled or baked.—*Ibid*.

TANSY AMBER CAKES.—Blanch a pound of Almonds,
steep them in a pint of cream, pound them in a mortar,
add to them the yolks of twelve and whites of six eggs,
put in half a pint of juice of spinage and a quarter of
a pint of juice of Tansy, add to it grated Bread ;
sweeten it with sugar to your palate fry it in sweet
Butter and keep it stirring in the Pan till it is of a
good thickness strew sugar over it and serve it up.—
From *The Receipt Book of John Nott*, Cook to the
Duke of Bolton, 1723.

To MAKE AN APPLE TANSY.—Pare your apples, cut them in thin round Slices, fry them in Sweet Butter ; then beat half a score of eggs with a quart of cream, the juice of spinage and Tansy of each a quarter of a pint, and a little Rose-water ; when these are all beaten together pour them on your apples.—*Ibid.*

A GOOD TANSY.—Take seven eggs and leaving out two whites, and a pint of Cream some Tansy, Thyme, Sweet Majoram, Parsley, Strawberry leaves all, shred very small a little nutmeg, add a plate of grated white Bread, let these be mixed all together, then fry them but not too brown.—*Ibid.*

TANSY PANCAKES.—Put four spoonfuls of flour into an earthen pan, and mix it with half a pint of cream to a smooth batter, beat four eggs well and put in, with two ounces of powdered sugar, and beat all well together for a quarter of an hour ; then put in two spoonsful of the juice of spinach and one of tansy, a little grated nutmeg, mix all well together, and fry them with fresh butter ; garnish them with Seville oranges cut in quarters, and strew powdered sugar over them.—*The New Art of Cooking*, by Richard Briggs, many years Cook at the Globe Tavern, Fleet Street, the White Hart Tavern, Holborn, and at the Temple Coffee House, 1788.

To MAKE A PLAIN TANSY.—Take a fine stale penny loaf and cut the crumb in thin shaves ; put it in a bowl, then boil a mutchkin of cream, and when boiled pour it over the bread, then cover the bowl with a plate, and let it lie a quarter of an hour ; then mix it with eight eggs well beaten, two gills of the juice of spinage, two spoonfuls of the juice of tansy and sweeten it with sugar, nutmeg, and a little brandy : rub your pan with butter and put it in it ; then keep it stirring on the fire till it is pretty thick ; then put it in a butter'd dish ; you may either bake it, or do it in the driping pan under roasted meat.—From *The Receipt Book of Elizabeth Cleland*, 1759.

TARRAGON

Tarragon is a comparative newcomer in the herb garden, for it was first grown (and then only in the Royal gardens) in Tudor days. Evelyn says that " the tops and young shoots like those of Rocket must never be excluded from sallets. 'Tis highly cordial and friendly to the head, heart, and liver." One old herbalist gives the strange advice that when tarragon is a foot high it should be taken up and put back into the same hole in order to make it grow better !

French tarragon is a native of the South of Europe but the kind most commonly grown in this country is Russian tarragon, which is a native of Siberia. Both the tarragons like a sunny aspect and poor dry soil. Increase by root division or propagate (in warmth) from cuttings.

TARRAGON VINEGAR.—Strip the Tarragon from the

stalks, put it into a Pot with White-wine and Vinegar, in equal quantities ; stop it up close and keep it for use.

THISTLE

Both the milk thistle and the blessed thistle were used by our ancestors, the former as a vegetable and the latter as a tonic, and Evelyn, in his *Acetaria*, says that to a salad of thistle leaves " the late Morocco Ambassador and his retinue were very partial." The leaves of the milk thistle shorn of their prickles were not only an ordinary ingredient in a salad, but they were also boiled, and Tryon says of them, " they are very wholesome and exceed all other greens in taste." They were also added to Pottages, baked in pies, like artichoke bottoms, and fried. Culpepper advises one to " cut off the prickles, unless you have a mind to choke yourself," but in olden days both the scales and the roots were eaten. The young stalks, peeled, were eaten both fresh and boiled.

MILK THISTLE STALKS.—The young stalks about May being peeled and soaked in water to extract the bitterness, boiled or raw are a very wholesome sallet eaten with oyl, salt and pepper. Boil them in water with a little salt till they are very soft and so let them dry to drain. They are eaten with fresh butter melted not too thin and this a delicate and wholesome dish.

Other stalks of the same kind may be so treated as the Bur being tender and disarmed of its prickles.— John Evelyn, *Acetaria*, 1699.

THYME

" I know a bank whereon the wild thyme blows,
  Where oxlips and the nodding violet grows ;
  Quite over canopied with lush woodbine,
  With sweet musk roses and with Eglantine."
  Midsummer Night's Dream, II. ii.

Thyme is, perhaps, the " cleanest " smelling herb
and even in winter it seems to radiate the warmth and
sunlight it has absorbed during the hot summer months.
Like fox-glove and wood-sorrel, wild thyme has always
been a favourite with fairies ; and bees, too, love
thyme. One old herbalist tell us " the owners of Hives
have a perfite foresight and knowledge what the
increase or yeelde of Honey will bee everie yeare by
the plentifull or small number of flowers growing and
appearing in the Thyme about the summer solstice."

Only an exceptionally dense person is insensible
to the joy of walking over acres of thyme on the Surrey
hills in midsummer, when the bees in thousands are
robbing the thyme of its honey. Amongst the Greeks
thyme was an emblem of courage, and the very name
of the herb signifies courage. The Romans gave it
as a remedy for melancholy, and in this country the
aromatic thyme tea was always administered to sickly
persons to revive and refresh them. In Lancastrian
days ladies frequently embroidered a bee hovering
over thyme on the scarves they gave their knights. All
the varieties of thyme should be grown in a herb
garden. The lemon-scented variety is the most
delicious, and it is the hardiest. In an old description

of the gardens at Deepdene near Dorking, one reads :
" There are twenty-one sorts of thyme in the garden
which may seem a second Eden—where under heaven
can be a sweeter place ? " Like violets, thyme will
only grow in a pure atmosphere, and " they joy to be
placed in a sunny and open place." There are, perhaps, no more health-giving herbal drinks than the
old sage and balm and thyme teas, and they should be
taken all through the spring and summer. Thyme is
exceptionally good for people with weak lungs. It
was the pleasant custom in olden days to strew dried
sweet-smelling herbs amongst furs and winter clothes
and dried thyme imparts a delicious fragrance.

Dried rosemary and dried thyme with freshly
ground cloves is an excellent mixture.

THYME TEA.—On two large handfuls of the leaves
pour a pint and a half of boiling water.

TO ENABLE ONE TO SEE THE FAIRIES.—A pint of
sallet oyle and put it into a vial glasse ; and first wash
it with rose-water and marygolde water ; the flowers
to be gathered towards the east. Wash it till the oyle
becomes white, then put into the glasse, and then put
thereto the budds of hollyhocke, the flowers of marygolde, the flowers or toppes of wild thyme the budds
of young hazle, and the thyme must be gathered near
the side of a hill where fairies use to be ; and take the
grasse of a fairy throne ; then all these put into the
oyle in the glasse and sette it to dissolve three dayes in
the sunne and then keep it for thy use.—Receipt
dated 1600.—Ashmolean Museum, Oxford.

VALERIAN

Valerian is still " officinal " but it is no longer used as a pot-herb. Gerard tell us, " It hath been had (and is to this day, among the poore people of our Northern parts) in such veneration amongst them, that no broths, pottage, or physicall meats are worth anything if Setwall were not at an end : whereupon some woman Poet or other hath made these verses :

> " They that will have their heale,
> Must put Setweell in their keale.' "

All the varieties of valerian were used as remedies and it was supposed to be a plant antagonistic to witches.

VIOLET

> " Violets dim,
> But sweeter than the lids of Juno's eyes."
>
> *Winter's Tale*, IV. iv.

> " From the meadows your walks have left so sweet
> That, whenever a March wind sighs,
> He sets the Jewel print of your feet
> In violets blue as your eyes."
>
> TENNYSON.

> " Nature . . . . .
> Who never negligently yet
> Fashioned an April violet
> Nor would forgive, did June disclose
> Unceremoniously the rose."
>
> W. WATSON.

In mediæval flower symbolism the violet signifies the humility of Our Lord. The violet had for centuries also been the emblem of constancy, and there is an old English sonnet in which the lines occur—

> " Violet is for faithfulnesse
> Which in me shall abide."

Both in ancient and modern days, in the East and the West, the violet has always been a favourite flower. There is an old Eastern proverb : " The excellence of the violet is as the excellence of El Islam above all other religions." The French people from the earliest days have always loved violets. In Troubador days at Toulouse the prize awarded to the author of the best poem was a golden violet, and Eleanor of Aquitaine refers to this old custom in " Becket " :—

> " You know I won the violet at Toulouse."

From the earliest times herbalists have lauded the virtues of the flowers and leaves of violets. Pliny bestowed high praise on them, and amongst the Persians and Romans violet wine was a favourite beverage. In Tudor days syrups, conserves, and paste of violets were much recommended for delicate people, and the leaves were used in salads and pottages. It is the sweet-smelling wild violet (not the dog violet) which possesses the virtues.

VIOLET TEA.—Half a pint of boiling water poured on a handful of the fresh or dried leaves.

VIOLET LEAVES, at the entrance of spring fried brownish and eaten with Orange or Lemon Juice and Sugar is one of the most agreeable of all the herbaceous dishes.—John Evelyn, *Acetaria*, 1699.

To MAKE SIRROP OF VIOLETS.—First gather a great quantity of violet flowers and pick them clean from the stalkes and set them on the fire and put to them so much rose-water as you think good. Then let them boil all together untill the colour be forth of them. Then take them off the fire and strain them through a fine cloth, then put so much suger to them as you thinke good, then set it againe to the fire until it be somewhat thick and put it into a violet glasse.—*The Good Housewife's Jewell*, 1585.

To MAKE HONEY OF VIOLETS.—The Honey of Violets is made like the honey of Roses, making three infusions, and the first infusion being strained, boyle as much honey with it, and at the last scumme it.—*The Charitable Physitian*, by Philbert Guibert, Physitian Regent in Paris, 1639.

See under Honey of Roses.

CONSERVE OF VIOLETS, THE ITALIAN MANNER.—Take the leaves of blew Violets separated from their stalks and greens, beat them very well in a stone Mortar, with twice their weight of sugar, and reserve them for your use in a glass vessel.—*The Queen's Closet Opened*, by W. M. Cook to Queen Henrietta Maria, 1655.

To MAKE VIOLET CAKES.—Wet double refin'd Sugar, and boil it, till it is almost come to Sugar again ; then put into it Juice of Violets, put in Juice of Lemons this will make them look red ; if you put in Juice and Water it will make them look green. If you will have them all

blue, put in the Juice of Violets without the Lemon.—
From *The Receipt Book of John Middleton*, 1734.

VIOLET TABLET.—Steep violet flowers in lemon
juice till the colour is deep enough. Add sugar and
boil to candy height and cut into cakes before it is
quite cold.

VIOLET SYRUP.—Macerate two pounds of fresh
violets in five pints of distilled water for twenty-four
hours. Strain the liquor through a cloth, and add
double refined sugar and boil to a syrup.

VIOLET VINEGAR.—Infuse violet flowers in ordinary
vinegar.

WOODRUFF

Why has dried woodruff gone out of fashion ? Time
seems to have no effect on it, and for years the whorl-
like leaves retain their exquisite perfume. Perhaps
one sees woodruff in gardens so seldom because it is
only the dried leaves which have such a lovely scent.
Formerly, dried woodruff leaves were put in quantities
in the pierced boxes of sweet scents, which were so
fashionable for perfuming rooms in Queen Elizabeth's
day. Gerard says of woodruff, that " hanged up in
houses, it doth very well attemper the aire, coole and
make fresh the place to the delight and comfort of
such as are therein." It was one of the most commonly
used herbs in garlands for church decorations, and it

was always put in sweet bags for the linen press. Its bruised leaves were laid on cuts, and woodruff tea was esteemed an " excellent cordial drink."

WOODRUFF TEA is made of the whole herb (leaves and flowers). On a large handful pour a pint of boiling water.

See also under Strawberry.

WOOD-SORREL

" There is a bank (I love it well)
    Where climbs the sorrel of the wood,
Here breathes, how frail ! a puce veined bell
    There snowy droops its crumpled hood.
With knotted roots of tinctured strings
    A tender tapestry it weaves,
While folding back like soft green wings
    The lappets of its cloven leaves."

CHARLES A. FOX.

Wood-sorrel has a number of pretty names—Alleluia, Lugula, Cuckoobread, Fairy Bells, Stubwort. It owes the last name to the fact that it so frequently grows over the stumps of old trees. Parkinson tells us, " It is called by the apothecaries in their shoppes Alleluia and Lugula, the one because about that time it is in flower, when Alleluya in antient times was wont to be sung in the Churches ; the other came corruptly from Juliola as they of Calabria in Naples doe call it. The name cuckoobread, by which many children call it now, it owes to the fact that it flowers when the cuckoo's note is most heard. Formerly, both the leaves and flowers were a common ingredient in salads.

AN EXCELLENT AND WHOLESOME WATER-GRUEL WITH WOOD-SORREL AND CURRANTS.—Into a posset of two quarts of water, besides the due proportion of beaten oat-meal, put two handfuls of Wood-sorrel a little chopped and bruised, and a good quantity of picked and washed currants, tyed loosely in a thin stuff bag (as a bolter cloth). Boil these very well together seasoning the Composition in due time, with salt nutmeg Mace, or what else you please, as Rosemary, etc., when it is sufficiently boiled strain the Oat-meal and press out all the Juyce and humidity of the Currants and Herbs, throwing away the insipid husks ; and season it with Sugar and Butter ; and to each Porrenger-full two spoonfuls of Rhenish Wine, and the yolke of an Egg.—*The Closet of Sir Kenelm Digby Opened*, 1669.

WORMWOOD

" Water of wormwoode is gode. . . . Grete lordes among the Saracenys usen to drinke hitt."—*Fifteenth Century MS., Herbal.*

" What savour is better, if physicke be true
For places infected than Wormwood and Rue ? "
TUSSER, *Five Hundred Points of Good Husbandry*, 1580.

There is an old tradition that wormwood sprang up in the track of the serpent as it writhed along the ground when driven out of Paradise. Wormwood was formerly one of the herbs put amongst clothes to keep away moths, and Culpepper tells us, " this herb Wormwood being laid among cloaths will make a moth scorn to meddle with the cloaths as much as a lion scorns to meddle with a mouse or an eagle with a fly." Sir John Hill was very scornful of those who used any variety of wormwood except the Roman : " No such herb is brought to market : they sell sea worm-wood, a nauseous bitter in its place, and the true medicine, though possessed of all its virtues, has thus lost much credit. All the time there is no plant more hardy than true Roman wormwood, none more easily propagated in the open ground ; but the physician overlooks the abuse, and long neglect has made the other a universal substitute."

To make Sugar of Wormwood, Mint, Aniseed, or any other of that Kinde.—Take double refined Sugar, and doe but wet it in fair water, or Rose-water, and boyle it to a Candy, when it is almost boyled take it off, and stir it till it be cold ; then drop in three or four drops of the oyls of whatsoever you will make and stir it well ; then drop it on a board being before sifted with Sugar.—*The Queen's Closet Opened*, by W. M., Cook to Queen Henrietta Maria, 1655.

To make Wormwood-Water.—Bruise half a Pound of Liquorish, and half a Pound of Anniseeds well, and put them into two Gallons of port Wine ; put in also two or three Handfuls of Roman Wormwood ; let them infuse for twelve Hours, then distil them in an

Alembick ; or you may infuse the Ingredients in Brandy and distil them.—*Ibid.*

To make Wormwood-Wine.—Take two Pounds of dry'd Wormwood, two gallons of Rhenish Wine, let the Wormwood lye in it to digest for three or four Months, shaking the Vessel often ; when it is settled, decant the clear Tincture for use.—*Ibid.*

Wormwood Brandy.—Put an ounce of these flowers with a pint of Brandy and let it stand six weeks. There will be a tincture produced of which a tablespoon should be taken in half a gill of water.—Sir John Hill, *The British Herbal*, 1772.

YARROW

" I rose early in the morning yesterday,
I plucked yarrow for the horoscope of thy tale
In the hope that I might see the desire of my heart
Ochone there was seen her back towards me."

An old " raum " sung in the Hebrides.

The old song quoted above refers to the story of a certain bard who fell in love with a girl in Stornaway, who married another. He was always conjuring up her image, and every Wednesday he composed a song to her till he pined away and became so small that his father had to carry him in a creel on his back. Yarrow from time immemorial has been used in incantations and by witches, and as late as the seventeenth century a witch was tried for using it.   Yarrow is an aboriginal English plant, and by many country people is still accounted one of the most valuable of our British herbs, and they still drink the old Yarrow tea for colds and rheumatism.

YARROW TEA.—On a large handful of the roots, leaves and flowers of yarrow pour one pint of boiling water.

CHAPTER III

OF SALLETS

" In Health, if Sallet Herbs, you can't endure,
Sick, you'll desire them, or for Food or Cure."

Old Proverb.

" Cold herbes now wholsom bee :
But let no blood in any wise :
By running stream and shadow tree,
Thy booke thou mayest well exercise."

July, *Ram's Little Dodoen,* 1606.

" We present you a taste of our English garden Housewifry in
the matter of Sallets. And though some of them may be vulgar
(as are most of the best things) yet we impart them to show the
Plenty, Riches, and variety of the Sallet-Garden. And to justify
what has been asserted of the possibility of living (not unhappily)
on Herbs and Plants according to Divine institution."—JOHN
EVELYN, *Acetaria,* 1699.

" STOCK-DOVES, pheasants and partridges," one old
herbalist says, " are the best sallet-gatherers in the
way of picking tender young sallets, and in their crops
we find the very tenderest of young buds, and even
first rudiments of several plants." Though we may
not care to include in our modern salads all the green
food picked by these birds, we might with advantage
re-introduce the herbs and flowers our forefathers used.
Some of their salads, as may be seen in the receipts,
were very magnificent affairs indeed, and the principal
ornament of the banqueting table, but even the ordinary

ones with their numerous daintily arranged ingredients and " strewings " of edible flowers must have been fascinating to look at. John Evelyn was a great authority on salads, and he tells us that " the Potagère was in such reputation that she who neglected her kitchen garden (for that was still the good woman's Province) was never reputed a tolerable Housewife . . . she was never surprised, had all at hand and could in a trice set forth an handsome sallet." Indeed, it required much skill and judgment to mingle the ingredients of " a brave sallet " as it must be done, " not only so as to agree with the Humours of those who eat them but so that nothing should be suffered to domineer, so should none of them lose their Gust, Savour, or Vertue. These must be in correct proportions, the cool and refreshing to extinguish thirst, attemper the Blood, repress Vapours, the Hot, Dry, Aromatic Cordial and friendly to the Brain, the bitter and mordaunt, the mild and insipid, animated with the piquant and brisk. In the composure every Plant must bear its part and they must fall into their places like the Notes in Music, and there must be nothing harsh or grating. And tho' admitting some discords (to distinguish and illustrate the rest), striking in the more sprightly and sometimes gentler Notes, reconcile all Disconancies and melt them into an agreeable composition."

As Evelyn says, it takes a wise person to be a sallet-gatherer ; " I can by no means approve of the extravagant Fancy of some, who tell us that a Fool is as fit to be the gatherer of Sallets as a wise man. Because say they one can hardly choose amiss provided the Plants be green, young and tender. Sad experience shows how many fatal mistakes have been made by those who took hemlock for aconite, cow weed for Chervil, Dog's Mercury for Spinach, whose dire effects have been many times sudden death and the cause of mortal accidents to those who have eaten them unwittingly, and even if not poisonous, some of these wild and unknown Plants may annoy the Head and Brain. It is not surprising, therefore, that divers Popes and Emperors had learned Physicians for their ' Master-Cooks,' " Those who were foolish enough to raise salad herbs out of season on hot-beds the old herbalists condemned. " These forward Plants and Roots are but for the wanton Palate, and being unnaturally raised cannot but produce malignant and ill effects. We prefer the honest industrious Country Man's Field and the Good Wife's Garden, where they are legitimately born and without forcing Nature."

The number and variety of the ingredients in the old salad would astonish most modern cooks. Even in the seventeenth century, Evelyn deplored how far we were behind the French and Italians, " who gather anything almost that is tender to the very tops of Nettles, so as every Hedge affords a sallet (not unagreeable), and seasoned with Vinegar Salt and Oil, which gives it both the Relish and Name of Salad—Ensalada —as with us of Sallet from the sapidity which renders, not Plants and Herbs alone, but men themselves pleasant and agreeable." And why should we not revive these excellent old salads ? Why do not our modern cooks decorate our salads with strewings of rose petals, violets, primroses, gillyflowers, cowslips, and the flowers of elder, orange, rosemary, red sage, angelica, nasturtium, wild thyme, bugloss and marigold. All these flowers, and many others, are full of virtue and most wholesome. That they might not be wanting in winter salads many of them were preserved in vinegar or candied, and sometimes instead of having the flowers whole they were chopped and mingled together. Besides the flowers, which were the most ornamental part, " the furniture, and materials," consisted of an astonishing number of roots, stalks, leaves and buds, which we never think of using. We know it was the opinion of James II's head gardener that there should be at least thirty-five ingredients in an ordinary salad. He would have had a poor opinion of the modern gardener's contribution to the salad bowl. Numbers of roots were included, such as the elecampane, daisy, fennel, angelica, rampion, parsnip, carrot, and they were frequently blanched or candied, or simply boiled and added when cold or pickled. Then for the green there were sowthistle leaves, to which Evelyn tells us the Ambassador from Morocco and his Retinue were so partial, young spinach and wild succory leaves, tansy (" very sparingly because of its domineering relish and much fitter for the pan, being qualified with the juices of other ' fresh herbs ' "), young primrose and violet leaves, tarragon and rocket leaves, the tops of red sage (" with their flowers they retain all the noble properties of the other aromatic plants—a plant endued with so many wonderful properties as that the assiduous use of it is said to render men immortal "), the young tops of hyssop, thyme, marigold and marjoram, Jack-by-the-hedge or Sauce alone, the tips of leeks (" a little shred comes not amiss in composition "), lettuce (" Galen saith it breeds the most laudable blood, and the great Emperor

Augustus attributing his recovery of a dangerous sickness to them, it is reported he erected a statue and built an altar to this noble plant "), young mallow leaves, mercury, salad burnet, purslane, cornsalad, cowslip leaves, cresses (" quickening the torpid spirits when the tender leaves flowers and seeds are laudably mixt with the colder Plants "), young basil, borage and bugloss leaves, chervil (" never to be wanting in sallets as long as they may be had, being exceedingly wholesome and chearing the spirits "), samphire (" you cannot provide too much of this excellent ingredient "), ox-eye daisy leaves, plantain and yarrow, vine tendrils, wood sorrel, young cabbage leaves shred finely, and scurvy grass. Ashen key, broom and elder buds pickled were all common ingredients, and sometimes they had the candied buds of flowers. Evelyn was somewhat contemptuous of beet-root, and describes it as being " of quality cold and moist, but sometimes commendable with wine and pepper." Evidently the English did not serve it shred, for like other writers he comments on the Italian and French custom of paring it, " contrived into curious figures to adorn their sallets."

And then what care must be taken in preparing the salad ! " Let your Herby ingredients be exquisitely cull'd and cleansed of all worm eaten slimy cankered dry spotted or any ways Vitiated Leaves. And then that they be rather discreetly sprinkled than over much sob'd with spring water (could a French chef be more particular ?) especially lettuce. After washing let them remain a while in the cullender to drain the superfluous moisture and lastly swing them all together gently in a clean coarse Napkin. Then the Oyl must be very clean, not highly coloured nor yellow, but with an eye rather of a pallid olive green without smell or the least touch of rancid or indeed of any other sensible taste or smell at all—but smooth, light and pleasant upon the tongue. The vinegar to be of the best wine vinegar and impregnated with the infusion of clove gilliflowers, Elder Roses, Rosemary, Nasturtium and thus enriched with the Virtues of these Plants. The Salt to be of the brightest and only enough put in to give them the grateful saline acrid. The sugar to be of the best refined. The mustard (a noble ingredient) to be of the best Tewkesbury or else composed of the soundest and weightiest Yorkshire Seed, exquisitely sifted winnow'd and free from the husks, a little (not over much) dry'd by the fire, temper'd to the consistence of a pap with Vinegar in which shavings of the Horse Radish have been steeped. Then cutting an onion and putting it into a small earthen gally pot or some thick glass of that shape pour the Mustard over it and close it very well with a cork. There be who preserve the Flower and Dust of the bruised seed in a well-stocked glass to temper and have it fresh when they please. But what is yet by some esteemed beyond all these is composed of the dry'd seeds of the Indian Nasturtium reduced to Powder finely bolted, from time to time made fresh as indeed all other mustard should be. The seeds to be pounded in a mortar or bruised with a polished cannon bullet in a large wooden Bowl or Dish or which is most preferred ground in a quern provided for this purpose only. The pepper whether white or black not to be bruised to too small a dust. Better than ordinary Pepper is the root of the Burnet saxe-

frage and extolled by some beyond all other peppers
and very wholesome." For " strewings " and " aroma-
tises," they used grated orange and lemon rind or
saffron (a noble cordial, but so apt to prevail above
everything, we little encourage it admittance into our
sallet). To all this they added the yolks of fresh and
new-laid eggs boiled only moderately hard and mashed
or cut into quarters to eat with the Herbs.

For the actual making of the salad the clearest
directions are given. No good modern cook uses a
knife in preparing a salad, and the old herbalists were
equally particular. If a knife were necessary it must
be of silver. Then the " sallet-dishes " must be of
Porcelain or the Holland Delft ware, " neither too deep
nor shallow. There must be a Dish in which to beat
and mingle the liquid vehicles and a second to receive
the crude Herbs upon which they are to be poured
and then with a Fork and Spoon kept continually
stirr'd till all the Furniture be equally moistened.
Some who are Husbands of their oyl pour at first the
oyl alone as more apt to communicate and diffuse
its slipperiness than when it is mingled and beaten
with the acids which they pour on last of all. 'Tis
incredible how small a quantity of oyl (in this quality
like the gilding of Wyer) is sufficient to imbue a very
plentiful assembly of sallet Herbs. Your Herbs being
handsomely parcell'd and spread on a clean Napkin
before are to be mingled together in one of the earthen
glas'd dishes. Take of clear and perfectly good olive
oyl three parts, of sharpest vinegar (sweetest of all
condiments), lemon or juice of orange one part, and
therein let steep some slices of horse-radish with a
little salt : Some in a separate dish of vinegar gently

bruise a pod of pepper straining both the vinegars apart to make use of either or one alone or of both as they best like. Then add as much Tewkesbury or other dry mustard grated as will lie upon a half-crown piece. Beat and mingle all these very well together but pour not on the oyl and vinegar till immediately before the sallet is ready to be eaten. And then with the yolks of two new laid eggs squash and bruise them all into mash with a spoon and lastly pour it all upon the Herbs stirring and mingling them till they are well and thoroughly imbued not forgetting the sprinkling of Aromatic and such flowers mentioned and garnishing the Dish with the thin slices of Horse Radish, Red Beet or Berberries, etc. The liquids may be made more or less acid as is most agreeable to your taste.

" These Rules and Prescriptions duly observ'd you have a sallet for a Table of six or eight persons."

Salads in those days must have been artistic triumphs, and no wonder one herbalist writes, " Let none despise our Sallet Dresser or disdain so clean innocent an sweet and naturall a Quality." Then looking back to a still more halycon age he adds regretfully, " All the world were eaters and composers of sallets in its best and brightest age."

SALLET FOR FISH DAIES.—Onions in flakes laid round about the dishe ; with minced carrots laid in the middle of the dish, with boyled hips in five parts like a oken leafe made and garnished with tansey long cut with oyle and vinegar.—*The Good Housewife's Jewell,* 1585.

TO MAKE A SALLET OF ALL KINDE OF HEARBS.—

Take your hearbes and picke them very fine into faire water and pick your flowers by themselves and washe them all cleane and swing them in a strainer and when you put them into a dish, mingle them with Cowcumbers or Lemmons payred and sliced and scrape sugar and put in ginger and oyle and throwe the flowers on the top of the Sallet.—*Ibid.*

DIVERS SALLETS BOYLED.—Parboyle spinnage and chop it fine, with the edges of two hard Trenchers upon a board, or the backs of two chopping knives then set them on a chafing dish of coales with butter and vinegar ; Season it with Cinnamon, Ginger, Sugar and a few parboyled currans. Then cut hard egges into quarters and garnish it withall and serve it upon sippets. So you may serve Burrage, Bugloss, Endive, Succory, Coleflowers, Sorrel, Marigold leaves, Water cresses, Leekes boiled, Onions, Rocket. Parboyle them and season them all alike : whether it be with Oyle and Vinegar, or Butter and Vinegar, Cinnamon, Ginger, Sugar, and Butter : egges are necessary or at least very good for all boyled sallets.— John Murrell, *The Ladies Practice*, 1621.

SALLETS OF FLOWERS preserved in Vinegar and Sugar as either Violets, broome flowers, or gillyflowers of all kindes.—G. Markham, *The English Husbandman*, 1615.

A brave WARMING SALAD FOR WINTER.—Spinnage, Sorrel, lettuce, and a few onions, then add oyl, vinegar, and salt, balm, pepper grass, mint, endive, young green buds of coleworts and garlic.—Tryon, *A Treatise of Cleanness in Meats*, 1692.

SALLET-ALL-SORTS.—The Almonds blanch'd in cold water, cut them round and thin and so leave them in cold water. Then have pickled Cucumbers, Olives, Capers, Berberries, Red-Beet. Buds of Nasturtium, Broom, etc., Purslan stalk, Sampier, Ash-keys, Walnuts, Mushrooms, with raisins of the Sun ston'd, citron and orange peel. Strew them over with any candy'd flowers and so dispose of them in the same Dish both mixt and by themselves. To these add Marrows, Pine kernels and of Almonds four times as much of the rest with some Rose-water. Here also come in the Pickled Flowers and Vinegar in little china Dishes. And thus have you an universal winter Sallet or an All sort in compendium fitted for a City Feast and distinguished from the Gran Sallet which should consist of the green blanched and unpickled under a stately Pennash of Sellery adorn'd with Buds and Flowers.—John Evelyn, *Acetaria*, 1699.

OTHER GRAND SALLET.—All sorts of Good herbs, the little leaves of red sage, the smallest leaves of Sorrel, and the leaves of Parsley picked very small, tear some white cabbage leaves, the youngest and smallest leaves of spinage, some leaves of burnet, the smallest leaves of lettice, white endive and chervil all finely picked, washed and swung in a strainer, or clean napkin and well drained from the water, then dish it in a clean scoured dish and about the center capers, currans, olives, lemons cerved and slic'd, boiled beet-roots,

carved and slic'd and dished round also, with good oyl
and Vinegar.—*The Art and Mystery of Cookery.*
Approved by the fifty-five years' experience and industry of Robert May in his Attendance on several
persons of great honour, 1671.

A GRAND SALLET OF DIVERS COMPOUNDS.—Take
green purslane and pick it leaf by leaf, wash it and
swing it in a napkin, then being dished in a faire clean
dish, and finely piled up in a heap in the midst of it,
lay round about the center of the sallet, pickled capers,
currans, and raisins of the Sun, washed picked mingled
and laid round about it ; about them some carved
cucumbers, in slices or halves and laid round also.
Then garnish the dish brims with borage or clove
gillyflowers or otherways with cucumber peels, olives,
capers, and raisins of the Sun, then the best sallet oyl
and wine vinegar.—*Ibid.*

AND NOW, IF YOU WILL MAKE A CROWNED, OR
GRAND SALLET, YOU MAY DO THIS.—Take a Ballotin,
or great Citron, cut off the two ends, as if you would
slice him out, then raise in his rind very even with
a great Knife to the very white : then raise up the meat
or white of your Fruit the thickness of a Crown-piece,
keeping your knife turning round the Fruit at that even
thickness, till you come to the heart or seeds of your
Fruit, then throw it into fair water, and when this is
done take a clean Napkin and spread it upon a Table
very even, then upon this Napkin you must lay your
Meat of the Ballotin, and there carve it neatly into what
Form or Figure you think fit, that may serve to make

a Crown, but the help of a Steel Saw which hath been
cut ; the French say cut in the day, that is, that you
may see clearly through it, and you are to take notice,
that you are to begin the work at the lower end of the
Crown, and pursue it to the middle and finish it at
the top or head. But because there are many sorts
of Crowns, you are to take notice that a Royal Crown
is to be cut at the top with crosses and Flower-de-
Luces. And you may take notice, by the way, that
thus you may make any Crown or Crownet, as big or
as little as you please, this being left to your own
discretion.

And when you have done carving and cutting of
your Figures for a Crown, and drawn and pick'd out all
the loose pieces, that your Work may show itself, then
put your Crown into cold water, and take fair Lemons
and Oranges, cut off the two ends and take off the Pill
to the white at their full bigness and height, to the
thickness of a Crown-piece, and throw them into fair
water, let them lye a little then take them out again and
cut them into what Figures you please, but at their
full length : to make a half-crown, you must have about
fifteen of these of both sorts, which will suffice to set
round the brims of a Plate.

Then you must have all sorts of good sallet herbs,
and to make a Bed of them, when they are cut indif-
ferent small, upon the hollow of a large brim'd Plate,
and garnish them with Beet-roots, and when that
great Crown hath been taken up and let run a little,
place him hansomly upon your bed of Herbs, at what
bigness you please, and garnish him within with all
sorts of good herbs, then Rasp the Rinds of green
Citron, and make a kind of a Rock within the Crown

In Apothecary's Garden

upon the herbs to that height that it may come a little above the Crown, and the Crown seem as if it were made fast about the Rock, but do not forget to garnish your works of the Crown with the seeds of Granandes that are very red.

Then take your little Crowns out of the Water, and let them run, and place them round about the great one upon little beds of good sallet herbs or Beet-roots, and fill them within with good herbs, and on the top of each a little of your green Citron or Lemon Rasped like a Rock, and they should be garnished also with the seeds of Granades, Pistaches, and sweet Almonds, and hansomely ranged and mingled, first an Orange than a Lemon ; thus garnish and set about your great Crown what garniture you please, for delight, between each little Crown : this will be pleasing to the Eye, set it in the middle of a Table, and ought to be served with Orange-Flowers-Water, and rasped Sugar over it.—From *The Receipt Book of John Middleton,* Cook to the Duke of Bolton, 1734.

To make a Grand Sallad for the Spring.— Take cowslip buds, violet-flowers and leaves ; young lettuce, spinach, Alexander Buds, Strawberry leaves, water cresses, each apart by themselves and then take also Capers, Olives, Samphire, Cucumbers, Broombuds, Raisins and Currans parboiled, Almonds blanched, Barberries and other pickles, then lay a Turnip or some other hard thing for a Standard in the middle of the Sallad, let it be formed like a Castle made of Paste washed over with the Yolks of Eggs and within it a Tree made in like manner and coloured with green Herbs and stuck with flowers ; you must also have annexed to it twelve supporters round it, sloping to it, and fastened to the Castle ; then having made four rings of Paste, each bigger than the other, the Biggest must compass the Castle and reach within three inches of the Feet of your supporters ; the second must be within two inches of that, and so place as many as you think convenient and according to the size of your dish, that they may be like so many Steps, one above another, then place one sort of your salad round on the uppermost Ring, and so on till you come to the Dish, laying a several sort on every one ; then place all your Pickles from the Sallad to the Brim of the Dish each by itself, then garnish your Dish with all things suitable to the Season. These grand Sallads are only for great Feasts. Remember that in Autumn your standard ought to be the Resemblance of a Castle carved out of Carrots and Turnips ; in the winter a tree hung with Snow, in Summer a green Tree.— From *The Receipt Book of John Nott*, Cook to the Duke of Bolton, 1723.

SALLAD FOR WINTER.—Take a hard cabbage, and with a sharp knife shave it as thin as possible and serve it up with oil, mustard and vinegar.

Or else take corn sallad and Horse radish scrap'd fine, dish it handsomely and serve it with oil and vinegar.—Mrs. Glasse, *The Art of Cookery made Plain and Easy*, 1784.

BROCCOLI IN SALLAD.—Broccoli is a pretty dish by way of Sallad in the middle of a table. Boil it like asparagus ; lay it in your dish, beat up with oil and vinegar and a little salt. Garnish with nasturtium buds.—*Ibid.*

To make a Grand Sallet for the Spring.—Your Gardener, or those that serve you with herbs, must supply you with all manner of Spring-Sallets, as buds of Cowslips, Violets, Strawberries, Primrose, Water-cresses, young Lettuce, Spinnage Alexander-buds, or what other things may be got, either backward or forward in the Spring ; having all these things sever-ally and apart, then take of themselves Sampier, Olives, Capers, Broom-buds, Cowcumbers, Raisons and Currans parboyled, blanched Almonds, Barberries, or what other pickles you can obtain ; then prepare your standard for the middle of your dish ; it may be a waxed tree, or a standard of Paste (like a Castle), being washed in the yolks of eggs, and all made green with herbs ; as also, a tree within that, in the like manner may be made, with Paste, made green, and stuck with Flowers, so that you may not perceive it, but to be a tree, with about twelve supporters round, stooping to, and fastened in holes in your Castle, and the other end bending out to the middle of your dish ; they may be formed with Paste ; then having four rings of Paste, the one bigger than another (like unto hoops), your biggest must come over your Castle, and reach within three inches of the foot of your supporter, the second to be within two inches of that and so place as many as you please gradually, that they may be like as many steps going up to a Cross ; you may have likewise four Belconies in your Castle with four Statues of the four Seasons ; this done, place your Sallet, around of one sort on the uppermost ring, or step, so round all the other till you come to the dish, with every one a several sort ; then place all your pickles from that to the brims of your dish severally, one answering another. As for example, if you have two of white, and two of green, let them be opposite, the white against the white, and the green against the green, and so all the other ; so your dishes bottom being wholly covered below your Mount, garnish your dish with all kind of things suitable, or afforded by the Spring ; your Statues ought to have every one a Cruitt placed in their hands, two with Vinegar and two with Oyl ; when this Sallet is made, let it be carried to the Table, and set in its place ; and when the guests are all placed, unstop the Cruitts, that the Oyl and Vinegar may run on the Sallet ; these Cruits must be glasses not a quarter of a pint apiece, sized over on the outside, and strowed with flowers : After the same manner may you make your Sallet in Summer, Autumn, or Winter ; only take those Sallets that are then in season, and changing your standard ; for in the Summer, you ought to resemble a green tree ; and in the Autumn, a Castle carved out of Carrots and Turnips ; in the Winter, a Tree hanged with Snow : This only is for great Feasts, and may inform the Practitioner in such Feasts, for the honour of his Master, and benefit of himself. The paste that you make your Castle or Standard with, must be made of Rye.

There is nothing of more constant use in our sallets than *good* Vinegar so we think it not amiss to give the following (much approv'd) Receipt.

VINEGAR.—To every gallon of Spring water, let here be allowed 3 lbs. of Malaga-Raisins. Put them

in an earthen Jarr and place them where they may have
the hottest sun from May till Michaelmas. Then
pressing them well Tun the liquor up in a very strong
iron-hoop'd Vessel to prevent its bursting. It will
appear very thick and muddy when newly pressed but
will refine in the Vessel and be as clear as wine. Thus
let it remain untouch'd for three months before it be
drawn off and it will prove excellent Vinegar.—John
Evelyn, *Acetaria*, 1699.

To MAKE MUSTARD.—The best way of making Mustard is this : Take of the Best Mustard-seed (which is
black) for example a quart. Dry it gently in an oven,
and beat it to subtle powder, and searce it. Then
mingle well strong Wine-vinegar with it, so much that
it be pretty liquid, for it will dry with keeping. Put
to this a little Pepper beaten small (white is the best)
at discretion, and put a good spoonful of sugar to it
(which is not to make it taste sweet, but rather quick,
and to help the fermentation), lay a good Onion in the
bottom, quarters if you will, and a Race of Ginger
scraped and bruised ; and stir it often with a Horse-
radish root cleansed, which let always lie in the pot,
till it have lost its vertue, then take a new one. This
will keep long and grow better for a while. It is not
good till after a month.

Some think it will be the quicker, if the seed be
ground with fair water, instead of vinegar, putting
store of Onions in it.

My Lady Holmeby makes her quick fine Mustard
thus : Choose true Mustard seed ; dry it in an oven,
after the bread is out. Beat and searce it to a most
subtle powder. Mingle Sherry sack with it (stirring

it a long time very well, so much as to have it of a fit consistence for Mustard) then put a good quantity of fine Sugar to it, as five or six spoonfuls, or more, to a pint of Mustard. Stir and incorporate all well together. This will keep good a long time. Some do like to put to it a little (but a little) of very sharp Wine-vinegar.—*The Closet of Sir Kenelm Digby Opened*, 1669.

CHAPTER IV

HERB POTTAGES

" In pottage without herbs there is
Neither goodness nor nourishment."

Book of Iago ab Dewi.

" We cannot make so much as a little good Pottage without Herbes, which give an admirable relish and make them wholsom for our Bodies."—W. COLES, *The Art of Simpling*, 1656.

A COOLING POTTAGE.—Take Borage, Mallows, Fumitory, Violet Leaves, Beetes, Great Raisins (the stones taken out), Prunes and a little Dill. Seethe these in pottage and eat thereof.—*The Good Housewife's Handmaid*, 1588.

HERB POTTAGE.—Take Elder buds, nettle tops, clivers and watercress, and what quantity of water you please proportionable to your quantity of herbs, add oatmeal according as you would have it in thickness and when your water and oatmeal is just ready to boyl, put your Herbs into it, cut or uncut as you like best ; take a Ladle and lade it and then you may eat it with the herbs or strain it adding a little butter, salt and bread. The best will be not to eat it till it is somewhat cooled and not past as hot as milk from the cow. You are to remember not to let it boyl at all. This is a brave, wholsom, cleansing sort of pottage far beyond what is commonly made.—T. Tryon, *The Good Housewife*, 1692.

ANOTHER SORT OF HERB POTTAGE.—Take water and oatmeal, make it boyling hot on a quick fire then take Spinnage, corn sallet and mint cut them and put a good quantity into it. Let it stand on the fire till it be ready to boyl and then lade it to and fro five or six minutes, then take it off and let it stand awhile that the oatmeal may sink to the bottom then strain it adding butter, salt and bread and when it is about Blood warm eat it. This is a gallant sublime pottage . . . it chears and comforts the Spirits, breeds good Blood and makes the whole body lightsom.

The same method you ought to follow in making all sorts of gruels and herb pottages, be the Herbs of what Nature they will, for the boyling of Herbs not only in pottage but for any other use of Food was not invented by wise seers into the Arcana of Nature, for it does as it were totally destroy the pure volatile spirits and balsamick vertues, as also the strong warming properties thereof. For this cause raw Herbs are much better. This is the way the wise, healthy, long-lived Antients prepared their herbs, who made them one of their principal Foods. Boyling any sorts of Herbs does in a moment's time either suffocate or evaporate the volatile Spirits of them and then all the sweet, pleasant, cleansing virtues are gone.—*Ibid*.

GARLIC OR ONION POTTAGE.—Take water and oatmeal, stir it together and when it is ready to boyle bruise as much garlick or onion as you please, to make it either strong or weak, put this bruised garlick into your boyling hot gruel and brew it to and fro with your ladle that it may not boyl, for five or six minutes ; then take it off and let it stand a little, then add butter, salt and bread and eat it as warm as your Blood. Tis a brave, warm, cleansing Gruel, nothing so strong and nauseous as that which is boyled for this way you do extract the finer and purer parts of the garlic, and leaves the strong, nauseous Qualities behind, but on the contrary much boyling, or boyling according to custom, does destroy the good cleansing vertues and awakens the Evil.—*Ibid.*

To make Spinage Pottage.—Take nothing but the Heart, or Soundest Part of the Spinage ; mince it fine, and stew it in a Pipkin with Pease-soop, an onion stuck with Cloves, a Carrot, and other Seasoning Ingredients. Set your Crusts a soaking, scrape in some Parmesan, and dress your Pottage : Garnish it with Sticks of Cinnamon round about, and lay one in the middle, or fry'd Bread or an Onion.—*The Queen's Closet Opened*, by W. M., Cook to Queen Henrietta Maria, 1655.

Soup de Santé for Fish Days.—Take Celery, Endive, Sorrel, a little Chevril and cabbage-lettuce well picked and washed, mince them down with a knife, squeeze the water from them, put them into a saucepan, toss them up in Butter with a little Onion, take off all the fat, then put to them a little water from boiled Peas, and let them boil till they are tender ; then put in half-a-spoonful of flower and keep moving it till it is brown. Then put in some good Fish-broth and a glass of wine, season it with Salt, pepper, an onion stuck with cloves, shred Parsley and a faggot of savoury Herbs, lay in the middle of your Soop-dish a French roll fried having taken the crumb out at the bottom, cover the Bottom of your dish with the crust of French Rolls, set it over a chafing dish of coals, lay the herbs upon them and then pour the soop upon your crusts and herbs, let it stand a while to simmer, and soak the Bread. Garnish it with Turnips and Carrots and serve it up hot.—From *The Receipt Book of Joseph Cooper*, Cook to Charles I, 1654.

BROWN POTTAGE OF HERB ROOTS.—Take carrots and turnips and cut them in Dice, flour them and fry them Brown in clarify'd Butter ; drain them from the Fat, and put to them of meagre broth and make a brown gravy from them. Then take celery, endive, spinach, sorrel, lettuce, parsley and onions, chop these together, not too small, put to them as much of your gravy as will fill your dish. When you fry your Turnips and Carrots pulp some of them and put that in to help thicken your soup. Make a few force-meat balls of soft herbs worked up into Bread and Eggs and season'd and put in ; Stove all well together. Put in French Bread fry'd and dish it. Put a Manchet, stoved, in the middle and garnish with Scalded Spinach and Sliced Lemon.—*Ibid.*

POTAGE MAIGRE.—Take four quarts of Spring water, two or three onions stuck with some Cloves, two or three slices of lemon peel ; Salt, whole white Pepper,

Mace, a Raze or two of Ginger tied up in a fine cloth (Lawn or Tiffany), and make all boil for half an hour. Then having Spinage, Sorrel, White Beet, chard a little cabbage a few small tops of Cives (Chives) wash'd and pick'd clean shred them and cast them into the Liquor, with a pint of blue pease boild soft, and strained with a bunch of sweet herbs, the top and bottom of a French roll, and so suffer it to boil during three hours and then dish it with another small French roll and Slices about the Dish. Some cut Bread in slices and frying them brown (being dried) put them into the Pottage just as it is going to be eaten.

The same herbs clean, washed, broken and pulled asunder only being put into a close cover'd pipkin, without any other water or liquor will stew in their own juice and moisture. Some add an whole onion which after a while should be taken out, remembering to serve it with salt or spice, and serve it up with Bread and a piece of fresh Butter.—John Evelyn, *Acetaria*, 1699.

ELDER LEAVES.—Though the leaves are somewhat rank of smell and so not commendable for Sallet they are otherwise (as indeed is the entire shrub) of the most sovereign virtues, and the Spring buds and tender leaves excellently wholesome in Pottage.—*Ibid.*

TO MAKE SOOP IN THE SPRING, WHEN THERE IS NO SELERY NOR ENDIVE.—Take twelve Cabbage Lettuce, six green Cucumbers, pare them and take the Cores out, cut both Cucumbers and Lettuce in little Bits about an Inch long, scald them off in boiling Water, and put

them to clear, strong Broth ; let them boil Tender
with a Handful of Green Pease. Let your garnishing
be Cucumbers and Lettuce. Use no thickening in
this Soop. So serve it.—*The Receipt Book of Patrick
Lamb*, Master Cook to Charles II, James II, William
and Mary, and Queen Anne, 1716.

To make Carrot Soup.—Boil your carrots, cleanse
them, beat them in a mortar or wooden tray, put them
into a pipkin with Butter, white Wine, Salt, Cinnamon,
Sugar, shred Dates, boil'd currants. Stew these well
together. Dish them on Sippets, garnish with hard
Eggs in Halves or Quarters and scrape in Sugar.—From
The Receipt Book of John Nott, Cook to the Duke of
Bolton, 1723.

To make Meagre Broth for Soop with Herbs.—
Set on a Kettle of Water and put in two or three crusts
of Bread and all sorts of Good Herbs, season it with
Salt put in Butter and a bunch of Sweet herbs, boil it
for an hour and a half, then strain it through a Sieve
or Napkin. This will serve to make Lettuce Soop,
Artichoke Soop, Asparagus Soop, Succory Soop, and
Soop de Santé with Herbs.—*Ibid*.

To make Potage the French way.—Take hard
lettuce, sorrel and chevril of each a like Quantity or
any other Herbs you like as much as half a peck will
hold pressed down, pick them, wash and drain them.
Put them in a Pot with fresh butter, then add water,
Salt, some whole cloves and a crust of Bread and

when it is boild take out the crust of bread and put in
the yolks of a couple of eggs well beaten and stir
together over the fire. Lay in a Dish some slices of
Bread. Pour it in, serve it up.—*Ibid.*

POTTAGE WITHOUT THE SIGHT OF HERBS.—Mince
several sorts of sweet herbs very fine—Spinage, Parsley,
Marigold flowers, Succory, Strawberry and Violet
Leaves. Pound them with oatmeal in a Mortar. Boil
your oatmeal and herbs in broth and serve.—*Ibid.*

TO MAKE A POTTAGE FOR ONE OR TWO PERSONS.—
Take four Handfuls of Pot-herbs, pick'd, wash'd, and
cut small, two or three Onions cut small likewise,
three or four Leeks, Half an Ounce of fresh Butter or
Bacon, four Spoonfuls either of fine Flour, pounded
Rice, Oatmeal, or peel'd Barley, a Dram of Salt, and
a little Pepper ; boil the whole in three Quarts of
Water, which must be reduced to a Pint and a Half,
and kept for use. You may make, at the same time,
Pottage enough for three or four days.—*The Modern
Cook*, by Vincent la Chapelle, Chief Cook to the
Prince of Orange, 1744.

A MOISTENING AND COOLING BROTH WITH HERBS.—
Take some Leaves of Sorrel, Beet, Lettuce, Purslane,
and Chevril, two large handfuls of each, pick, wash
and cut them all small, let them boil with a Crust of
Bread and two Drams of fresh Butter in two Pints of
Water, which when half boiled away is to be taken off
and strained through a Sieve.—*Ibid.*

To MAKE POTTAGE OF CHOPPED HERBS.—Mince very fine Spinage, Chives, Parsley, Marigold-flowers, Succory, Strawberry and Violet Leaves, stamp them with Oatmeal in a Bowl, put chopped Greens in with it : you may either put Broth or Water to them ; if Water, boil a good Piece of Butter in it ; put sipets in the Dish, and pour it over them.—From *The Receipt Book of Elizabeth Cleland*, 1759.

CHAPTER V

HERB PUDDINGS

" Thus have you receipts for herb puddings."

To MAKE A GREEN PUDDING.—Take a penny loafe of stale bread. Grate it put to it halfe a pound of Sugar, a grated nutmeg, as much salt as will season it, three-quarters of a pound of Beef suet shred very small, then take sweet herbs, the most of them Marrigold, shred the herbs very small mix all well together then take two eggs and work them up together with your hand, and make them into round balls and when the Water boyls put them in, serve them. Rose-water, sugar and butter for sauce.—*The Compleat Cook*, 1655.

To MAKE TARTS CALLED TAFFITY TARTS.—First wet your paste with Butter and cold water and roule it very thin, also then lay them in layes and between every lay of apples strew some sugar and some lemond pill, cut very small. If you please, put some Fennel seed to them ; then put them into a stoak hot oven, and let them stand an houre in or more, then take them out and take Rose-water and Butter beaten together and wash them over with the same and strew fine sugar upon them, then put them into the Oven againe, let them stand a little while and take them out.—*Ibid.*

To MAKE A GREEN BOILED PUDDING OF SWEET

HERBS.—Take and steep a penny white loaf in a quart of cream and onely eight yolks of eggs, some currans, sugar, cloves, beaten mace, dates, juice of spinage, saffron, cinnamon, nutmeg, sweet marjoram, tyme, savory, minced very small and some salt, boil it with beef-suet, marrow (or none).—Robert May, *The Art and Mystery of Cookery*, 1671.

A TART OF ARTICHOKE CREAM WITH SUGAR.—When your artichoke bottoms are well boiled beat them in a mortar and strain them through a cullendar with butter, the yolks of two eggs raw, salt, cinnamon sugar and green citron, put them into a Patty pan sheeted with fine Paste, but do not cover it all and when it is baked ice it over with Sugar and Orange-flower water and so serve it away.—*A Perfect School of Instructions for the Officers of the Month*, by Giles Rose, one of the Master Cooks to Charles II, 1682.

A TART OF BEET ROOTS.—First roste your Beet roots in the Embers and peel them very well, cut them in pieces and give them a boil with a glass of white wine and then beat them in a Morter, with a piece of Sugar, a little Salt, and Cinnamon, and put them into fine paste with some green citron rasped and a piece of Butter and do not cover it, but when it is baked, serve it with perfumed Sugar and Orange flowers.—*Ibid.*

TANSY PUDDING.—Take the gratings or slices of three Naples biscuits put them into ½ pint of cream with twelve fresh eggs four of the whites cast out, strain the rest and break them with two spoonfuls of rose-water a little salt and sugar, and half a grated nutmeg. And when ready for the pan put almost a pint of the juice of Spinnach, Beets, Corn sallet, green corn, violet or primrose tender leaves (for any of these you may take your choice) with a very small sprig of tansy and let it be fried so as to look green in the dish. Dish with a strew of sugar of the juice of Orange. Some affect to have it fried a little brown and thick.—*Ibid.*

SPINAGE PUDDING.—Take a sufficient quantity of Spinage, stamp and strain out the juice ; put to it grated Manchet ; the yolks of three eggs, some Marrow shred small, nutmeg, sugar, some Corinths (if you please), a few Carraways, Rose or Orange-flower water (as you like best) to make it grateful. Mingle all with a little boiled Cream and set the Dish or Pan in the Oven with a garmint of Puff Paste. It will require but very moderate baking.—*Ibid.*

PUDDING OF CARROT.—Pare off some of the crust of Manchet bread and grate off half as much of the rest as there is of the root, which must also be grated. Then take half a pint of half Cream or New Milk half a Pound of fresh Butter Six new laid Eggs (taking out three of the Whites) mash and mingle them well with the Cream and Butter. Then put in the grated Bread and Carrot with near half a Pound of Sugar and a little Salt ; some grated Nutmeg and beaten Spice and pour all into a convenient dish or pan buttered to keep the ingredients from sticking or burning ; set it in a quick oven for about an Hour. And so have you a Composi-ion for any Root Pudding. The Sauce is a little rose-water with Butter beaten together and sweetened with the Sugar Caster.—*Ibid*.

TART OF HERBS.—An herb tart is made thus : Boil fresh cream or milk with a little grated Bread or Naples Biscuit (which is better) to thicken it, a pretty quantity of Chevril, Spinach, Beet (or what other herb you please) being first parboil'd and chop'd. Than add Macaron or Almonds beaten to a paste, a little sweet Butter the yolk of five eggs (three of the whites rejected). To these add some Corinths plump'd in milk or boild therein. Sugar and Spice at discretion and stirring it all together over the Fire, bake it in the Tart Pan.— *Ibid*.

A FLOWER PUDDING.—Mince cowslip flowers, clove, gillyflowers, rose petals and Spinach of each a handful, take a slice of Manchet (white bread) and scald it with cream. Add a pound of blanch'd Almonds pounded small with Rose-water, a quarter of a Pound of Dates sliced and cut small, the yolks of three eggs, a handful of Currants and sweeten all with Sugar. When boiled pour Rose-water over and scrape Sugar on. Then serve up.—From *The Receipt Book of John Nott*, Cook to the Duke of Bolton, 1723.

TO MAKE A CARROT PUDDING.—Boil a couple of middling Carrots till they are three quarters boil'd, then shred them very small and mix them with an equal quantity of grated Bread and a pound of Beef-suet shred small, some Cream, half a dozen Eggs, half a Nutmeg, a little Salt and Sugar to your Palate either boil or bake it. If boil'd sauce it with Butter, Lemon Juice and Sugar.—*Ibid.*

POTATOE PUDDINGS, MADE WITH SWEET-MEATS. (From Mr. Moring of Temple Bar).—Take some clean Potatoes, boil them tender and when they are so, and clean from their Skins, break them in a Marble Mortar, till they become a Pulp; then put to them, or you might beat with them some slices of candy'd Lemons and Oranges, and beat these together with some Spices, and Lemon-Peel Candy'd. Put to these some Marrow, and as much Sugar, with Orange-flower Water, as you think fit. Mix all together, and then take some whole candy'd Orange-Peels, and stuff them full of the Meat, and set them upon a Dish in a gentle Oven; when they have stood half an hour serve them hot, with a Sauce of Sack and Butter, and fine Sugar grated over them.—R. Bradley, *The Country Housewife and Lady's Director,* 1732.

HERB PUDDING.—Take oatmeal groats a quart and soak them all night in three pints of milk, and then the next day break in twelve or fourteen Eggs, season it with Pepper, Salt, Cloves, Mace and Ginger. Then take some Spinach, some Parsley, some Burrage, some Beet Leaves, and some Leek Blades. Mince in a little Thyme and sweet Majoram. Cut the Herbs but not too small. Put in a pound of Raisins and a pound of Currants. Put in a little Flour to bind it and mix it all very well together. Boil it in a cloth buttered and floured and mingle with it a pound and a half of good Beef Suet. Tye it very close in your Cloth and boil it very well and when well boiled serve it with plain thick Butter.—From *The Receipt Book of Charles Carter*, Cook to the Duke of Argyll, 1732.

To make Herb Dumplings.—Take a Penny Loaf, cut off the out Crust, and the rest in Slices, put to it as much hot Milk as will just wet it, take the Yolks and Whites of six Eggs, beat them with two Spoonfuls of powder Sugar, Half a Nutmeg, and a little Salt, so put it to your Bread ; take Half a Pound of Currants well cleaned, put them to your Eggs, then take a Handful of the Mildest Herbs you can get, gather them so equal that the Taste of one be not above the other, wash and chop them very small, put as many of them in as will make a deep Green (don't put any Parsley amongst them, nor any other strong Herb) so mix them all together, and boil them in a Cloth, make them about the Bigness of middling Apples ; about Half an Hour will boil them ; put them into your Dish, and have a little Candy'd Orange, White-wine, Butter and Sugar for Sauce.—Sarah Jackson, *The Director*, 1754.

CHAPTER VI

HERB DRINKS AND HOME-MADE WINES

" And then she took him into a room of the eighteenth century, which no longer exists, there or elsewhere save in name. It was the still room, and on its shelves stood the elixirs and cordials of ancient time :—The Elderberry Wine, good, mulled and spiced at Christmas time ; the Blackberry Wine ; the home-made Distilled Waters ; Lavender Water ; Hungary Water ; Cyprus Water, and the Divine Cordial itself, which takes three seasons to complete, and require all the flowers of Spring, Summer and Autumn."—
W. BESANT.

POSSET OF HERBS.—Take a fair scoured skellet, put in some milk into it and some rosemary ; the rosemary being well boiled in it, take it out and have some ale or beer in a pot, put to it the milk and sugar (or none).

Thus of thyme, cardus, camomile, mint or marigold flowers.—*The Art and Mystery of Cookery*. Approved by the fifty-five years' experience and industry of Robert May in his attendance on several persons of great honour, 1671.

MULLED CLARET.—Put into a double saucepan half a pint of water and when nearly boiling add a small handful of borage, 6 cloves, a pinch of nutmeg and a bay leaf and a teaspoon of mixed spice. Bring to the boil, stir in until dissolved three tablespoons of sugar and then remove from the fire. In another pan boil half a pint of water with 6 cloves, a little spice and two dessert spoons of sugar. Pour a bottle of claret into the first pan and bring to the boil again, stirring occasionally but do not lift the lid too often. If not spicy enough add a very little from the second saucepan until the flavour is to your liking.

An Excellent Drink.—Take a handful of fennel roots, as much parsley roots, half a handful of Borage roots and put out the pith of all the said roots, then take half a handful of pennyroyal, as much of violet leaves, as much succory and endive, hollyhock leaves, mallow leaves and red garden mints, of all these the like quantity as of these next before, half a handful of liquorice sticks scraped, bruised and beaten to fine powder, a gallon of fair running water. Boyle therein all these simples and boyle these seeds with them, that is—three spoonfulls of anniseeds, as much fennel seedes, the like of coriander seed and cummon seed, a good handful of Dandelion rootes and so boyle altogether from a gallon to a pottle.—*The Good Housewife's Jewell*, 1585.

To make a Tysand.—Take borage, sorrell, endive, cinquefoil, two or three handfuls of barley, then take halfe a handful of red fennell rootes, and a quantity of liquorice, sugar candie, figges, dates, great Raisins ; boyle all together from a gallon to three pintes and strain.—*The Good Housewife's Handmaid*, 1588.

The Drinke.—Take Rosemary with Tyme and

seeth them in faire water, with as much sugar as will make it sweet, from a quart to a pint. Use the quantity of hearbes according to your discretion so that it may savour well of the hearbes and so use it nine mornings— six or seven spoonfuls at a time.—*Ibid*.

Rosa-solis.—Take of the Herbe Rosa-Solis, gathered in Julie, one gallon, picke out all the blacke moats from the leaves ; Dates, halfe a pound, cinamon ginger, cloves of each one ounce ; fine sugar, a pound and a halfe ; red Rose-leaves, greene or dryed, foure hand-fuls ; steep all these in a gallon of good *Aqua Composita*, in a glasse close stopped with wax, during twenty dayes : shake it well together once every two days. Your sugar must be powdered, your spices bruised onely, or grossely beaten ; your Dates cut in long slices, the stones taken away.

If you adde two or three graines of Amber-greece, and as much Musk, in your glasse, among the rest of the ingredients, it will have a pleasant smell. Some adde the Gum Amber, with corell and pearle finely powdered and fine leafe-gold. Some used to boile Ferdinande-buck in Rose-water till they have pur-chased a faire, deep, crimson colour ; and when the same is cold, they colour their Rosa-Solis and *Aqua Rubea* therewith.—Sir Hugh Platt, *Delights for Ladies*, 1594.

Spirit of Wine (tasting of what vegetable you please). —Macerate Rosemary, Sage, sweet Fennell seeds, Lemmon or Orange pills, etc., in spirit of wine a day or two, and then distil it over again, unless you had rather have it in his proper colour, for so you shall have it upon the first infusion without any further distillation, and some young Alchymists doe hold these for the true spirits of vegetables.—*Ibid.*

How to make a Souveraigne Water that Master Doctor Stevens, Physitian, a man of great knowledge and cunning did practice and used of long experience and therewith did very many cures, and kept it always secret, till of late, a little before his death, a special friend of his did get it in writing of him.

Take a gallon of good Gascoine Wine, then take ginger, camomile, cinnamon, nutmegs, cloves, mace, annis seeds, fennell seeds, carroway seeds, of every of them a dramme, then take sage, minte, red Roses, Tyme, Pellitory of the Wall, wild margerum, Rosemary, wild Tyme, Camomile, and lavender of every one of them one handfull, then beat the spices small, and bruise the hearbes, and put all into the wine, and let it stand twelve hours, stirring it divers times ; then still it in a Limbeck, and keepe the first pinte of the water, for it is the best, then will come a seconde water, which is not so good as the first.

The vertues of these waters be these—it comforteth the spirites, and preserveth one greatly, and whoso useth this water ever and anon and not too ofte it preserveth him in good liking and shall make one seeme young very long. You must take one spoonfull of this water fasting.—John Partridge, *The Treasurie of Commodius Conceits and Hidden Secrets*, 1586.

To make a Hordeat or Mundified Barley.— Take two ounces of French Barly, boyle it upon a cleare fire in three quarters of a pint of water three or four houres, until that there bee but a porringer of liquor left, then straine it without pressing the Barly ; then peele and beate in the morter two ounces of sweet Almonds, pouring this liquor upon them as aforesaid, then straine and presse them very hard, and boyle it a little, and dissolve in it two ounces of fine sugar, and take it when you goe to bed.

There are those also that beat their Barly in the Morter with the Almonds, and presse it hard, which you may doe if you please.—*The Charitable Physitian*, by Philbert Guibert, Physitian Regent in Paris, 1639.

DR. BUTLER'S CORDIAL WATER against Melancholy, etc. Most Approved.—Take the flowers of Cowslips, Marigolds, Pinks, Clove gillyflowers, single stock gillyflowers, of each four handfuls, the flowers of Rosemary, Damask Roses, of each three handfuls, Borage and Bugloss flowers, and Balm leaves, of each two handfuls, put them in a quart of Canary wine into a great bottle or jugge close stopped with a cork, sometimes stirring the flowers and wine together, adding to them Anniseeds bruised one dram, two nutmegs sliced, English Saffron two pennyworth ; after some time infusion, distil them in a cold still with a hot fire, hanging at the nose of the Still Ambergreece and Musk, of each one grain, then to the distilled water put white sugar-candy finely beaten six ounces, and put the glass wherein they are, into hot water for one hour.   Take of this water at one time three spoonfuls thrice a week, or when you are ill.   It cureth all Melancholy, fumes, and infinitely comforts the spirits.—*The Queen's Closet Opened*, by W. M., Cook to Queen Henrietta Maria, 1655.

THE HEARBS TO BE DISTILLED FOR USQUABATH.—
Take Agrimony, Fumitory, Betony, Bugloss, Wormwood, Hart's tongue, Carduus Benedictus, Rosemary,
Angelica, Tormentil, of each of these for every
gallon of Ale one handful, Anniseeds and Liquorice well bruised half a pound. Still all these together,
and when it is stilled you must infuse Cinamon,
Nutmeg, Mace, Liquorice, Dates, and Raysins of
the Sun, and Sugar what quantity you please.
The infusion must be till the colour please you.—
Ibid.

TO MAKE HYPOCRAS.—Take four gallons of Claret
Wine, eight ounces of Cinamon, and Oranges, of Ginger,
Cloves, and Nutmegs a small quantity, Sugar six
pound, three sprigs of Rosemary, bruise all the spices
somewhat small, and so put them into the Wine, and
keep them close stopped, and often shaked together
a day or two, then let it run through a jelly bagge twice
or thrice with a quart of new milk.—*The Queen's
Closet Opened*, by W. M., Cook to Queen Henrietta
Maria, 1655.

A COMFORTABLE CORDIAL TO CHEER THE HEART.—
Take one ounce of conserve of gilliflowers, four grains
of the best Musk bruised as fine as flower, then put
into a little tin pot and keep it till you have need to make
this Cordial following :—Take the quantity of one nutmeg out of your tin pot, put to it one spoonful of
Cinnamon-water, and one spoonful of the Sirup of
Gilliflowers, Ambergris, mix all these together, and
drink them in the morning, fasting three or four

hours, this is most comfortable.—*A Choice Manual of Secrets in Physick*, by Elizabeth Grey, Countess of Kent, 1653.

HYDROMEL AS I MADE IT WEAK FOR THE QUEEN MOTHER.—Take eighteen quarts of spring water, and one quart of honey, when the water is warm put the honey into it. When it boileth up, skim it very well and continue skimming it as long as any scum will rise. Then put in one Race of Ginger (sliced in thin slices), four Cloves, and a little sprig of green Rosemary. Let these boil in the liquor so long till in all it have boiled one hour. Then set it to cool, till it be blood-warm, and then put to it a spoonful of Ale-yest. When it is worked up, put it into a vessel of a fit size, and after two or three days, bottle it up. You may drink it after six weeks or two months.—*The Closet of Sir Kenelm Digby Opened*, 1669.

To MAKE HYPOCRAS PRESENTLY.—Take twelve drops of Oyl of Cloves, eight of Oyl of Nutmegs, and five of Oyl of Cinamon. Put them into a large strong drinking glass, and mingle well with them two ounces of the purest double refined sugar in powder. Then take twenty drops of Rosewater in a spoon, and in it a little Ambergris, and a little Musk, and then pour that to your former Composition and work all well together ; and if you find the matter too moist, knead some more sugar amongst it. If you put a little of this Composition into a quart of Wine, and make it sweet with sugar besides, it will taste like excellent Hypocras.—*Ibid.*

APPLE DRINK WITH SUGAR, HONEY, ETC.—A very pleasant drink is made of Apples, thus :—Boil sliced Apples in water to make the water strong of Apples, as when you make to drink it for coolness and pleasure. Sweeten it with sugar to your taste, such a quantity of sliced apples as would make so much water strong enough of apples, and then bottle it up close for three or four months. There will come a thick mother at the top, which being taken off, all the rest will be very clear, and quick and pleasant to the taste, beyond any Cider. It will be the better to most taste, if you put a very little Rosemary into the Liquor, when you boil it and a little Limon peel into each bottle, when you bottle it up.—*Ibid.*

CINAMON WATER.—Make about a quart of water boil and take it from the fire and break into it about a quarter of an ounce of cinamon with a quarter of a pound of sugar, and let it stand till it be cool. Then strain it out through a clean cloth and so set it to cool and drink it when you please.—*A Perfect School of Instructions for the Officers of the Month*, by Giles Rose, one of the Master Cooks to Charles II, 1682.

HYPOCRAS OF WHITE WINE.—Take about three quarts of the best white wine, a pound and a half of sugar, an ounce of cinamon, two or three leaves of sweet margerum, two grains of whole pepper, let all this pass through your bag with a grain of Musk, two or three slices of lemon when it hath stood and infused altogether the space of three or four hours. That of Claret may be made the same way.—*Ibid.*

WINE FOR THE GODS.—Take two great lemons, peel them and cut them in slices with two Pippens pared and sliced like your lemons, put all this into a dish with three quarters of a pound of sugar in powder, a pint of Burgundy Wine, six cloves, a little orange-flower water. Cover this up and let it steep two or three hours then pass it through a bag as you do Hypocras and it will be most excellent.—*Ibid.*

GOOD ADVICE TO ALL ENGLISH PEOPLE TO MAKE A DRINKE THEMSELVES, WHICH THEY MAY DRINK AS THEY DRINK COFFEE, CHOCOLET AND TEA.—Take a quart of spring or conduit water, and boil it till it wastes one third part, when you have so done, your water being boiling hot, put in twenty or thirty leaves of good Sage, and half the quantity of Rosemary, with fifteen or twenty grains of good English Saffron, and let it infuse hot as before, for about a quarter of an hour close stopped ; then pour it out clear from the Ingredients, drink it as hot as you can, taking about a quarter or half a pint of it at a time, sweetened with a little white sugar ; and question not but the benefits you will receive will be far more and better this spring and hereafter than you have ever done by those liquors that so many commend ; but the Virtues of these Plants are so universally known to be of such admirable Qualities, that I shall say the less in the Praise of them, but something I shall say of them that they are the best Plants that grow in this Island, which is a Climate and Country which I may boldly say is so well furnished with Herbs and Plants which for Virtue and Goodness is not inferior to any Country in the whole World, and these I have pitched upon are of its choicest

Product.—From *The Receipt Book of Henry Howard*, Free Cook of London and Cook to the Duke of Ormond, 1710.

RED HIPPOCRAS.—Put a gallon of Claret into an earthen vessel, put to it two pounds of sugar beaten in a mortar, a dozen of sweet almonds stampt with a glass of brandy ; add to the infusion a dram of cinnamon, a little long pepper, four grains of white pepper, a blade of Mace, and some Coriander seeds, all these bruised. Cover the vessel close and let all these infuse for an hour, stirring it often with a spoon, that the sugar may dissolve and incorporate. Then add a glass of milk, and pass all through the straining bag.—From *The Receipt Book of Charles Carter*, Cook to the Duke of Argyll, 1732.

TO MAKE MILK-WATER.—Take a pound of Wormwood, Spear-mint, Balm, and two pounds of Carduus shred a little, put them into a still, with two gallons of milk, and distil them gently, it is an excellent drink to quench thirst.—*Ibid*.

Another Way.—Take a handful of Spear-mint, two handfuls of Wormwood, and Carduus, cut them, pour upon them a quart of canary ; let them stand all night to infuse, the next day put them into a cold Still, with two gallons of milk or clarified whey, and distil it as long as it runs good.—*Ibid*.

A CORDIAL MINT WATER.—Strip Mint from the stalks, weigh two pounds of the leaves and tops, add two pounds of Raisins of the Sun stoned, of Carraway seeds, and anniseeds of each two ounces and half a pound of Liquorice sliced thin ; infuse these in two gallons of good Claret, and distil it in an Alembick or cold Still ; let it drop on some fine Sugar through a Bag of Saffron.—*Ibid.*

CURRANT WATER.—Take a pound of currants to a quart of water, that you must squeeze in the same water and put in about four or five ounces of sugar, being well mixed put it through a straining bag until it be clear. Put in a cool place and give it to drink.—L. Lemery, *A Treatise of all sorts of Foods,* 1745.

RASPBERRY WATER.—Take a pound of raspberries to a quart of water, if the raspberries be good, three quarters of a pound will be sufficient with five ounces of sugar ; it needs no lemon. The sugar being melted put it through a straining bag until it runs clear, put in a cool place and give it to drink.—*Ibid.*

APPLE, PEACH OR PEAR WATER.—In a quart of water put five or six apricots, peaches or pears according to their bigness augmenting or diminishing ; cut them in pieces into the water. Boil them in it, put in four or five ounces of sugar.

Being cold put it through a straining bag until it be clear. Put it to cool and give it to drink.—*Ibid.*

TO MAKE ORANGE-FLOWER BRANDY.—Take a gallon of French Brandy, boil a pound of orange flowers a little while, and put them in, save the water and with that make a syrup to sweeten it.—E. Smith, *The Compleat Housewife*, 1736.

THE SAFFRON CORDIAL.—Fill a large still with marigold flowers, adding to them of nutmegs, mace, and English Saffron, of each an ounce ; then take three pints of muscadine, or Malaga sack, and with a sprig of rosemary dash it on the flowers ; then distil it off with a slow fire, and let it drop on white sugar-candy, draw it off till it begins to be sour ; save a pint of the first running to mix with the other waters on an extraordinary occasion, mix the rest together to drink it by itself. This Cordial is excellent in fainting and for the small-pox or ague ; take five or six spoonfuls at a time.—*Ibid.*

BLACK CHERRY WATER FOR CHILDREN.—Take six pounds of black cherries and bruise them small, then put to them the tops of rosemary, sweet marjoram, spearmint, angelica, balm, marigold flowers, of each a handful, dried violets an ounce, aniseeds and sweet fennell seeds, of each half an ounce bruised ; cut the herbs small, mix them together, and distil them off in a cold still. This water is excellent for children, giving them two or three spoonfuls at a time.—*Ibid.*

TO MAKE WHITE CAUDLE.—Take four spoonfuls of oatmeal, two blades of mace, a piece of lemon-peel, cloves and ginger, of each a quarter of an ounce ; put these into two quarts of water, and let it boil about an hour, stirring it often ; then strain it out, and add to every quart half a pint of wine, some grated nutmeg and sugar.—*Ibid.*

To make Bitters.—Take a quart of the best Frencn Brandy, a quarter of an ounce of Saffron, half an ounce of gentian roots sliced thin, two pennyworth of Cochineal, and a small quantity of orange-peel, put them in a bottle, and let them stand two or three days.— Sarah Jackson, *The Director*, 1754.

Seed Water.—Take a spoonful of Coriander seed, half a spoonful of carraway seed, bruised and boiled in a pint of water, then strain it, and bruise it with the yolk of an egg ; mix it with sack and double refined sugar, according to your palate.—*The New Art of Cookery*, by Richard Briggs, many years Cook at the Globe Tavern, Fleet Street, the White Hart Tavern, Holborn, and at the Temple Coffee House, 1788.

Orange Shrub.—Break a hundred pounds of loaf sugar in small pieces, put it into twenty gallons of water, boil it till the sugar is melted, skim it well, and put it in a tub to cool ; when cold, put it into a cask, with thirty gallons of good Jamaica Rum, and fifteen gallons of orange juice (mind to strain all the seeds out of the juice), mix them well together, then beat up the whites of six eggs very well, stir them well in, let it stand a week to fine, and then draw it off for use. By the same rules you may make any quantity you want.— *Ibid.*

WINE A DELICIOUS SORT.—Cut a couple of Pippens and a couple of Lemons into slices into a Dish, with half a pound of fine Sugar ; a quart of good red Port Wine, half a dozen Cloves, some Cinnamon powdered, and Orange-Flower water ; cover these and let them infuse for three or four hours ; then strain it through a bag, and give it a flavour with Musk or Amber, as you please.—From *The Receipt Book of John Nott*, Cook to the Duke of Bolton, 1723.

LEMON WINE.—Take a dozen of large Malaga Lemons, pare off the Rind, cut the Lemons and squeeze out the Juice, put the Rind to steep, and add to it two quarts of Brandy ; let it stand in an earthern Vessel for three Days close stopped, then squeeze another dozen of Lemons, and add a gallon of Spring water to them, and as much sugar as will sweeten the whole to your palate. Boil the Water, the lemons and the Sugar together, and let it stand till it is cool ; then add to it a quart of White Wine, and the other Lemon and Brandy, and having mixed them together, run it through a Flannel Bag into the Vessel you would keep it in, in which let it stand three months and bottle it off for use. Let the Bottles be well cork'd and kept cool, and it will be fit to drink in a month or six weeks.—From *The Receipt Book of Charles Carter*, Cook to the Duke of Argyll, 1732.

DOCTOR HARVEY'S PLEASANT WATER-CIDER, whereof he used to drink much, making it his ordinary drink. —Take one Bushel of Pippins, cut them into slices with the Parings and Cores ; boil them in twelve gallons of water, till the goodness of them be in the water ; and that consumed about three gallons, then put it into an Hypocras-bag, made of cotton ; and when it is clear run out and almost cold, sweeten it with five pounds of Brown Sugar, and put a pint of Ale-yest to it, and set it a working two nights and days. Then skim off the yest clean, and put it into bottles, and let it stand two or three days, till the yest fall dead at the top ; then take it off clean with a knife, and fill it up a little within the neck (that is to say that a little about a finger's breadth of the neck be empty, between the superficies of the Liquor, and the bottom of the stopple), and then stop them up and tye them, or else it will drive out the corks. Within a fortnight you may drink of it. It will keep five or six weeks.—*The Closet of Sir Kenelm Digby Opened*, 1699.

To MAKE RASPBERRY WINE.—Take a gallon of good Rhenish Wine, put into it as much Rasberries very ripe as will make it strong, put it in an earthen pot, and let it stand two days ; then pour your Wine from the Rasberries, and put into every bottle two ounces of sugar. Stop it up and keep it by you.—*The Queen's Closet Opened*, by W. M., Cook to Queen Henrietta Maria, 1655.

To MAKE RASBERY WINE.—Putt a gallon of Sack into an Earthen Vessell and fill it thick with rasberys cover it up close let it stand 3 or 4 Dayes then runn it through a Jelly bag to every quart 3 quarters of a pound of lose Sugar let it Stand till it has don working take off the Scum from the top to the bottom bottle it close and let it Stand.

Spread yeast on both Sides of a Tost. Put in your wine cover it close to work—So you must doe by all your Wines.—*MS. Book of Receipts* by Thomas Newington, 1719.

SEVERAL SORTS OF MEATH, small and strong.— (Small). Take ten gallons of water, and five quarts of honey, with a little Rosemary, more Sweet-bryar, some Balme, Burnet, Cloves, less Ginger, Lemon Peel, Tun it with a little Barm; let it remain a week in the barrel with a bag of Elder-flowers, then bottle it.

(2) (Small). Take ten quarts of water, and one of honey, Balm a little; Mint, Cloves, Limon-peel, Elder-flowers, a little Ginger; wrought with a little yest, bottle it after a night working.

(3) (Strong). Take ten gallons of water, thirteen quarts of honey, with Angelica Borrage and Bugloss,' Rosemary, Balm, and Sweet-bryar, pour it into a barrel, upon three spoonfuls of yest; hang in a bag Cloves, Elder-flowers and a little Ginger.—*The Closet of Sir Kenelm Digby Opened*, 1699.

TO MAKE WHITE METHEGLIN.—Take of Sweet-bryar a great handful; of Violet-flowers, Sweet-marjoram, Strawberry-leaves, Violet leaves, and one handful, Agrimony, Bugloss, Borrage, and half a handful Rosemary; four branches, Gillyflowers (the Yellow wall-flowers with great tops), Anniseeds, Fennel, and Caraway, of each a spoonful, two large Mace. Boil all these in twelve gallons of water for the space of an hour; then strain it, and let it stand until it be Milk-warm.

Then put in as much honey as will carry an Egge to the breadth of sixpence at least ; then boil it again, and scum it clean ; then let it stand, until it be cold ; then put a pint of Ale-barm into it, and ripen it as you do Beer, and tun it. Then hang in the midst of the vessel a little bag with a Nutmeg quartered, a Race of Ginger sliced, a little Cinnamon, and mace whole, and three grains of Musk in a cloth put into the bag amongst the rest of the Spices. Put a stone in the bag, to keep it in the midst of the Liquor. This quantity took up three gallons of honey ; therefore be sure to have four in readiness.—*Ibid.*

METHEGLIN (Composed by myself out of sundry receipts).—In sixty gallons of water, boil ten handfuls of Sweet-bryar leaves ; Eyebright, Liverwort, Agrimony, Scabious, Balme, Wood-bettony, Strawberry-leaves, Burnet, of each four handfuls ; of Rosemary, three handfuls ; of Mint, Angelica, Bayes and Wild-Thyme, Sweet Marjoram, of each two handfuls ; six Eringo roots. When the water hath taken out the virtue of the herbs and roots, let it settle, and the next day pour off the clear, and in every three gallons of it boil one of honey, scumming it well, and putting in a little cold water now and then to make the scum rise, as also some Whites of Eggs. When it is clear scummed, take it off, and let it cool, then work it with Ale-yest ; tun it up, and hang in it a bag with Ginger, Cinamon, Cloves and Cardamon, and as it worketh over, put in some strong honey drink warmed. When it works no more, stop it up close.

In twenty gallons of water boil Sweet-bryar leaves, Eye-bright, Rosemary, Bayes, Clove-gillyflowers, of each fine handfuls, and four Eringo-roots. To every two gallons and a half of this decoction, put one gallon of honey ; boil it, etc. When it is tunned up, hang in it a bag containing five handfuls of Clove-gilly-flowers, and sufficient quantity of the spices above.

In both these receipts, the quantity of the herbs is too great, the strong herbs preserve the drink, and make it nobler. Use Marjoram and Thyme in little quantity in all.—*Ibid.*

To make Turnip Drink.—Pound your turnips and press them through a Hair-bag ; then let it stand a Day or two in the open Tun, or only covered with a cloth or boards to keep it from the Dust, or in a Hogs-head or other Vessel not quite full, with an open Bung, till the more gross parts subside ; then draw it off, and put it into the Vessels you design to keep it in longer, leaving them about an eighth part empty. Let the Vessels stand in a Cellar, with the Bung open, or covered only with a loose Cover, that there may be a free evaporation of the volatile particles of the Liquor. If you make this drink in very cold Weather, it will be requisite to treat the Liquor in a Copper, something more than Blood-warm to make it ferment ; or you may put the yeast to it for the same purpose.—From *The Receipt Book of John Nott*, Cook to the Duke of Bolton, 1723.

Raisin Wine.—Take twelve pounds of Raisins of the Sun and stone them, six pounds of White sugar, the juice of a dozen Lemons and the peels of six, put

them into a pot with a cover with twelve gallons of
water, let them boil for half an hour ; then take them
off the Fire, and let them stand close covered for three
or four Days, stirring it twice a day, then strain it
and bottle it up close for use, but do not fill the Bottles
quite full, lest it should break them, set them in a cool
place, and in a Fortnight's time you may drink it. If
you make your wine when they are in season you may
add cowslips or clove-gillyflowers.—*Ibid.*

MORELLO WINE.—Take twenty-four Pound of Morello Cherries pull off the stalkes, and bruise them so
that the stones may be broken, press out the juice and
put it to nine or ten gallons of White-Wine. Put the
skins and the stones in a Bag and let them be hung in
a Cask so as not to touch the bottom of it and let it
stand for a month or more. You may also put in spices
if you please but the wine will be very pleasant without
them.—*Ibid.*

MUM.—Take thirty-two gallons of water, boil it till
a third part is wasted, brew it according to Art with
three Bushels and a half of Malt, half a Bushel of ground
Beans, and half a Bushel of Oatmeal when you put it
into your Cask do not fill it too full and when it begins
to work, put in a pound and a half of the inner rind of
Fir, half a pound of tops of Fir and Birch instead of
the inward Rind. Our English Mum-makers use
Sassafras and ginger, the Rind of Walnut Tree, Elecampane Root, Water Cresses, and Horse Radish root
rasp'd, Betony, Burnet, Marjoram, Mother of Thyme,
Pennyroyal of each a small handful, Elder-flowers a

handful, of Blessed Thistle a handful, of Barberries bruised half an ounce, of Cardamums bruised an ounce and a half. All these ingredients are to be put in when the liquor has wrought a while and after they are in let it work over the Vessel as little as may be when it has done working. Fill up the cask and put into it five new-laid eggs not broken nor crack'd, stop it close and it will be fit to drink in two years.—*Ibid.*

To MAKE MEAD.—Set three gallons of water on the fire, put in Balm, Lemon, Thyme, Sweet Marjoram, and Rosemary, let them boil some time, then put in five or six handfuls of Borrage and Bugloss, and when they have boiled a little take them off, strain them and set the liquor by to settle for a Night. Then to every gallon of liquor add three Pound of Honey; put on the Fire, boil and scum as long as any scum rises; then take thirty cloves, two ounces of Nutmegs, and six ounces of Ginger, beat them, put them in a Bag and boil them in the liquor, a little before you take it off the Fire. Then empty it into a vessel, put to it a pint and a half of Ale yeast, lay a sheet over it and a Blanket upon that. Let it work sufficiently, then tun it, hang the Bag of Spice in the Cask, and stop it up close for six or seven weeks; then bottle it off with some sugar.—*Ibid.*

To MAKE WHITE MEAD.—Put a handful of Thyme, Rosemary, Sweet Briar, Eyebright, Wood Betony, Scabious, Roman Wormwood, Agrimony (of each a like quantity), and steep for twenty-four hours in a Wooden bowl, uncovered, then boil them in another water till it be very high coloured; then change the water and boil them till it is coloured green, and as long as any green mess remain, then set it by for twenty-four hours more. Then strain the liquor from the Herbs and put a Pound of Honey to every two Quarts of the liquor and when it will bear an egg to three pence breadth above the water work it together till the Honey is all dissolved ; then let it settle for a Night ; the next day boil it with the shells and whites of half a dozen eggs ; then strain it, set it by to cool ; then put it up into the Cask, then bruise cinnamon, nutmeg, cloves, mace, and put them in a Bag and hang them in the Cask and stop it up.

If you would have it fit to drink in a little time, beat together the whites of three or four eggs ; add to them a spoonful of yeast, two spoonfuls of Honey, and put them into the Cask and then temper some Clay with Bay salt and stop it up close.—*Ibid.*

CHERRY WINE.—Pick off the stalks and stone your cherries, press out the juice, and to each gallon put two pounds of Sugar, put it in a Cask, set it a working, and when it has done, stop it up for two months, then bottle it off, putting a little Sugar, and after it has stood six weeks, it will be fit for use.—From *The Receipt Book of Charles Carter*, Cook to the Duke of Argyll, 1723.

CHERRY WINE.—Pick your cherryes from the Stalks break them very well but not to brake the Stone to every gallon of cherryes a quart of water. Set them over the fiare let them boyle a little. Straine them out to every gallon of wine put half a pound of Sugar.

Spread some yeste upon a toste put it into low warme cover it up close let it Stand all night to worke then put it in your vessell and when it has don working Stope it close doune let it Stand a month then bottle it put some lose Sugar in each bottle corke it close and it will be ripe in a month.—*MS. Book of Receipts*, by Charles Thomas Newington, 1719.

GOOSEBERRY WINE.—Let your Gooseberries be gathered before they are too ripe, and to every twelve pounds of gooseberries take six pounds of Sugar and a gallon of Water. Stamp the Gooseberries and let them steep in the Water twenty-four Hours; then strain them and put the liquor into a Vessel, and let it stand close stopped up for two or three Weeks, and if it prove fine, draw it off, otherwise let it stand a Fortnight longer, and then bottle it; but rack it off, or use Isinglass if it be not sufficiently fine.

PEARL GOOSEBERRY WINE.—Bruise the Gooseberries and let them stand all night; the next morning let them be squeezed or pressed out, set the Liquor to settle for six or eight hours, then pour off so much as is clear, and to every gallon of Liquor put three pounds of double-refined Sugar, broken into small lumps. Put all into the Vessel with a bit of Isinglass and stop it up. Let it stand three months, and then bottle it, slipping in a Lump of double-refined Sugar into each Bottle. This is called the fine Gooseberry Wine.— *Ibid.*

DAMSON WINE.—Put two pounds and half of Sugar

to every gallon of Water ; boil them for three-quarters of an Hour, and scum them very well, and to every gallon put five pints of Damsons stoned. Boil them till the Liquor is of very fine colour, then strain it through a fine sieve, work it for three or four days in an open Vessel, then pour it off from the Lees and work it in that Vessel as long as it will work, then stop it up for six or eight months ; at which time, if it be fine, you may bottle it off, and it will keep a year or two.—*Ibid.*

BLACK CHERRY WINE.—Boil three gallons of Spring water for an Hour, then bruise twelve pounds of Black cherries ; but don't break the stones ; pour the Water boiling hot on the Cherries ; stir the Cherries well in the Water, and let it stand for twenty-four Hours ; then strain it off, and to every gallon put near two pounds of good Sugar, mix it well with the Liquor, and let it stand one Day longer ; then pour it off clear into the Vessel, and stop it close. Let it be very fine before you draw it off in Bottles.—*Ibid.*

MORELLO CHERRY WINE is made after the same manner, the fruit being picked and bruised without breaking the stones. This mash being let stand in an open Vessel for twenty-four hours, must be afterwards press'd in a Hair Bag, twenty-two pounds of fine sugar put to every gallon of Liquor, and after it has done working, being stopp'd up close for three or four months, it may be bottled and will be fit for drinking in two months.—*Ibid.*

APRICOT WINE.—Take twelve pounds of ripe

Apricots, stone and pare them fine, put six pounds of good Sugar into seven quarts of Water, boil them together and as the scum rises take it off, and when it has been well scummed, slip in the Apricots, and boil them till they become tender, then take them out, and if you please you may put in a Sprig or two of flowered Clary, and let it have a boil or two more, and when it is cold Bottle it up, and in six months it will be fit for drinking; but the longer it is kept the better it will be, for it will hold good for two years and more. After it has been Bottled a Week, you should try if there be any settlement, and if so, pour the liquor off into fresh Bottles, which may be afterwards separated again as it grows fine. The Apricots that are taken out may be made into marmalade, and will be very good for present spending; but will not keep long, unless they be used as in Preserving.— *Ibid.*

To make Frontiniac Wine.—Take six gallons of water and twelve pounds of White Sugar, and six pounds of Raisins of the Sun cut small; boil these together an hour; then take of the Flowers of Elder, when they are falling off and will shake off, the quantity of half a peck; put them in the liquor when 'tis almost cold, the next Day put in six spoonfuls of Syrup of Lemons and four spoonfuls of Ale-yeast, and two days after put in a Vessel that is fit for it, and when it has stood two months, bottle it off.—E. Smith, *The Compleat Housewife*, 1736.

To make English Champayne or the fine Currant

WINE.—Take to three gallons of water nine pounds of Lisbon Sugar ; boil the water and Sugar half an hour scum it clean, then have one gallon of Currants, pick'd but not bruised, pour the liquor boiling hot over them and when cold, work it with half a pint of balm two days ; then pour it through a Flannel or Sieve, then put it into a barrel fit for it with half an ounce of Isinglass well bruised ; when it is done working, stop it close for a month, then bottle it, and in every bottle put a small lump of double-refined Sugar. This is excellent Wine and has a beautiful colour.—*Ibid.*

TO MAKE SARAGOSSA WINE OR ENGLISH SACK.—To every quart of water, put a sprig of Rue and to every gallon a handful of Fennel roots, boil these half an hour, then strain it out and to every gallon of this Liquor, put three pounds of Honey ; boil it two hours and scum it well, and when it is cold pour it off and turn it into a Vessel, or such Cask as is fit for it ; keep it a year in the Vessel and then Bottle it. 'Tis a very good sack.—*Ibid.*

MOUNTAIN WINE.—Pick out the big stalks of your Malaga Raisins, then chop them very small, five gallons to every gallon of Spring water, let them steep a Fortnight or more, squeeze out the Liquor, and barrel it in the Vessel fit for it ; first fume the Vessel with Brimstone ; don't stop it up till the hissing is over.—*Ibid.*

BIRCH WINE.—The season for procuring the liquors

from the Birch trees is in the beginning of March, while the sap is rising, and before the leaves shoot out ; for when the sap is come forward and the leaves appear, the juice, by being long digested in the bark, grows thick and coloured, which before is thin and clear.

The method of procuring the juice is by boring holes in the body of the tree, and putting in fossets, which are commonly made of the branches of elder, the pith being taken out. You may, without hurting the tree, if large, tap it in several places, four or five at a time ; and by that means save from a good many trees several gallons every day. If you have not enough in one day, the bottles, in which it drops, must be cork'd close, and rosined or waxed ; however, make use of it as soon as you can. Take the sap and boil it as long as any scum rises, skimming it all the time, to every gallon of liquor put four pounds of good sugar, and the thin peel of a lemon ; boil it afterwards half an hour, skimming it very well ; pour it into a clean tub, and when it is almost cold, set it to work with yeast spread upon a toast. Let it stand five or six days, stirring it often, then take such a cask as will hold the liquor ; fire a large match dipped in brimstone and throw it into the cask, stop it close till the match is extinguished ; tun your wine, and lay the bung on light till you find it has done working ; stop it close and keep it three months, then bottle it off.—*Ibid.*

QUINCE WINE.—Gather the quinces when dry and full ripe. Take twenty large quinces, wipe them clean with a coarse cloth, and grate them with a large grater or rasp, as near the core as you can, but none of the core ; boil a gallon of spring water throwing your quinces in, and let it boil softly a quarter of an hour, then strain them well into an earthen pan on two pounds of double-refined sugar ; pare the peel of two large lemons, throw in and squeeze the juice through a sieve, and stir it about till it is very cool ; then toast a little bit of bread, very thin and brown, rub a little yeast on it, let it stand close-covered twenty-four hours ; then take out the toast and lemon, put it up in a keg, keep it three months and then bottle it. If you make a twenty gallon cask let it stand six months before you bottle it. When you strain your quinces you are to wring them hard in a coarse cloth.—*Ibid.*

TURNIP WINE.—Take a good many turnips, pare, slice, and put them in a cyder-press, and press out all the juice very well ; to every gallon of juice put three pounds of lump sugar ; have a vessel ready, just big enough to hold the juice ; put your sugar into a vessel ; and also to every gallon of juice half a pint of brandy ; pour in the juice, and lay something over the bung for a week, to see if it works ; if it does, you must not bung it down till it has done working ; then stop it close for three months, and draw it off in another vessel ; when it is fine, bottle it off.—*The New Art of Cookery*, by R. Briggs, many years Cook at the Globe Tavern, Fleet Street, the White Hart Tavern, Holborn, and now at the Temple Coffee House, London, 1788.

CURRANT WINE.—Gather your currants on a fine dry day, when the fruit is full ripe, strip them, put them in a large pan, and bruise them with a wooden pestle ; let them stand in a pan or tub twenty-four hours to ferment ; then run it through a hair sieve, and do not let your hand touch the liquor, to every gallon of this liquor put two pounds and a half of white sugar, stir it well together, and put it into your vessel ; to every six gallons put in a quart of brandy, and let it stand six weeks ; if it is fine, bottle it ; if it is not, draw it off as clear as you can into another vessel, or large bottles, and in a fortnight bottle it in small bottles.—*Ibid*.

RED CURRANT WINE.—Four gallons of cold water to four of bruised currants, picked carefully from their stalks ; let them stand together for four days, then strain them off, mix three pounds and a half of brown sugar or white sugar which is greatly to be preferred, to each gallon of diluted currant juice ; stir it well, then put it into a Cask and add also a piece of toasted bread spread over with yeast which will ferment it ; after this is over bring it up very light and it will be ready for bottling off in six months and for domestic use after six months keeping in the bottle.

The white currant alone produces the best wine when it is clear like Champayne and sparkles as much, but it is oftener made of red currants when it has the appearance of mountain grape wine, or the two are mixed together. These home made wines are an excellent substitute for the more expensive foreign provided they were kept a sufficient length of time and properly fermented.—R. Thornton, *The Family Herbal*, 1810.

BLACK CURRANT WINE.—The Currants should be gathered on a dry day when quite ripe ; strip them, put them into a large pan, bruise them with a wooden pestle and let them stand twenty-four hours to ferment, then rub it through a hair sieve, but do not let the hand touch the liquor. To every gallon of this liquor stir in two pounds and a half of white sugar, and put it into a vessel, to every six gallons add one quart of brandy, and let it stand six weeks, if fine bottle it ; if not, draw it off clear into another vessel or large bottles, and in a fortnight bottle it up for use.—*Ibid.*

RAISIN WINE.—To one gallon of water put six gallons of sun raisins, let it stand in a tub twelve days, stir frequently, press the raisins as dry as possible, and put the liquor into a Cask of the proper size : to ten gallons put a quart of brandy, if you wish to make it very rich you may put seven pounds of raisins to a gallon and dissolve five pounds of sugar-candy in the liquor, before you put it into the barrels ; when thus made it must stand longer and is scarcely inferior to any foreign wine.—*Ibid.*

ORANGE BRANDY.—Four quarts of the best pale brandy, two and a half pounds fine white sugar, the juice of twelve Seville oranges, the rinds of ten, and a quart of milk. Put the brandy into a large jar or open vessel with a cover. Add the juice and rind of the oranges and then the sugar. Heat the milk and pour it boiling over the other ingredients in the pan. Let the liquid remain six or eight days, stirring thoroughly each day, strain into bottles and cork well.—E. G. Hayden, *Travels round our Village*.

BLACK CURRANT WINE.—To every three quarts of juice allow the same amount of water unboiled, and to every three quarts of the liquid add three pounds very pure moist sugar. Put all into a Cask, reserving a little for filling up. Place the cask in a warm, dry room, the liquid will ferment of itself. Skim off the refuse when fermentation ceases, fill up with the reserved liquid when it has ceased working, pour in three quarts of brandy to four quarts of wine. Bung it close for nine months, then bottle it and strain the thick part through a Jelly bag, when it also can be bottled. Keep ten or twelve months before drinking.—*Ibid*.

SLOE GIN.—To every gallon of Sloes add the same quantity of good gin and one pound of white sugar, more or less according as the liquor is desired sweet or not. Crush the fruit in a jar, take out and crack the stones, replace them in the jar, add the sugar, pour over the gin. Cork or cover the jar lightly and leave it to stand for a month, when strain and bottle.—*Ibid*.

GINGER WINE.—Ten gallons of water, sixteen pounds of lump sugar, five pounds raisins, the whites of six eggs well beaten, Mix cold and then boil skimming well. Add one and a half pounds bruised white ginger. Boil 20 minutes. Take the thinly peeled rinds of seven lemons and pour the liquor on to them. When cold tun with two spoonfuls of yeast. Take a quart of the liquor and put to it two ounces isinglass shavings, whisk when still warm and pour into the barrel. The next day stop it up and in three weeks bottle. It will be ready for use in three months. March is said to be the best month for making ginger wine.

CHAPTER VII

ADDITIONAL RECEIPTS

A SURRUP FOR THE PRESERVATION OF LONG LIFE, RECOMMENDED RO THE RIGHT HONBLE MARY COUNTESS OF FEVERSHAM BY DR. PETER DUMOULIN OF CANTERBURY JUNE YE 2, 1682.

An Eminent Officer in the great Army with the Emperor Charles the 5th sent into Barbary had his quarters there Assigned him in an Old Gentlemans House with whom by mutuall Offices of Humanity he soone contracted a Singular Friendship. Seeing him looke very Old yet very Fresh and Vigorous he asked him how old he was he answered he was 132 years old that till Sixty Yeares of Age he had been a good Fellow takeing litle care of his health but that then he had begun to take a spoonfull of Surrup every morning fasting which ever since had keept him in health being Desired to impart that Receipt to his Guest he freely granted it and the officer being returned to his Country made use of that Surrup and with it Preserved him Self and many more yet kept the Receipt Secret till haveing attained by his Surrupe Ninety two years of Aige he made a Scruple to keep it Secreet any Longer and publisht it for the Common good.

A receipt for the Surrup of Long Life to be done in the Moone of May.

Take of the juice of mercury eight pound of the juice of Burridg two pounds of the juice of Buglosse two pounds mingle these with twelve pounds of Clarrified

Honey the whitest you can gett let them boyle together a boyling and pass through a Hypocras Bag of New flannell Infuse in three pints of White Wine a Quarter of a pound of gentian Root and half a pound of Iris Root or blew Flower de Lis let them be infused twenty-fouer houers then Strain without Squeezing. Put the liquor to that of the herbs and Hony boyle them well together to the consistance of a Surrup you must order the matter so that one thing stays not for the other but that all be ready together.

A spoonfull of this Surrup is to be taken every Morning Fasting. *MS. Book of Receipts*, by Thomas Newington, 1719.[1]

[1] Several recipes have been quoted from this interesting MS. book written by a butler—Thomas Newington—200 years ago. His introductory letter to his collection of " Receips " is well worth quoting and I give it below.

MADAM,

Perhaps you may wonder to see your Receips they increase in Bulk and Number Especily when you consider that they come from me who can not make pretentions to things of this nature but haveing in my hands som Excelent Manuscripts of Phisick, Cookery Preserves, etc., which were the Palladium of Many Noble Familyes I did Imagine that by blending them together which in themselves were so Choice and valuable they would magnifie and Illustrate each other. I have taken great care in this Transcription that nothing might be omitted which ought to be incerted. I question not but you will much improve what I here lay before you.

Madam, I might well fear lest these my rude and unpolished lines Should offend you but that I hope your goodness will rather Smile at the faults commited then censure them. However I desire your Ladyships pardon for prescuting things so unworthy to your View and Accept the Goodwill of him who in all Duty is bound to be

Your Ladyships
Most Humble and most Obeiant
Sarvant,

Brighthelmstone,   THOMAS NEWINGTON.
May the 20. 1719.

AN OYNTMENT FOR ALL KIND OF ACHES TO BE MADE IN MAY.—Take of Sage Leaves of Rue of each a pound of wormwood of bay leaves of each half a Pound all these purely pickt in the heat of the Day. Cutt them Small and beat them in a mortar then take three Pound of Sheeps Suet New from the Sheepe cold mince it small and put it in the mortar to the herbs and then beat them together till Such time that the Suet be not seene and that the Herbs and it be all of one coloure then take it out and put it into a cleane basson and put thereto two Quarts of Oyle of Olive and work the Oyle with your hands into the hearbs untill it be all of one softness then put it into an Earthern pott and Cover it Close So let it stand Eight Dayes then Seeth it in a fair Brass Pott with a Soft fire untill the Strength of the herbs begon and this you shall perseive when it is sodden enough to take a Spoonfull or two of the same and put it into a new canvis Cloath and so wring the Juice of the Herbs into a Sausor and if at the last wringing their com any liquor like a brown matter then it is not sodden enough for if it were there woold come nothing but cleare Oyntment and this way you Shall perseive all other Oyntments when you have Soden it Streyne it into a Cleane Earthen Pott for that will keep it best when you use this Oyntment to any sore lay a warme Cloath to the Soare when you have anointed it. Chang not the first Cloath for any Cleane at any time three ounces of Oyle of Spike to be mingled amongst it.—*Ibid.*

A MEDDICINE THAT WAS SENT BY YE QUEENS MAJ^{TI} TO YE LORD MAYOR OF LONDON FOR YE PLAGUE.— Take Sage of Vertue herb grace Elder leaves Red

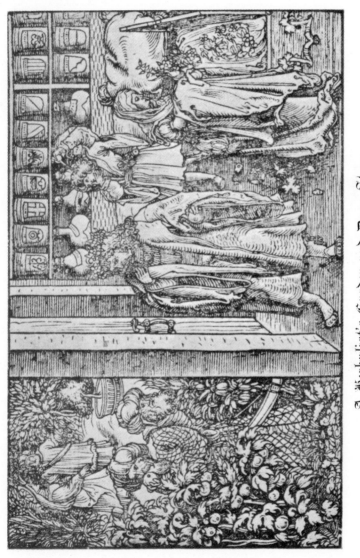

A Herbalist's Garden and Drug Store

bramble leaves and Stamp them together Seeth them in a quart of white Wine and a quantity of white wine Vinegar Streyne them together drink thereof evening and morning i Spoonful Nine dayes together after the first Spoonfull thee shall be made Safe for 24 days and after the 9th Spoonfull for a whole yeare by the grace of God and if it happen that the Party be sick of the Plague before he have drunke of this medicine then take the water of Scabious i Spoonfull of bettony Water i Spoonfull a quantity of Treackell, put it all together and it will drive out the Venome but if the botch appear then take bramble leaves Elder leaves and Musstard Seed Stamp them together and make a playster therof and lay it on the Sore this will draw out the venome and heale the Patient.—*Ibid.*

A MILK WATER.—Take Strawberry leaves Violet leaves Sorrell Cinquefoile Planten (plantain) Borrage Bugloss balme saxifrage and maiden hare of each of them a good handfull Coriander seeds Carriway Seeds and Liquorrise of each of them an ounce Sweet margerom and Rosemary of each a Small handfull nutmeg half an ounce Mace two drams Cloves one dram bruise all the herbs together in a Stone Mortar beat the Seeds likewise and Squeeze and Slice the liquoriss and bruise it a little and put all those Ingredients into a gallon of New Milk then put it all into your Still and distill off the next day. Drink of this water three or fouer Ounces Morning and Evening sweetened with Duble Refine Sugar.

This water is excelent against the heat of the livor and all hott Distempers and very good to comfort the Vitall Spirrits.—*Ibid.*

THE GREEN OYLE TO BE MADE IN MAY CALLED OYLE OF CHARITY.—Take Red Sage Rosemary Spanish lavender with the broad leafe and bawme Camomile Valerian of each fouer ounces wormwood two ounces gather them in a hott Sunny day and wipe them upon a Cloath but do not wash them then cut them very Small and put them into a Convenient Vessell or a Glass if you have it and put to it a quart of the Purest Oyle you can gett and tye it up very close letting it Stand in the Sunn a fortnight or three weeks Stirring it once in three or fouer days then put it into a Skillet and boyle it for a quarter of an hour or more and Strain out all the herbs as hard as you can wring them and put into the Oyle half the same quantity of herbs againe and let them Stand as before three or four dayes in the Sun then Sett them on the fire which must be very gentle and let them boyle very Softly till your Oyle be of a perfect Green Colour then straine out your herbs and let your Oyle stand all night in a Pewter basson then Sett the basson on a Chaffing Dish of Coles and let your Oyle boyle a little while and Scum it as long as anything does rise and then take it of and let it Stand till it be cold then take up a litle Glass of the uppermost and keep it for speciall uses the rest put into a Glass and if there be water at the bottom putt it away and so keep it for your use.

The Virtues of this Oyle. It is good to anoint and tent all wounds for it will Search to the bottom it will Dead the proud flesh that growes in a wound it Draws out thornes and Splinters and it is excellent for bruises in any part of the body to anoint the place or to give inwardly to Drink tenn or twelve drops for a man

or woman half as much to a Child in a Spoonfull
of Possett Drink made with Ale or White Wine.—
Ibid.

DR. TWIN'S ALMOND MILK.—Boil two quarts of
water, then let it stand till it is clear ; put in Strawberry Plants, both Leaf and Roots, and Violet Leaves,
of each a large handful and a large Root of Sorrel, le
them all be well wash'd ; put in two ounces of Raisins
of the Sun ston'd and a crust of white Bread. Boil all
these with fifty Almonds blanched and beaten ; draw
an Almond Milk, sweetened with Sugar to your Palate.
From *The Receipt Book of John Nott*, Cook to the Duke
of Bolton, 1723.

TO MAKE LEACH OF ALMONDS.—Take halfe a pound
of Sweete Almondes, and beat them in a mortar : then
straine them with a pinte of sweet milke from the cow :
then put to it one graine of musk, two spoonfuls of
Rose-water, two ounces of fine Sugar, the weight of
three whole shillings of Isinglasse that is very white,
and so boyle them : then let all tun thorow a strainer
then may you slice the same and so serve it.—Sir Hugh
Platt, *Delights for Ladies*, 1594.

BALLS FOR LENT.—Grate white bread, nutmeg, salt,
shred parsley, a very little thyme, and a little orange or
lemon-peel cut small ; make them up into balls with
beaten eggs, or you may add a spoonful of Cream ;
and roll them up in flour, and fry them.—E. Smith,
The Compleat Housewife, 1736.

To MAKE BISCUITS OF RED BEET-ROOTS : FROM THE
SAME ; CALL'D THE CRIMSON BISCUIT.—Take the Roots
of Red Beets, and boil them tender, clean them and
beat them in a Mortar with as much Sugar, finely
sifted ; some Butter ; the Yolks of hard Eggs, a little
Flower ; some Spice, finely beaten, and some Orange-
Flower water, and a little Lemon-juice. When
they are well mixed, and reduced to a Paste, make
them into Cakes, and dry them in a slow Oven.—
R. Bradley, *The Country Housewife and Lady's Director*,
1732.

How TO DRAW THE BLOUD OF HEARBES.—Stamp the
hearbe, put the same into a large glasse, leaving two
parts emptie (some commend the juice of the hearbe
only) nip or else lute the glasse very well : digest it in
balneo 15 or 16 daies, and you shall find the same very
red : divide the watrish part ; and that which remaineth, is the bloud or essence of the herb.—Sir Hugh
Platt, *Delights for Ladies*, 1594.

To MAKE PARSLEY, SAGE, THYME, SAVORY, AND
LEMON THYME BUTTER.—Clarify your Butter, then
mix it with a little of the oil of any of the Herbs, till
the Butter is strong enough to your taste or liking.
Then mix them well together. This is a great Rarity
and will make the Butter keep a long time. This will
be better than eating the Plants with Bread and Butter
by taking Butter newly made and working it well from
its water milk and wheyish Parts before you put in
the Oils.—From *The Receipt Book of John Nott*, Cook
to the Duke of Bolton, 1723.

How to make sundry sorts of most dainty Butter, having a lively taste of Sage, Cinnamon, Nutmegs, Mace, etc.—This is done by mixing a few dropps of the extracted oyle of Sage, Cinnamon, Nutmegs, Mace, etc., in the making up of your Butter : for Oyle and Butter will incorporate and agree very kindly and naturally together. And how to make the said oyles, with all necessarie vessels, instruments and other circumstances by a most plaine and familiar description ; see my " Jewel house of Art and Nature," under the Title of " Distillation."—Sir Hugh Platt, *Delights for Ladies*, 1594.

To make Almond Butter.—Blanch your Almonds, and beate them as fine as you can with faire water, two or three houres, then strain them through a linen cloth, boile them with Rose-water, whole mace and aniseeds, till the substance be thick : spread it upon a faire cloath, dressing the whey from it, after let it hang in the same cloath some few houres, then strain it and season it with Rose-water and sugar.—Sir Hugh Platt, *Delights for Ladies*, 1594.

To make Fairy Butter.—Take the Yolks of four hard Eggs, and half a Pound of Loaf Sugar beat and sifted, half a Pound of fresh Butter ; bray them in a clean Bowl with two spoonfuls of Orange-flower Water ; when it is well mixed, force it through the corner of a thin Canvas Strainer in little Heaps on a Plate. It is a very pretty Supper Dish.—From *The Receipt Book of Elizabeth Cleland*, 1759.

To make a Caudle for Sweet Pies.—Take two Gills of White Wine, a little Nutmeg, Sugar and Lemon-peel ; put it on the Fire, and when it is scalding hot, beat the Yolks of two Eggs, and mix them with a little cold Wine ; then mix all together ; keep it stirring till it is scalding hot, then take it up and pour it over the Pye or Tart.—From *The Receipt Book of Elizabeth Cleland*, 1759.

To make Flummery Caudle.—Take a Mutchkin of fine Oatmeal, put to it two Chopins of Water, let it stand twelve Hours ; then strain it into a Skellet with a little Mace and Nutmeg ; set it on the Fire and keep it stirring, and let it boil a quarter of an Hour ; if it is too thick put in more Water, and let it boil longer ; add to it a Mutchkin of White Wine, the juice of a Lemon or Orange, and a Bit of Butter : Sweeten it to your Taste, let it have one Boil. You may put in the Yolks of two Eggs, but let it not boil after you put in the Eggs ; let it be scalding hot, keep it stirring till you dish it.

Cinnamon Tostes.—Cut fine thin tostes, then toste them on a gridiron and lay them in ranks in a dish, put to them fine beaten cinnamon mixed with Sugar and some claret, warm them over the fire and serve them hot.—Robert May, *The Art and Mystery of Cookery*, 1671.

To fry Cucumbers for Mutton Sauce.—You must brown some Butter in a pan, and cut the cucumber

in thin slices ; drain them from the Water, then fli
them into the pan, and when they are fried browɪɪ,
put in a little pepper and salt, a bit of onion and gravy,
and let them stew together, and squeeze in some juice
of lemon ; shake them well and put them under
your mutton.—E. Smith, *The Compleat Housewife*,
1736.

To make Paste of Flowers of the Colour of
Marble tasting of Natural Flowers.—Take every
sort of pleasing flowers, as Violets, Cowslips, Gillyflowers, Roses, or Marygolds, and beat them in a
Mortar, each flower by itself with Sugar, till the Sugar
become the Colour of the flower, then put a little Gum
Dragon steept in Water into it, and beat it into a
perfect paste ; so when you have half a dozen colours,
every flower will take of his nature, then rowl the Paste
therein, and lay one peece upon another, in mingling,
so rowl your paste in small rowls as bigge and as long
as your finger, then cut it off the bigness of a small nut,
overthwart, and so rowl them thin, that you may see
a knife through them, so dry them before the fire, till
they be dry.—*The Queen's Closet Opened*, by W. M.,
Cook to Queen Henrietta Maria, 1655.

To Candy all kind of Flowers in Wayes of the
Spanish Candy.—Take double refined sugar, put it
into a posnet with as much rose-water as will melt it,
and put into it the pappe of half a roasted apple, and
a grain of musk, then let it boyl till it come to a candy
height, then put in your flowers being picked, and so
let it boyl, then cast them on a fine plate, and cut

inwayes with your knife, then you may spot it with gold and keep it.—*A Choice Manual of Secrets*, by Elizabeth Grey, Countess of Kent, 1653.

To Candy all manner of Flowers in their Natural Colours.—Take the flowers with the stalks, and wash them over with a little Rose-water, wherein Gum-Arabick is dissolved; then take searsed sugar, and dust over them, and set them a drying on the bottom of a sieve in an oven, and they will glister as if it were Sugar-Candy.—William Rabisha, *The Whole Body of Cookery Dissected*, 1675.

To dish up Fruits and preserved Flowers.—Take a large Dish, cover it with another of the same bigness, and lay the uppermost all over with Almond paste; inlaid with white, red, green, blue or white Marmalad in the Figures of Banks of Flowers. Then take branches of candy'd Flowers and stick them upright in the Paste in as handsome orders as you can, then erect little Bushes covered with Paste, and upon them fasten preserved Apples, Apricochs, Currants, Gooseberries, Peaches, Pears, Plums, etc., and for Leaves you may make use either of coloured Paste, Parchment or Horn. This will be very proper in winter.—*Ibid.*

To keep Flowers all the Year.—Put Gum Arabic into Rose-water, to make it sticky; take what sorts of flowers you please and drop them into the liquor, swing the liquor off and set them in a sieve to dry in the sun.—*Ibid.*

To pickle Flowers.—Take Flowers of any sort, put them into a Gallypot with their weight in Sugar, and to each pound of sugar put a pint of Vinegar.— *Ibid*.

To make Syrups of any Flowers.—Clip your flowers and take their weight in Sugar ; then take a gallypot, and put a row of flowers and a strewing of sugar, till the pot is full ; then put in two or three spoonfuls of the same syrup or still'd water ; tie a cloth on the top of the pot, put a tile on that, set your gallypot in a Kettle of water over a gentle fire, and let it infuse till the strength is out of the flowers, which will be in four or five hours ; then strain it through a flannel, and when it is cold bottle it up.—E. Smith, *The Compleat Housewife*, 1736.

To Sugar all sorts of small Fruits.—Beat the white of an egg and dip the fruit in it, let it lie on a cloth that it may not wet ; then take fine sifted sugar and rowl the Fruit in it till it is quite covered with sugar and lay it on a sieve in a Stove or before a Fire to dry it well ; it will keep well a week.—From *The Receipt Book of Mrs. Mary Eales*, Confectioner to Queen Anne, 1719.

To make French Puffes with greene Hearbes.— Take Spinage, Parsley, Endife, a sprigge or two of Savory, mince them very fine : season them with Nutmeg, ginger and sugar. Wet them with eggs according to the quantity of the Hearbes, more or lesse. Then take the Coare of a Lemmon, cut it in round slices very thinne : put to every slice of your lemmon one spoonfule of this stuffe. Then fry it with Sweet lard in a Frying-panne as you frye Egges, and serve them with Sippets or without, sprinckle them eyther with White-wine or Sacke, or any other wine, saving Rennish-wine. Serve them eyther at Dinner or Supper.—John Murrel, *A New Book of Cookerie*, 1621.

To MAKE GOOSEBERRY VINEGAR.—Take gooseberries full syse, bruise them in a mortar, then measure them, and to every quart of gooseberries, put three quarts of water, first boiled, and let it stand till cold ; let it stand twenty-four hours ; then strain it thro' a canvas, then a flannel ; and to every gallon of this liquor put one pound of brown sugar ; stir it well, and barrel it up ; at three-quarters of a year old it is fit for use ; but if it stands longer it is the better. This vinegar is likewise good for pickles.—E. Smith, *The Compleat Housewife*, 1736.

MARROW AND HERB BALLS.—Take cooked marrow, a little thyme, winter avory and Sweet Marjoram, the yolks of three Eggs, a Quarter of a Pound of Sugar, a Quarter of a Pound of Currant, a little Rose-water and some Nutmeg. Work all these well together and put them into a pasty of Puff paste and fry them in sweet butter or lard.—*England's Newest Way in All Sorts of Cookery*, by Henry Howard, Free Cook of London, 1710.

How TO CANDY GINGER, NUTMEGS, OR ANY ROOT OR

FLOWERS.—Take a quarter of a pound of the best refined Sugar, which you can get : powder it : put thereto two Spoonfuls of Rose-water : dip therein your Nutmegs, Ginger, roots, etc., being first sodden in faire water till they bee soft and tender : the oftener you dip them in your sirup, the thicker the candy will bee, but it will bee the longer in candying : your sirup must be of such stiffness, as that a drop thereof, being let fall upon a pewter-dish, may congeale and harden being cold. You must make your sirup in a chafing-dish of coales, keeping a gentle fire. After your sirup is once at his full height, then put them upon papers presently into a store, or in dishes : continue for some tenne or twelve dayes, till you finde the candy hard, and glistening like diamonds : you must dip the red rose, the gilliflower, the marigold, the borage-flowers and all other flowers but once.—Sir Hugh Platt, *Delights for Ladies*, 1694.

AN OLIO FOR DAYS OF ABSTINENCE.—Put fresh broth and good Pea Soup into a Pot with Borage, Endive, Marigold, Sorrel or other Sweet Herbs grossly shred and some Spinage whole, likewise Turnips, Carrots, Onions and Cabbage cut in pieces, a little saffron, cloves, mace and nutmegs, etc. Add bottoms of Artichokes and Chestnuts (boiled and blanched) with a couple of Colleyflowers. Let them boil to-gether as long as is requisite. Add Yolks of eggs and then serve your olio with seppets of bread and garnished as you please.—From *The Receipt Book of John Nott*, Cook to the Duke of Bolton, 1723.

PARSNIP-CAKES.—Scrape some Parsnip-Roots, and

slice them thin, dry them in an Oven and beat them to Powder ; mix them then with an equal quantity of Flour, and make them up with Cream and Spices powder'd ; then mould them into Cakes, and bake them in a gentle Oven.—N.B. The Sweetness of the Parsnip Powder answers the want of Sugar.—R. Bradley, *The Country Housewife and Lady's Director*, 1732.

SWEETE CAKES WITHOUT EITHER SPICE OR SUGAR.— Scrape or wash your Parsneps cleane, slice them thinne, dry them upon Canvas or network frames, beat them to powder, mixing one third thereof with two thirds of fine wheate flower : make up your paste into coates, and you shall find them very delicate.—Sir Hugh Platt, *Delights for Ladies*, 1594.

POTATO PYE SWEET.—You must first boil them half enough, then make a good Puff-paste and lay in your Potatoes, and betwixt every one a Lump of Marrow rolled in Egg ; cut in some slices of Orange and Lemon-peel, and a little Sugar ; then make a Caudle with Cream and Eggs, and a little Sack, and when your Pye is bak'd, take off the Lid and pour all your Caudle over it.—From *The Receipt Book of Charles Carter*, Cook to the Duke of Argyll, 1732.

POTATO TART.—Take a pound and a half of potatoes, boil them and skin them and cut them in slices, not thin ; sheet a Dish with puff-paste, lay some citron in the bottom, lay over your potatoes, and season them with ginger, cinnamon, nutmeg and sugar ; then take the marrow of two Bones cut it into Pieces as big as Walnuts roll it in yolks of eggs and season it as the Potatoes ; lay it on them and between the Lumps of Marrow lay Citron and Dates sprinkle over some Orange flower or Rose-water. Draw up a quart of Cream with yolks of eggs pour all over it, bake it and stick over some Citron and serve it.—*Ibid.*

POTATO AND LEMON CHEESECAKES.—Take six ounces of potatoes, four ounces of lemon-peel, four ounces of sugar, four ounces of butter, boil the lemon-peel till tender, pare and scrape the potatoes, and boil them tender and bruise them ; beat the lemon-peel with the sugar then beat all and mix all together very well and let it lie till cold : put crust in your pattipans, and fill them little more than half full : bake them in a quick oven half an hour, sift some double refin'd sugar on them as they go into the oven ; this quantity will make a dozen small pattipans.—E. Smith, *The Compleat Housewife*, 1736.

TO MAKE BISCUITS OF POTATOES. (From Mrs. Mary Gordon).—Boil the Roots of Potatoes till they are tender ; then peel them, and take their weight of fine Sugar, finely sifted ; grate some Lemon-Peel on the Sugar ; and then beat the Potatoes and Sugar together, in a Stone Mortar, with some Butter, a little Mace, or Cloves, finely sifted, and a little Gum Dragon, steeped in Orange-Flower Water, or Rose-Water, till it becomes a Paste ; then make it into Cakes with Sugar, finely powder'd, and dry them in a gentle Oven.—

R. Bradley, *The Country Housewife and Lady's Director*, 1732.

POTATOE-PUDDING BAKED. (From Mr. Shepherd of Windmill Street).—Boil some fair Potatoes till they are tender ; then, when they are made clean, bruise them in a Marble Mortar, till they become a Paste, with some Mace powder'd, some Sugar and the Pulp of Oranges, with a Naples Biscuit or two grated in, and a large Carrot grated. Add to these some Orange-Flower Water ; and when all these are well mix'd, put to them some butter'd Eggs, with some slices of Butter aid upon your Pudding, when it is put into the Dish, or Pan. A little baking will serve for it ; and when it is enough, serve it hot, with a garnish of Sliced Lemon or Orange. Some will put this into a Paste, but not cover it over.—*Ibid*.

TO MAKE A WHYTE-SYLLABUB.—Put a Pint of White-wine, and a Pint of Mulberry, or black Cherry Juice, into a wooden Bowl ; add also a Pint of Cream, sweeten it with Sugar, and put in a large perfumed Comfit, put a Branch or two of Rosemary stript from the Leaves, among some Willow-twigs peeled, and wind a Lemon-peel about your Willow-twigs, etc. together very well, and melt the butter in a little thick cream. Then stir your Syllabub well together, and whip it up till it froths, take off the Froth with a Spoon, and put it into your Glasses, and squeeze some Spirit of Lemon-peel between every Layer of Froth, and let it stand till the next Day before you eat it.—*Ibid*.

A WORCESTERSHIRE SYLLABUB.—Fill your Syllabub-pot with Cyder, put in a good Quantity of Sugar, and a little Nutmeg ; stir these well together, then put in as much thick Cream by two or three Spoon-fuls at a time, as if you were milking it ; then stir it round very gently, and let it stand two Hours, then eat it.

If it be in the Field, only milk the Cow into the Cyder, etc. and so drink it.—*Ibid*.

To make Syrop of all Kinde.—Take Bugloss, Borage, white Endive, of each one handefull, of Rose-marie, Tyme, Hysope, winter saverie, of each half a handefull, seethe them (being first broken betweene your handes) in three quartes of water into three pintes, then streine it and put in the liquor whole cloves an ounce, powder of cinnamon halfe an ounce, powder of ginger a quarter of an ounce, one nutmeg in powder, of sugar halfe a pound or more : let them seethe upon a soft fire, well stirred until it come to the thick-ness of live honey, then keep it in galley-pots. If you put one pint of Malmsey in the second seething it will be better. When it is perfect have sixe graines of fine Muske in powder, stir it amongst your Syrop, as yee put it into the Galley-pot and cover it.

This Syrop will last many yeeres and is excellent. it comforteth the braine and sinewes.—John Partridge, *The Treasurie of Commodious Conceits and Hidden Secrets*, 1586.

To make Taffaty-Cream.—Beat the Whites of eight Eggs up to a froth with Rose-water, skim off the Froth, and put it into a Quart of Cream, and set it

on the Fire to boil, but keep it continually stirring ;
then having beaten the Yolks of eight Eggs very well,
slip them into the Cream, and stir it a little ; then take
it off the Fire, and stir it still, sweeten it with Sugar,
pour it out, and set it by to cool.—*The Complete
Family Piece*, 1737.

A TART OF GREEN SPROUTS AND HERBS.—Take your
green sprouts, and give them a scald and lay them a
draining, then mince them small and also the herbs
(such as you please) season with Beef marrow an onion
stuck with Cloves and some thin slices of Bacon,
cover it up with the same paste and when it is baked
put in some gravy, the juice of Lemon and serve it
away.—From *The Receipt Book of Patrick Lord
Ruthven*, 1655.

TO MAKE A SPRING TART.—Gather such Buds, in
the Spring of the year, that are not bitter ; also the
Leaves of Primroses, Violets and Strawberries ; take
also a little young Spinage, boil them, drain them in
a Colander ; then chop them very small, and boil them
over again in Cream ; add to them Naples bisket
grated, and so many Yolks and Whites of Eggs as will
make the Cream very thick, colour all green with the
Juice of Spinage ; season with Salt, Nutmeg, Cinnamon and Sugar, and bake it in Puff-paste, or otherways.—From *The Receipt Book of John Nott*, Cook to
the Duke of Bolton, 1723.

TO MAKE A SWEET-SOUR TART.—Boil a quarter of
a Pound of Sugar in a Glass of Verjuice or Lemon-

juice, and when it is wasted half, put to it some Cream, with the Yolks of half a dozen Eggs, Orange-flowers, Lemon-peel candy'd, grated ; a little beaten Cinnamon, and a little Butter. Put these into a Tart made of fine Paste, and bake it without a Lid.—*Ibid*.

TATTES OR BALDE MEATES FOR FISH DAIES.—Take your dish and anoint the bottom well with butter, then make a fine past to the bredth of the dish and lay it on the same dish upon the butter, then take Dates, Spinnage, and Cabbadges, or white Lettuce, cutting them fine in long pieces, then take the yolks of eight raw eggs and six yolks of hard eggs with small raisins and a little cheese fine scraped, and grated bread and three or four dishes of Butter melted and when you have brought it together season it with sugar and cinnamon, ginger and salt. Then lay it upon your fine paste spreading it abroad, then the cover of the fine paste being cut with prettie work then set it in your Oven bake it and when it is enough then at the serving of it you must newe past the cover with butter and so scrape sugar upon it and then serve it forth.—*The Good Housewife's Jewell*, 1585.

TURNIP BREAD (" of which we have eaten at the Greatest Persons Tables hardly to be distinguished from best of wheat ").—Let the turnips first be peeled and boiled in water till soft and tender. Then strongly pressing out the juice mix them together and when dry (beaten or pounded very fine) with their weight of Wheat Meal season it as you do other bread and knead it up. Then letting the Dough remain a little to ferment fashion the paste into loaves and bake it like common bread.—John Evelyn, *Acetaria*, 1699.

TURNIP STALKS.—Take their Stalks (when they begin to run up to seed) as far as they will easily break downwards : Peel and tie them in Bundles. Then boiling them as they do Sparagus are to be eaten with melted Butter.—*Ibid.*

VINE LEAF FRITTERS.—Take a dozen of the smallest Vine Leaves you can get, cut off the stalks, put them in a deep dish, pour in a glass of brandy, and grate the rind of a lemon over them, and about two ounces of powder sugar, mix a gill of Cream with two eggs and flour to a stiff batter, and mix with them ; have a pan of boiling hog's-lard, minding that the leaves have plenty of batter on both sides ; put them in and fry them quick on both sides of a light brown, lay them on a sieve to drain, then put them in a dish, sprinkle powder sugar over them, and glaze them with a hot iron.—*The New Art of Cookery*, by Richard Briggs, Head Cook successively to Charles II, James II, William and Mary, and Anne, 1788.

AN EXCELLENT CONCEIT UPON THE KERNELS OF DRIE WALNUTS.—Gather not your Walnuts before they be full ripe, keep them without any art untill Newyeare's tide, then break the shells carefully, so as you deface not the kernels ; (and therefore you must take choise of such nuts as have this shell) whatsoever you find to come away easily, remove it : steepe these kernels in

conduit water, forty-eight houres, then will they swell
and grow very plumpe and faire, and you may pill
them easily, and present to any friend you have for
a Newyeare's gift ; but being pilled, they must be
eaten within two or three houres, or else they lose their
whitenesse and beautie, but unpilled they will last two
or three daies faire and fresh. This of a kinde gentle-
woman, whose skill I doe highly commend, and whose
case I doe greatly pittie ; such are the hard fortunes
of the best wits and natures in our daies.—Sir Hugh
Platt, *Delights for Ladies*, 1594.

To DESTROY BROWN MOLES ON THE SKIN.—4 ozs.
dried tops of rosemary, 4 ozs. dried leaves of sage, 4 ozs.
dried flowers of lavenders, $\frac{1}{2}$ oz. cloves, 3 drachms of
camphor, 6 pints distilled Vinegar. Macerate 14 days
with heat, then filter and it is ready for use.
Apply a drop twice a day to the moles until they
are removed.

To MAKE A WHITE-POT.—Boil a Quart of Cream with
large Mace, let it stand till it is almost cold ; then beat
the Yolks of eight Eggs, and put them into the Cream
with Salt and Sugar to your Taste. Lay thin Slices
of White Bread in the Bottom of the Dish, and lay
on them sliced Dates, Raisins of the Sun, or what
Sweet-meats you please, with bits of Marrow, or of
fresh Butter ; then lay another Layer of Bread, Fruit,
etc., till the Dish is full, grating Nutmeg between every
Layer ; then put in your Cream, and lay Slices of
Bread and Bits of Butter on the top of all, and bake it.—
From *The Receipt Book of John Middleton*, 1734.

MAY BLOSSOM FLAVOURING.—Fill a pint bottle with freshly gathered may blossoms, picked when most of the blossoms are only half out. When the bottle is full fill up with the best brandy. Cork well and leave for two days. The flowers will have sunk considerably ; get more blossoms and fill up. Continue like this till the bottle will hold no more. Then cork and run wax over the cork and put in a dark cupboard for at least six months. This is a delicious flavouring and tastes like the smell of newly opened may blossoms.

FRENCH " TISANES "

TISANE DE QUATRE FLEURS.—Lime flowers, orange flowers, borage and camomile. Half a pint of boiling water poured on to a heaped dessertspoon of these dried flowers.

In spite of its name *tisane de quatre fleurs* has sometimes more ingredients. Dried violets, for instance, are frequently added.

TISANE DE VERVEINE.—Three leaves of verbena in a cup of boiling water.

TISANE DE TILLEUL.—Pick the flowers when they begin to open. Dry and keep in air-tight tins. Boil a dessertspoonful of the dried flowers in half a pint of water for a few seconds. Leave to infuse quarter of an hour and then strain. A few orange-flowers added are an improvement.

TISANE D'ORANGE.—Half a pint of boiling water poured on to a dessertspoonful of dried orange flowers.

For sleeplessness two tablespoonfuls of orange-flower water—not the flowers—in a tumbler of warm water. If beaten up with the white of an egg this is " lait au poule."

TISANE DES VIOLETTES.—Half a pint of boiling water poured on to half an ounce of the fresh flowers. If dried flowers are used, less than half an ounce.

CHAPTER VIII

OF THE PICKING AND DRYING OF HERBS

" Aristotell the prince of philosophers sayeth in maneye places, that everye science is of the kynde of good thynges. But notwithstanding the operation sometyme is good, sometyme evell, as the science is chaunged to a good or to an evell ende, to which it worketh."—*The boke of the secrets of Albertus Magnus of the vertues of herbes, stones and certaine beastes*, 1569.

ALL the northern nations had runes or charms for the picking of herbs, but unfortunately most of these have been lost, for as nearly all the manuscripts were written by monks they omitted the old pagan charms. There are traces of Scandinavian mythology to be found in the oldest herbals, but of the runes nothing remains, with the rare exception of perhaps the name of an idol, such as Leleloth, given after the names of the four Apostles. In the Penitential of Theodore, Archbishop of Canterbury, one of the oldest books of penalties for offences against the laws of the Church, there are given the penalties to be imposed on those who practised the old heathen rites connected with plants and trees, and when the monks transcribed herbals they substituted Christian prayers for the old charms. Some of these prayers are very beautiful, and the following dates back to at least the fourteenth century, and is probably much older—

" Haile be thou holie hearbe
Growing on the ground
All in the mount of Calvarie
First wert thou found.
Thou art good for manie a sore
And healest manie a wound
In the name of sweete Jesus
I take thee from the ground."

It would be easy to fill a book with these extracts
of the prayers to be said when gathering herbs. For
example, in one old herbal one finds, " For the delirious.
When day and night divide, then sing thou in the
Church, litanies, the names of the hallows (Saints)
and the Pater Noster. With the song go thou near the
herbs and go thrice about them, and when thou takest
them go again to the Church with the same song and
sing twelve masses over them and over all the drinks
which belong to the disease in honour of the twelve
Apostles." Then, again, in making use of sorrel or
dock, " Sing twelve times the Psalm miserere mei
Deus and Gloria in excelsis Deo and the Pater Noster
. . . when day and night divide then drink the dose
and wrap thyself up warm." In another herbal, " For
much travelling overland lest a man tire. Let him take
mugwort in his hand and put it in his shoe lest he
should be weary. And when he will pluck it before
sunrise let him first say, ' Tollam te artemisia ne lassus
sim in via.' Sign it (with the sign of the Cross) when
thou pullest it up." When picking celandine, " Sing
over it nine Pater Nosters and at the ninth at ' Deliver
us from evil,' take it up." In the later herbals one finds
more general instructions : " Make mention of the
passion and grief and the name of the thynge for the

which thou doest gather it and the selfe herbe lay on
wheat or barley." Again a godly prayer, " Thine Hand
vexeth, Thine Hand vexeth."

Although so little remains of the old charms there is
more evidence of pagan worship in the old belief of
the influence of the sun, moon, and other celestial
bodies on the herbs. Every herb was supposed to be
under the influence of one of these bodies, and they
must be in a favourable position when the herb was used.
Herbs under the dominion of the Sun must never be
picked except with gold or a stag's horn—(emblems of
the sun's rays). There are many herbalists to-day
(and many gardeners too for that matter) who firmly
believe in sowing all seeds when the moon is waxing,
but the rest is now regarded as mere superstition.
Perhaps in another century science will have discovered
that there is a great deal in these old beliefs. William
Coles, in his *Art of Simpling* (1656), is very scornful of
the old herbalists in this matter. " And now I have
done with the setting of Plants, give me leave to speak
somewhat of the gathering them also : Some of the
Antients, and divers Modern writers which have pro-
fessed Astrology, have noted a Sympathy between
the Sunne, Moon, and some principal Starres, and
certain Plants, and so they have denominated some
Herbes Solar, and some Lunar, and such toyes put
into great words. Amongst which Master Culpepper
(a man now dead, and therefore I shall speak of him
as modestly as I can, for were he alive, I should be more
plain with him) was a great stickler ; And he, forsooth,
judgeth all men unfit to be Physicians who are not
Artists in Astrology, as if he and some other Figure-
flingers, his companions, had been the only Physicians

in England, whereas for ought I can gather, either by
his Books, or learne from the report of others, he was
a man very ignorant in the form of Simples. Many
Books indeed he hath tumbled over, and transcribed
as much out of them, as he thought would serve his
turne (though many times he were therein mistaken),
but added very little of his owne. . . . Herbs are
more antient than the Sunne, or Moon, or Starres,
they being created on the fourth day whereas plants
were the third. Thus did God even at first confute
the folly of those Astrologers, who goe about to
maintain that all vegetables in their growth are enslaved
to a necessary and unavoidable dependence on the
influences of the Starres. Whereas Plants were, even
when Planets were not."

And now to turn to more practical matters ! Nearly
all herbs are at their best when they are going to flower.
The young tops and flowers contain more virtues than
the older leaves. They should always be picked when
the dew has well dried off them, but before the sun is
at its hottest. No herbs should ever be dried in the
sunlight, as this extracts so much of their virtue.
They should be hung in small bunches in a dark, dry
place, with paper over them to keep off the dust, and
as soon as they are perfectly dry they should be
powdered and put into airtight tins, or preferably, in
well-corked bottles. If in the latter they should be
kept in the dark. There is no comparison between the
flavour of herbs kept in bags and those in bottles, for
the former naturally lose more than half their goodness
One of the easiest ways of drying herbs if you have no
proper drying-shed is to hang them in bunches in a cool
oven. Flowers for pot-pourri should be dried spread

out on wire sieves so that the air can circulate all round
them, below as well as above. If necessary cover with
butter muslin to prevent petals, etc., blowing about.
No writer has put more concisely the directions for
picking herbs than old Sir John Hill. " When the
whole plant dies the root is seldom of any value, but
when the root remains many years, sends up many
shoots in the Spring, it commonly has great virtue.
There is very little to be expected in the roots of annual
plants : their seeds for the most part contain their
greatest virtue. In others the root lives through the
Winter, and there arise from it large leaves in the
Spring before the stalk appears. These are to be distinguished from those which afterwards grow on the
Stalk, for they are more juicy, and for many Purposes
much better. When the leaves of any Plant are said
to be the part fittest for use they are not to be taken from
the stalk, but these large ones growing from the roots
are to be chosen, and these when there is no stalk if
that can be, for then only are they fullest of juice and
have their compleat virtue ; the stalk running away
with the nourishment from them. This is so much done
in some plants that although the Leaves growing from
Root were very vigorous before the stalk grew up they
die and wither as it rises. Nature in the whole growth
of plants tends to the production of their flowers
and seed, but when they are ripe the rest begins to
decay, having done its Duty, so that the time when
the entire Plant is in its most full Perfection is when
it is in the Bud when the Heads are formed for flowering, but not a single Flower has yet disclosed itself.
The tops of the plant are always preferable to the whole
Plant for immediate use. The time of the Day must be

when the morning Dew is dried away. This is a very material circumstance, for if they be cut wet with the Dew, Herbs will not dry well, and if they be cut at Noon Day, when the sun has made the Leaves flag, they will not have their full Power. Care must also be taken to cut them on a dry day, for the wet of Rain will do as much harm as that of Dew. When the Herbs are thus gathered they are to be looked over, the decayed Leaves picked off, and the dead ends of the stalks cut away. They are then to be tied up into small bunches, the less the better, and hung upon Lines drawn across the room where the windows and doors are to be kept open in good weather ; the Bunches are to be kept half a foot asunder, and they are to hang till perfectly dry. They are then to be taken softly down, without shaking off the Buds of the flowers, and laid evenly in a Drawer, pressing them down and covering them with paper."

A drying-shed is a very charming adjunct to a herb garden, and though it is not at all scientific, it is very delightful to see great bunches of herbs hanging up in the old-fashioned way. The most interesting drying-shed I know belongs to a herbalist who lives in a remote village in Devonshire. Her cottage, which looks as though it had been comfortably tucked up in its garden for centuries, is very tiny, and the garden, surrounded by a typical Devonshire bank, is full of herbs both wild and cultivated. The owner comes of the fine old English yeoman stock, and one never sees her without feeling it is a privilege to know any one with such beautiful old-fashioned manners. She is a tall, splendid-looking woman well over eighty, but not in the least bent, and it is obvious she has never known a moment's boredom. The least observant stranger would realise she was a silent person, and any child would very soon class her as one of those comfortable grown-ups who do not bother one with silly questions. To listen to her talking about her beloved herbs is a joy, and to see her working in the garden amongst them would rejoice the heart of any artist. But to return to her drying-shed. This is on the sunniest side of the house, and of course it is quite dark, as nothing is worse for herbs than to dry them where the sunlight can reach them. From the old beam which runs the length of the roof hang bunches of all the herbs she uses :—Meadowsweet, elder (in enormous quantities), tansy, thyme, sage (both the purple and the green), and many others. Then there are the boxes where she keeps the dried flowers—marigold, camomile and lime, coltsfoot, and quantities of lavender (which somehow always smells as though it had only just been picked). There are queer coloured bottles, too, full of all sorts of mixtures—decoctions of ground ivy, sloe gin, dandelion, sage and elder wine ; endless ointments, and lotions, for cuts and bruises.

No one who picks and carefully dries their own herbs ever wants to use bought herbs again. And even if you have a very beautiful herb garden don't neglect to make use of the wild herbs also. Remember the wise advice of a fifteenth-century herbalist who wrote, " Herbes that grow in the fieldes be bettere then those that growe in gardenes. And those that grow on the hillis be best."

CHAPTER IX

OF SWEET SCENTS

" Scents are the souls of flowers : they may be even perceptible in the land of shadows. The tulip is a flower without a soul, but the rose and the lily seem to have one."—JOUBERT.

" If odours may worke satisfaction, they are so soveraigne in plants and so comfortable that no confection of the apothecaries can equall their excellent Vertue."—JOHN GERARD, *The Herball*, 1597.

" Smells and other odours are sweeter in the Air at some distance. For we see that in Sounds likewise they are sweetest when we cannot hear every part by itself. . . . For all sweet smells have joined with them some earthly or crude odours and at some distance the sweet which is the more spiritual is perceived and the earthy reaches not so far."—BACON, *Sylva Sylvarum*

THE *Malmesbury Chronicle* tells us that when Hugh the Great, the father of Hugh Capet, asked in marriage the sister of King Athelstan of England, he sent her gifts of perfumes the like of which had never before been seen in England. We have always lacked the skill of the professional perfumers of the continent, but when English women were wise enough to make their own perfumes, sweet waters, washing-balls, pomanders, and sweet linen bags from their herb gardens, they were unrivalled. We know that at least as early as the twelfth century the French perfume-makers were of sufficient importance to be granted a charter, but there was no such trade in England for centuries later, and even in Chaucer's day it was only possible to buy perfumes from the mercers. From crusading days the far-famed perfumes of the East were valued gifts amongst the nobility of the continent, but in England they never found so much favour; and when perfumes became the fashion in Elizabeth's reign, it was to the herb garden the English women turned rather than to the products of Eastern lands. For at least two hundred years rose-water was the perfume most in request, and it was always used after banquets for washing the hands. When one remembers that as late as James I's reign it was regarded as foppish to use a fork, one realises that these salvers of rose or sweet waters must have been more of a necessity than a luxury. The custom of having scented gloves and jerkins was introduced by that Elizabeth dandy Edward de Vere, Earl of Oxford, on his return from Italy. Queen Elizabeth the same year had a pair of scented gloves, with which she was so delighted that they were painted in her next portrait, and she was mightily pleased when another courtier gave her a " gyrdle of pomanders." Excepting during the Puritan *régime* the use of perfumes in every way became rapidly so popular that all the small country houses soon had their still-rooms, and the delightful custom of scenting rooms with fragrant herbs was almost universal.

Of this custom Sir Hugh Platt in his *Garden of Eden* writes : " I hold it for a most delicate and pleasing thing to have a fair gallery, great chamber or other lodging, that openeth fully upon the East or West sun, to be inwardly garnished with sweet Hearbs and Flowers, yea and Fruit if it were possible. For the performance whereof, I have thought of these courses following. First, you may have fair sweet Marjerom, Basil, Carnation, or Rosemary-pots, etc., to stand loosly upon fair shelves, which pots you may let down at your pleasure in apt frames with a pulley from your Chamber window into your garden, or you may place them upon shelves made without the Room, there to receive the warm Sun, or temperate Rain at your pleasure, now and then when you see cause. In every window you may make square frames either of Lead or of Boards, well pitched within : fill them with some rich earth, and plant such Flowers or Hearbs therein as you like best ; if Hearbs, you may keep them in the shape of green borders, or other form. And if you plant them with Rosemary, you may maintain the same running up your windows. And in the shady places of the Room, you may prove if such shady plants as do grow abroad out of the Sun, will not also grow there : as sweet Bryars, Bays, Germander, etc. But you must often set open your Casements, especially in the day time, which would also be many in number ; because Flowers delight and prosper best in the open Air. You may also hang in the Roof, and about the sides of this Room, small Pompions or Cowcumbers, pricked full of Barley, first making holes for the Barley, and these will be overgrown with green spires, so as the Pompion or Cowcumber will not appear."

Extravagance in perfumes was never so great in England as in France where during the reign of Louis XV it reached its high-water mark. The court then was in truth *la cour parfumée*, and the strict rules of etiquette prescribed the use of a different perfume each day. Madame de Pompadour spent 500,000 livres a year on perfumes for the use of her household at Choisy. Nor have we in England raised the sense of smell to an art like the Breton peasant of whom Dideron tells us in his *Annales Archéologiques*. This peasant, after musing over the scents of the flowers in the fields, claimed to have discovered the harmonious relation between odours. He came to Paris to give a concert of perfumes, but they took him for a madman. Perhaps, like so many madmen, he was only in advance of his times ; and is not modern science returning to the ancient belief in the value of wholesome and refreshing scents ?

The old herbalists were never weary of teaching the value of the scents of our aromatic herbs. How great was the popular belief in rosemary to ward off infection may be gathered from the fact that during the great plague in Charles II's time small bunches of rosemary were sold for six and eightpence. Before the plague an armful cost but twelve pence. Till recently there were at least two curious survivals of this belief in herbal scents—the doctors' gold-headed cane which formerly contained a vinaigrette, and the little bouquets carried by the clergy at the distribution of the Maundy money in Westminster Abbey. " Physicians," wrote Montaigne, " might in my opinion draw more use and good from odours than they do. For myself, I have often perceived that according unto their strength and quality they change and alter and move my spirits and make strange effects in me, which makes me approve the common saying that the invention of the incense and perfumes in churches so ancient and so far diffused throughout all nations and religions had a special regard to rejoice, to comfort, to quicken, to rouse, and to purify our senses so that we might be the apter and readier unto our contemplations."

Artificial scents have had a long enough reign in England, and perhaps we shall be wise enough to return to the simple old home-made rose, lavender, jasmine and other sweet waters, the pomanders and scented wash balls of our great-great-grandmothers. And is not a garden full of fragrant herbs a perpetual delight ? Are there any bought scents so delicious and exhilarating as wild thyme, marjoram and rosemary ? There is something so clean and wholesome in them that one feels the old herbalists were right when they said that to smell these herbs continually would keep any one in perfect health. They are so full of sunshine and sweetness that it seems there can be no tonic like them, and it is curious how appreciative invalids are of sweet-scented herbs. Flower scents are often too heavy for them, but a bunch of fragrant herbs seems a perpetual joy. In London, where one can buy all the costliest and most beautiful flowers in or out of season, does anything bring a breath of the country air so perfectly as a boxful of lavender ? " There are few better places for the study of scents," says Mrs. Bardswell, " than the herb garden. Here fragrance depends more on the leaves of plants than on the flowers. One secret is soon discovered. It is the value of leaf-scents. Flower-scents are evanescent ; leaf-odours are permanent. On the other hand, leaf-odours though ready when sought, do not force themselves upon us, as it were, like flower-scents, which we must smell whether we will or no. Leaf-scents have to be coaxed out by touching, bruising or pressing ; but there they are. After all, that is the

great point, and long after the summer flower-scents
have departed we can enjoy the perfumes of the sweet-
leaved Herbs and plants such as Rosemary, Bay and
Thyme. Even when withered in the depth of winter,
how full of fragrance are the natural Herb gardens of
the south of Europe, where one walks over stretches
of dry Thyme and Lavender, every step crushing out
their sweetness."

A COMFORTABLE POMANDER FOR THE BRAINE.—Take
Labdanum one ounce, Benjamin and Storax of each
two drams, Damaske powder finely searced, one Dram,
Cloves and Mace of each a little, a Nutmeg and a little
Camphire, Muske and Civet a little. First heate your
morter and pestle with coales, then make them verie
cleane and put in your labdanum, beate it till it waxe
softe, put to it two or three drops of oyl of spike, and
so labour them a while : then put in all the rest finely
in powder, and worke them till all be incorporated,
then take it out, anoynting your hands with Civet,
roll it up and with a Bodkin pierce a hole thorow it.—
Ram's Little Dadoen, 1606.

A BAG TO SMELL UNTO FOR MELANCHOLY, OR TO
CAUSE ONE TO SLEEP.—Take drie Rose leaves, keep them
close in a glasse which will keep them sweet, then take
powder of Mints, powder of Cloves in a grosse powder,
and put the same to the Rose leaves, then put all these
together in a bag, and take that to bed with you, and it
will cause you to sleep, and it is good to smell unto at
other times.—*Ibid*.

TO RENEW THE SENT OF A POMANDER.—Take one

grain of Civet, and two of Musk, or if you double the
proportion, it will bee so much the sweeter ; grinde
them upon a stone with a little Rose-water ; and after
wetting your hands with Rose-water you may worke
the same in your Pomander. This is a sleight to passe
away an old Pomander ; but my intention is honest.—
Ibid.

How to gather and clarifie May-dew.—When
there hath fallen no raine the night before, then with
a cleane and large sponge, the next morning, you may
gather the same from sweet herbs, grasse or corne :
straine your dew, and expose it to the Sun in glasses
covered with papers or parchments prickt full of holes ;
straine it often, continuing it in the Sun, and in an
hot place, till the same grow white and cleare, which
will require the best part of the Summer.

Some commend May-dew, gathered from Fennell
and Celandine to be most excellent for sore eyes :
and some commend the same (prepared as before)
above Rose-water for preserving of fruits, flowers,
etc.—*Ibid.*

A delicate Washing-ball.—Take three ounces of
orace, halfe an ounce of Cypres, two ounces of *Calamus
Aromaticus*, one ounce of Rose leaves, two ounces of
Lavender flowers : beat all these together in a mortar,
searcing them thorow a fine Searce, then scrape some
Castill sope, and dissolve it with some Rose-water,
then incorporate all your powders therewith, by
labouring of them well in a mortar.—*Ibid.*

A Scottish Handwater.—Put Thyme, Lavender

and Rosemary confusedly together, then make a lay of thicke wine Lees in the bottom of a stone pot, upon which make another lay of the said hearbs, and then a lay of Lees, and then so forward : lute the pot well, bury it in the ground for six weeks ; distil it. A little thereof put into a bason of common water maketh very sweete washing water.—*Ibid.*

AN EXCELLENT DAMASK POWDER.—You may take of Rose leaves four ounces, cloves one ounce, lignum Rhodium two ounces, Storax one ounce and a halfe, Muske and Civet of each ten grains ; beat and in corporate them well together.—*Ibid.*

JESEMAIN WATER.—Take two handfuls of Jeseme flowers and put them into a flagon or earthen pot, put to them about a quart of fair water and a quarter of a pound of Sugar, let this stand and steep about half an hour, then take your water and flowers and pour them out of one vessel into another till such time as the water hath taken the sent and tast of the flowers, then set it in a cool place a cooling and you will find it a most excellent sented water.—*A Perfect School of Instructions for the Officers of the Month,* by Giles Rose, one of the Master Cooks to Charles II, 1682.

ORANGE-FLOWER WATER.—Take one handful orange flowers and put them to about a quart of water and a quarter of a pound of sugar and do with them as you did with your Jeseme.—*Ibid.*

KING EDWARD VI's PERFUME.—Take twelve spoon-

fulls of right red rose-water, the weight of six pence
in fine powder of sugar, and boyl it on hot Embers and
coals softly, and the house will smell as though it were
full of Roses, but you must burn the sweet Cypress
wood before, to take away the gross ayre.—*The Queen's
Closet Opened*, by W. M., Cook to Queen Henrietta
Maria, 1655.

To MAKE AN IPSWICH BALL.—Take a pound of fine
white Castill Sope, shave it thin in a pinte of Rose-
water, and let it stand two or three days, then pour
all the water from it, and put to it half a pinte of fresh
water, and so let it stand one whole day, then pour out
that, and put half a pinte more, and let it stand a night
more, then put to it half an ounce of powder called
sweet Marjoram, a quarter of an ounce of powder of
Winter Savoury, two or three drops of the Oyl of Spike,
and the Oyl of Cloves, three grains of Musk, and as
much Ambergris, work all these together in a fair
Mortar, with the powder of an Almond Cake dryed,
and beaten as small as fine flowre, so rowl it round in
your hands in Rose-water.—*Ibid*.

A MOST PRECIOUS OINTMENT FOR ALL MANNER OF
ACHES AND BRUISES ; AND ALSO FOR THE REDNESS OF
THE FACE.—Take Violet, Primrose, Elder, Cowslip,
leafs and flowers ; Sage, Mugwort, Ragweed, white
Lillies, St. Johnswort, Smallage, Marjoram, Lavender,
Sothernwood, Rosemary, Rose-leafs, Rue, Fetherfew,
Tansie, Lovage, Mint, Camomile, Thyme, Dill, Clary,
Oak of Jerusalem, Penyroyal, Hysop, Balm, White
Mint, Marygold, Peony-leafs, Bay-leafs, Saffron, each

one handful. Stamp all these in a Stone-mortar, as
you get them then put them into a Pottle of Sallet
Oyl, and so let them infuse there till you have
all the rest together ; for you cannot get them all
at one time, but get them as fast as you can. Then
put to them and the Oyl a quart of White Wine, and
set it over the fire, and boyl it to the Consumption of
the Wine ; then take it off and strain it ; then put it
into a glass and keep it for use. When you anoint
any sore with this do it by the fire side, chafing it well
in ; and then lay a Hog's-bladder next to it, and a
Linnen upon that.—*Receipts in Physick and Chirurgery*,
by Sir Kenelm Digby, 1668.

To make Sweet Water.—Take Damask Roses at
discretion, Basil, Sweet Marjoram, Lavender, Walnut
Leafs, of each two handfuls, Rosemary one handful,
a little Balm, Cloves, Cinamon, one ounce, Bay leaf,
Rosemary tops, Limon and Orange Pills of each a few ;
pour upon these as much White Wine as will con-
veniently wet them, and let them infuse ten or twelve
days ; then distil it off.—*Ibid.*

To make Perfumes to Burn.—Take half a pound of
Damask Rosebuds (the whites cut off), Benjamin three
ounces beaten to powder, half a quarter of an ounce of
Musk, and as much of Ambergris, the like of Civet.
Beat all these together in a stone Morter. Then put
in an ounce of Sugar, and make it up in Cakes, and
dry them in the Sun, or by the fire.—*Ibid.*

A delicate Wash-ball.—Take a quarter of a Pound

of *Calamus Aromaticus*, a quarter of a Pound of Lavender flowers, six ounces of Orris, two ounces of Rose leaves, and an ounce of Cypres ; pownd all these together in a Mortar, and rub them through a fine Sieve, then scrape Castile-soap, and dissolve it in Rose-water, put in your beaten Powder, pownd it in a Mortar, and make it up into Balls.—From *The Receipt Book of John Nott*, Cook to the Duke of Bolton, 1723.

A GOOD MOUTH-WATER.—Boil a Bit of Alum, six Ounces of black Thorn Bark slic'd, and a handful of red Rose Leaves, and a Quart of Water, and a quart of Claret, till it is wasted a third Part. Then put in two Handfuls of Scurvy-grass, the Peel of two Sevil Oranges, and as much powder'd Myrrh as will lie on a Shilling twice ; stir them well together, and when they boil up, strain it. A mouthful of this Water being held in the mouth as long as you can, once or twice a Day, is good for the Scurvy, makes the Gums grow up to the Teeth, and fastens them if loose.—*Ibid.*

To MAKE A POMANDER.—Take Benjamin, Labdanum and Storax of each an ounce. Then heat a mortar very hot and beat them all to a perfect paste adding four grains of Civet and six of musk. Then roll your paste into small beads, make holes in them and string them while they are hot.—From *The Receipt Book of John Middleton*, 1734.

A SWEET-SCENTED BATH.—Take of Roses, Citron peel, Sweet flowers, Orange flowers, Jessamy, Bays, Rosemary, Lavender, Mint, Pennyroyal, of each a sufficient quantity, boil them together gently and make a Bath to which add Oyl of Spike six drops, mush five grains, Ambergris three grains.—*Ibid.*

For a Bath.—Take of Sage, Lavender flowers, Rose-flowers of each two handfuls, a little salt, boil them in water or lye, and make a bath not too hot in which bathe the Body in a morning, or two hours before Meat.—*Ibid.*

A Perfume to Perfume any sort of Confections.—Take musk, the like quantity of Oil of Nutmeg, infuse in them Rose-water, and with it sprinkle your Banqueting preparations and the scent will be as pleasing as the taste.—*England's newest way in all sorts of Cookery,* by Henry Howard, Free Cook of London, 1710.

To make Spirit of Lilley of the Valley.—Gather your Lilley-of-the-Valley Flowers, when they are dry, and pick them from the Stalks ; then put a quarter of a pint of them into a Quart of Brandy, and so in proportion, to infuse six or eight days ; then distil it in a cold Still, marking the Bottles, as they are drawn off, which is first, second and third, etc. When you have distill'd them, take the first, and so on to the third or fourth, and mix them together, till you have as strong as you desire ; and then bottle them, and cork them well, putting a lump of Loaf-sugar into each Bottle.

This serves in the room of Orange-Flower Water in Puddings, and to perfume Cakes ; though it is drank as a Dram in Norway.—R. Bradley, *The Country Housewife and Lady's Director*, 1732.

For the Face.—Take a small Handful of Strawberry Leaves, as much Cinquefoil, the same quantity of Tansey or of Mallows, and four Handfuls of Plantane Leaves, pick them clean, put them into an Alembick, and also two quarts of Milk from the Cow, when it has dropp'd a quart, draw off no more. Wet a Linen Cloth in this distilled Water, and wash the Face with it, at Night in Bed, and several times in the Day if you please. The best time to make this Water in, is May. It may be kept in a glass Bottle the whole year.—From *The Receipt Book of Charles Carter*, Cook to the Duke of Argyll, 1732.

Another.—Take a quart of running Water, put it into an earthen Pipkin, with half an Ounce of white Mercury finely powdered, set it on the fire, keep it close covered, but when you are stirring it, let it boil till one half is wasted ; in the meantime boil the whites of three new-laid Eggs, for half an Hour or more, then slip them into the Liquor, when you have taken it off the Fire ; add to it some Juice of Lemons, and a quarter of a pint of New Milk, and two ounces of Almonds, blanched and pounded, and also a quarter of a pint of Damask Rose-water. Strain it, and let it stand three weeks before it is us'd, wash with it, and it will render the Face fair.—Ibid.

To make a Paste for the Hands.—Take half a pound of bitter Almonds, blanch and pound them, and as you are pounding them, put in a handful of ston'd Raisins, and pound them together till the Mass is well incorporated and very fine ; then add a Spoonful or two of Brandy, the same quantity of Ox Gall and two spoonfuls of brown Sugar, and the Yolks of a couple of small eggs, or of one large one ; and after these have all been beaten well together, except the Almonds, let it have two or three boils over the Fire, put in the Almonds. Put it up in a Gallipot, the next Day cover it close, keep it cool, and it will keep good half a year. —*Ibid*.

To CLEAN AND SOFTEN THE HANDS.—Take four Ounces of blanch'd Almonds beaten fine into a quart of Milk ; as soon as it begins to boil take it off, and thicken it with a couple of Yolks of Eggs, set it on the Fire again, let it be kept continually stirring both before and after the Eggs are put in ; when you take it off the Fire, add two small spoonfuls of Oil, and put it up in a Gallipot for use. A Bit of this about the Bigness of a Walnut rubbed about the Hands, the Dirt will rub off, and it will render them very soft and smooth. When you have used it, it will be proper to put on Gloves. If one Person only be to use it, half the quantity may suffice to be made at once, for it will not hold good above a Week.—*Ibid*.

To MAKE AN EXCELLENT PERFUME.—Take half a pound of Damask Rose Buds cut clear from the Whites, stamp them well, and add to them two large Spoonfuls of Damask Rose-water, put them into a Bottle, stop them close, let them stand all night, then take two

Ounces and a half of Benjamin, beat it fine, add twenty grains of Musk, and (if you please) as much Civet, mingle these with the Roses, beating all well together, make it up in little Cakes, and dry them between Sheets of Paper.—*Ibid.*

To make perfumed Wash-balls.—Dissolve Musk in sweet compounded Water, then take about the quantity of one Wash-ball of this Composition, and mix it together in a Mortar : Mix this well with your Paste, and make it up into Balls.—*Ibid.*

To make Perfumed Powder.—Take four ounces of Florence Orris, four ounces of dry'd Damask Roses, half an Ounce of Benjamin, a quarter of an Ounce of Storax, as much of yellow Saunders, half a dram of Cloves, and a little Citron Peel ; pound all these in a Mortar to a very fine Powder, put to them five pounds of Starch pounded, mix them well, sift it fine, and keep it dry for use.—*Ibid.*

To take away Freckles and Morphew.—Distil Elder Leaves in May, and wash with a Spunge with this Liquor Morning and Evening, and let it dry of itself.—*Ibid.*

Delicate Wash-balls.—Take four Ounces of the Flowers of Lavender, 4 ounces of *Calamus Aromaticus*, 2 ounces of Rose Leaves, 2 ounces of Cypress, and 6 Ounces of Orris ; pound all these together in a Mortar, then searse them through a fine searse, then having scraped a sufficient quantity of Castile Soap, dissolve it in Rose-Water, mix the Powder with them, beat and blend them well together, in a Mortar, then make them up into Balls.—*Ibid*.

To MAKE A SWEET-BAG FOR LINEN.—Take of Orris roots, sweet Calamus, cypress-roots, of dried Lemon-peel, and dried Orange-peel ; of each a pound ; a peck of dried roses ; make all these into a gross powder ; coriander-seed four ounces, nutmegs an ounce and a half, an ounce of cloves ; make all these into fine powder and mix with the other ; add musk and amber-gris ; then take four large handfuls of lavender flowers dried and rubbed ; of sweet-marjoram, orange-leaves, and young walnut-leaves, of each a handful, all dried and rubb'd ; mix all together, with some bits of cotton perfum'd with essences, and put it up into silk bags to lay with your Linnen.—E. Smith, *The Compleat Housewife*, 1736.

RECIPE FOR POT POURRI.—Thoroughly dry the flowers to be used. There must be no particle of moisture left as it would mould, and spoil the whole. The best flowers for the purpose are roses (damask) Moss-roses, and the old cabbage-roses best of all, lavender, clove carnations, woodruff, rosemary, violets, sweet-verbena and in fact any sweet-smelling flowers. Leaves of the sweet bay, Sweet Briar, Balm, Lemon, Thyme, and even a *little* Mint, are all good. The rind of a lemon or two, and the rind of Tangerine and oranges (cut in strips), may be added. Have ready a mixture composed of one pound of Kitchen Salt, half pound Bay salt, half oz. of Storax, 6 drachms of Orris root, a grated Nutmeg, half a teaspoonful of ground cloves, half a teaspoonful of all-spice and 1 oz. of oil of Bergamot. The Bay salt must be pounded and all the dry ingredients well mixed, then add the Bergamot, and mix again. Put a layer of this at the bottom of your jar, then a layer of dried flowers *alternately* and keep the jar *closed*. Turn it over frequently especially at first.[1]

EAU DE COLOGNE.—One pint rectified spirits, one ounce orange-flower water, two drams oil of bergamot, two drams oil of lemon, twenty minims oil of rosemary, twenty minims oil of neroli. Allow the mixture to stand for a couple of months, thoroughly shaking at intervals. Filter if necessary.—Mrs. Charles Roundell, *The Still-room.*

For Lavender Water, see under Lavender.

[1] Miss Lydia Fraser, of the Manse of Sprouston, Kelso, kindly gave me this excellent old Scotch Receipt.

" Thus have I ended my booke . . . and yf to some I shall seeme not fullye to have satisfied their desyres herein accordinge to their expectation or not so cunninglye have handled the same as the matter itself offereth and is worthy of, then I referre my selfe wholye to ye learned correction of the wise, desyrynge theym frendelye to geeve knowledge to the printer, or to me, and beinge detected of my fault, wyll wyllyngelye correct and amend the same : for well I wotte that no treatise can alwaies so workmanly be handeled but that somewhat sometimes may fall out amisse contrary both to the minde of the wryter and contrary to the expectation of the reader. Wherefore my petition to the gentle reader is to accept these my trevails with that minde I do offer them to thee and to take gentelye that I geeve gladly, in so doinge I shal thinke my paynes well bestowed and shal be encouraged hereafter to trust more, unto thy curtesye. And therefore I cravve at thy handes the thankefull acceptance of these rude labours of myne. The favour of God bee with thee alwayes."—Thomas Hill, *The Proffitable Arte of Gardeninge*, 1568.

AUTHORITIES

MSS. (Harleian 2378 ; Sloane 2584 ; Sloane 521 ; Harleian 5294 ; Harleian 4986 ; Harleian 1585 ; Additional MS. 17063 ; Sloane 282 ; Sloane 1201 ; Sloane 3215).

1440. The Feate of Gardening. MAYSTER JON GARDENER.

1525. Here begynnyth a new matter the whiche sheweth and treateth of ye vertues and propyrtes of herbes the whiche is called an Herball. Imprinted by me RICHARD BANCKES, etc.

1526. The grete herball whiche geveth parfyt knowlege and understandyng of all maner of herbes and there gracyous vertues whiche god hath ordeyned for our prosperous welfare and helth, for they hele and cure all maner of dyseases and sickenesses that fall or mysfortune to all maner of creatoures of god created, practised by many expert and wyse maysters. . . . Imprinted at London in Southwarke by me Peter Treveris dwellynge in the sygne of the wodows. In the yere of our Lorde god MDXXVI. the xxvii day of July.

1527. The virtuose boke of Distyllacion of the waters of all maner Herbes. . . . First made and compyled by the thyrte yeres study and labour of the most conynge and famous mayster of phisyke, Master JHEROM BRUNSWYKE. And now newly translated out of Duyche into Englysshe.

293

1548. The names of herbes in Greek, Latin, Englishe, Duche and Frenche with the commune names that Herbaries and Apotecaries use. WILLIAM TURNER.

1551. A new Herball, wherein are conteyned the names of Herbes in Greke, Latin, Englysh, Duch, Frenche, and in the Potecaries and Herbaries Latin, with the properties degrees and naturall places of the same, gathered and made by Wylliam Turner, Phisicion unto the Duke of Somersettes Grace. Imprinted at London, By Steven Myerdman and they are to be soolde in Paules churchyarde at the sygne of the sprede Egle by JOHN GYBKEN.

1560 ? The boke of secretes of Albartus Magnus.

1562. The seconde parte of William Turner's herball . . . with the vertues of the same herbes with diverse confutations of no small errours that men of no small learning have committed in the intreatinge of herbes of late yeares.

1567. A greene Forest. J. MAPLET.

1568. The Proffitable Arte of Gardeninge. THOMAS HYLL.

1573. Five Hundreth Points of Good Husbandry. TUSSER.

1576. A proper new Booke of Cookerie. RICHARD PYNSEN.

1577. The Gardener's Labyrinth. THOMAS HYLL.

1577. Joyfull Newes out of the newe founde worlde. Englished by J. FRAMPTON.

1578. A Niewe Herball or Historie of Plantes : wherein is contayned the whole discourse and perfect description of all sortes of Herbes and Plantes . . . their strange Figures, Fashions and Shapes : their Names, Natures Operations and Vertues : and that not only

of those which are here growyng in our Countrie
of Englande but of all others also of forrayne
Realmes. First set forth in the Doutche or Al-
mayne tongue by that learned doctor Rembert
Dodoens Physition to the Emperour. And now
first translated out of French into English by Henry
Lyte Esquyer.

1584. The Garden of Health : containing the sundry rare
and hidden vertues and properties of all kinds of
Simples and Plants. . . . Gathered by the long
experience and industry of WILLIAM LANGHAM,
Practitioner in Physicke.

1584. The Discoverie of Witchcraft. REGINALD SCOT.

1585. The Good Housewife's Jewel and rare Conceits in
Cookery. T. DAWSON.

1586. The Treasurie of Commodious Conceits and Hidden
Secrets. JOHN PARTRIDGE.

1587. An Herbal for the Bible. . . . Drawen into English
by THOMAS NEWTON.

1587. The Breviare of Health. ANDREW BOORD.

1588. The Good Housewive's Treasurie. EDWARD ALLDE.

1594. Delights for Ladies. SIR HUGH PLATT.

1594. The Jewell House of Art and Nature. Sir HUGH
PLATT.

1597. The Herball. JOHN GERARD.

1600. Maison Rustique, or the Countrie Farme. Compiled
in the French tongue by CHARLES STEVENS and JOHN
LIEBAULT. . . . And translated into English by
RICHARD SURFLET.

1606.   Ram's little Dodoen. W. RAM.

1615.   Country Contentments. GERVASE MARKHAM.

1615.   A Garden of Flowers. . . . Faithfully and truely trans-
    lated out of the Netherlandish originall into English
    for the common benefite of those that understand no
    other languages and also for the benefite of others.
    Newly printed both in the Latin and French tongues
    and all at the charges of the Author . . . CRISPIN
    DE PASSE.

1618.   A New Orchard and Garden. WILLIAM LAWSON.

1621.   A delightful daily exercise for Ladies and Gentlemen.
    JOHN MURRELL.

1625.   Sylva Sylvarum. FRANCIS BACON.

1626.   Adam out of Eden. ADOLPHUS SPEED.

1629.   Paradisi in Sole Paradisus Terrestris. A Garden of
    all Sorts of Pleasant Flowers Which Our English
    Ayre will Permitt to be noursed up : with A Kitchen
    Garden of all manner of herbes . . . and An
    Orchard. Collected by JOHN PARKINSON Apothecary
    of London.

1639.   A Discovery of Infinite Treasure hidden since the
    World's Beginning. GABRIEL PLATTES.

1639.   The Charitable Physitian. PHILBERT GUIBERT.

1640.   Theatrum Botanicum. JOHN PARKINSON.

1651.   Le Jardin de Plaisir. ANDRÉ MOLLET.

1652.   The Ladies Dispensatory. LEONARD SOWERBY.

1653.   The English Physitian or an Astrologo-Physical Dis-
    course of the Vulgar Herbs of this Nation. . . .
    NICHOLAS CULPEPPER.

1653. A choice Manuall or rare and select secrets in Physick and Chirurgery by ELIZABETH GREY, Countess of Kent.

1654. The Art of Cookery. JOSEPH COOPER (Cook to Charles I).

1655. The Queen's Closet Opened. W.M. (Cook to Queen Henrietta Maria).

1655. The Ladies Cabinet Opened. PATRICK, LORD RUTHVEN

1655. Healths Improvement. T. MUFFET.

1655. The Complete Cook.

1656. The Art of Simpling. An Introduction to the Knowledge and Gathering of Plants. WILLIAM COLES.

1659. The Compleat Husbandman. SAMUEL HARTLEB.

1664. The Compleat Gardener's Practice. STEPHEN BLAKE.

1666. Kalendarium Hortense. JOHN EVELYN.

1668. Choice and Experimental Receipts. SIR KENELM DIGBY.

1669. The Closet of Sir Kenelm Digby Opened. SIR KENELM DIGBY.

1670. The English Gardener. LEONARD MEAGER.

1671. The Art and Mystery of Cooking Approved by the Fifty-five Years' Experience and Industry. ROBERT MAY.

1675. The Queen-like Closet. WILLIAM RABISHA.

1677. The Curious Distillatory or the Art of distilling coloured liquors, spirits, oyls, etc., from vegetables, animals, minerals and metals. A thing hitherto known to few. THOMAS SHIRLEY, Physician in ordinary to Charles II.

1682. A Perfect School of Instructions for the Officers of the Month. GILES ROSE (Cook to Charles II).

1683. The Scots Gardener. JOHN REID.

1692. The Good Housewife. THOMAS TRYON.

1694. The Compleat Herbal of Physical Plants. J. PECHEY.

1699. The Compleat Gardner. By the famous Monsr. DE LA QUINTINYE, Chief director of all the Gardens of the French King. . . . Made English by JOHN EVELYN Esquire.

1699. Acetaria : A Discourse of Sallets. JOHN EVELYN.

1710. The English Herbal. WILLIAM SALMON.

1710. England's newest way in all sorts of Cookery. HENRY HOWARD (Free Cook of London).

1712. A Complete History of Drugs. PIERRE POMET.

1715. The Nobleman, Gentleman, and Gardener's Recreation. STEPHEN SWITZER.

1716. Royal Cookery or the Complete Court Cook. PATRICK LAMB (Head Cook successively to Charles II, James II, William and Mary and Anne).

1716. The Compleat Herbal of Tournefort, translated by J. MARTYN.

1719. The Queen's Royal Cookery. T. HALL.

1719. The Accomplished Lady's Delight. Mrs. MARY EALES (Confectioner to Queen Anne).

1723. The Receipt Book of John Nott (Cook to the Duke of Bolton).

1726. The Cooks and Confectioners Dictionary. JOHN NOTT (Cook to the Duke of Bolton).

1732. The Compleat City and Country Cook. CHARLES CARTER (Cook to the Duke of Argyll).

1732. The Country Housewife and Lady's Director. R. BRADLEY.

1734. Five Hundred Receipts. JOHN MIDDLETON.

1736. The Complete Housewife. E. SMITH.

1737. A curious Herbal. ELIZABETH BLACKWELL.

1737. The Complete Family Piece.

1739. New Treatise of Husbandry, Gardening and other Curious Matters. SAMUEL TROWELL.

1739. The Housekeeper's Pocket Book. SARAH HARRISON.

1744. The Modern Cook. VINCENT LA CHAPELLE (Chief Cook to the Prince of Orange).

1745. A Treatise of all Sorts of Food. L. LEMERY.

1750. The Prudent Housewife. Mrs. FISHER.

1754. The Director. SARAH JACKSON.

1759. A New and Easy Method of Cookery. ELIZABETH CLELAND.

1767. The Modern Art of Cookery. Mrs. ANNE SHACKLE-FORD of Winchester.

1772. Virtues of British Herbs. Sir JOHN HILL.

1780. Flora Londiniensis. W. CURTIS.

1784. The Art of Cookery. Mrs. GLASSE.

1788. The English Art of Cookery. RICHARD BRIGGS.

1789. The Compleat Kitchen Gardener. JOHN ABERCROMBIE.

1790. Historical and Biographical Sketches. R. PULTENEY.

1810. The Family Herbal. R. THORNTON.

1861. The Physicians of Myddvai. JOHN PUGHE.

1865. Leechdoms, Wortcunning and Starcraft. O. COCKAYNE

1881. A History of the Cries of London. C. HINDLEY.

1884. Botanique et Plantes Medicinales. A. BOSSU.

1885. Manuel d'histoire Naturelle Medicale. J. L. DE LANESSAN.

1893. Plant Atlas to my Water-cure. S. KNEIPP.

1896. Le Jardin de l'Herboriste. H. CONEVON.

1897. Herbal Simples. DR. FERNIE.

1899. Medical Works of the Fourteenth Century. G. HENSLOW.

1901. The Book of Herbs. Lady ROSALIND NORTHCOTE.

1904. The Fitzpatrick Lectures for 1903. J. F. PAYNE.

1910. A History of Gardening in England. The Hon. Lady CECIL.

1911. The Herb Garden. Mrs. BARDSWELL.

1912. The English Housewife in the Seventeenth and Eighteenth Centuries. R. M. BRADLEY.

1912. Transactions of the Bibliographical Society.

A CATALOGUE OF SELECTED DOVER BOOKS
IN ALL FIELDS OF INTEREST

A CATALOGUE OF SELECTED DOVER
BOOKS IN ALL FIELDS OF INTEREST

RACKHAM'S COLOR ILLUSTRATIONS FOR WAGNER'S RING. Rackham's finest mature work—all 64 full-color watercolors in a faithful and lush interpretation of the *Ring*. Full-sized plates on coated stock of the paintings used by opera companies for authentic staging of Wagner. Captions aid in following complete Ring cycle. Introduction. 64 illustrations plus vignettes. 72pp. 8⅝ x 11¼.   23779-6 Pa. $6.00

CONTEMPORARY POLISH POSTERS IN FULL COLOR, edited by Joseph Czestochowski. 46 full-color examples of brilliant school of Polish graphic design, selected from world's first museum (near Warsaw) dedicated to poster art. Posters on circuses, films, plays, concerts all show cosmopolitan influences, free imagination. Introduction. 48pp. 9⅜ x 12¼.
23780-X Pa. $6.00

GRAPHIC WORKS OF EDVARD MUNCH, Edvard Munch. 90 haunting, evocative prints by first major Expressionist artist and one of the greatest graphic artists of his time: *The Scream, Anxiety, Death Chamber, The Kiss, Madonna*, etc. Introduction by Alfred Werner. 90pp. 9 x 12.
23765-6 Pa. $5.00

THE GOLDEN AGE OF THE POSTER, Hayward and Blanche Cirker. 70 extraordinary posters in full colors, from Maitres de l'Affiche, Mucha, Lautrec, Bradley, Cheret, Beardsley, many others. Total of 78pp. 9⅜ x 12¼.   22753-7 Pa. $5.95

THE NOTEBOOKS OF LEONARDO DA VINCI, edited by J. P. Richter. Extracts from manuscripts reveal great genius; on painting, sculpture, anatomy, sciences, geography, etc. Both Italian and English. 186 ms. pages reproduced, plus 500 additional drawings, including studies for *Last Supper*, Sforza monument, etc. 860pp. 7⅞ x 10¾. (Available in U.S. only)
22572-0, 22573-9 Pa., Two-vol. set $15.90

THE CODEX NUTTALL, as first edited by Zelia Nuttall. Only inexpensive edition, in full color, of a pre-Columbian Mexican (Mixtec) book. 88 color plates show kings, gods, heroes, temples, sacrifices. New explanatory, historical introduction by Arthur G. Miller. 96pp. 11⅜ x 8½. (Available in U.S. only)   23168-2 Pa. $7.95

UNE SEMAINE DE BONTÉ, A SURREALISTIC NOVEL IN COLLAGE, Max Ernst. Masterpiece created out of 19th-century periodical illustrations, explores worlds of terror and surprise. Some consider this Ernst's greatest work. 208pp. 8⅛ x 11.   23252-2 Pa. $5.00

AN AUTOBIOGRAPHY, Margaret Sanger. Exciting personal account of hard-fought battle for woman's right to birth control, against prejudice, church, law. Foremost feminist document. 504pp. 5⅜ x 8½.
20470-7 Pa. $5.50

MY BONDAGE AND MY FREEDOM, Frederick Douglass. Born as a slave, Douglass became outspoken force in antislavery movement. The best of Douglass's autobiographies. Graphic description of slave life. Introduction by P. Foner. 464pp. 5⅜ x 8½.   22457-0 Pa. $5.50

LIVING MY LIFE, Emma Goldman. Candid, no holds barred account by foremost American anarchist: her own life, anarchist movement, famous contemporaries, ideas and their impact. Struggles and confrontations in America, plus deportation to U.S.S.R. Shocking inside account of persecution of anarchists under Lenin. 13 plates. Total of 944pp. 5⅜ x 8½.
22543-7, 22544-5 Pa., Two-vol. set $11.00

LETTERS AND NOTES ON THE MANNERS, CUSTOMS AND CONDITIONS OF THE NORTH AMERICAN INDIANS, George Catlin. Classic account of life among Plains Indians: ceremonies, hunt, warfare, etc. Dover edition reproduces for first time all original paintings. 312 plates. 572pp. of text. 6⅛ x 9¼.   22118-0, 22119-9 Pa.. Two-vol. set $11.50

THE MAYA AND THEIR NEIGHBORS, edited by Clarence L. Hay, others. Synoptic view of Maya civilization in broadest sense, together with Northern, Southern neighbors. Integrates much background, valuable detail not elsewhere. Prepared by greatest scholars: Kroeber, Morley, Thompson, Spinden, Vaillant, many others. Sometimes called Tozzer Memorial Volume. 60 illustrations, linguistic map. 634pp. 5⅜ x 8½.
23510-6 Pa. $7.50

HANDBOOK OF THE INDIANS OF CALIFORNIA, A. L. Kroeber. Foremost American anthropologist offers complete ethnographic study of each group. Monumental classic. 459 illustrations, maps. 995pp. 5⅜ x 8½.
23368-5 Pa. $10.00

SHAKTI AND SHAKTA, Arthur Avalon. First book to give clear, cohesive analysis of Shakta doctrine, Shakta ritual and Kundalini Shakti (yoga). Important work by one of world's foremost students of Shaktic and Tantric thought. 732pp. 5⅜ x 8½. (Available in U.S. only)
23645-5 Pa. $7.95

AN INTRODUCTION TO THE STUDY OF THE MAYA HIEROGLYPHS, Syvanus Griswold Morley. Classic study by one of the truly great figures in hieroglyph research. Still the best introduction for the student for reading Maya hieroglyphs. New introduction by J. Eric S. Thompson. 117 illustrations. 284pp. 5⅜ x 8½.   23108-9 Pa. $4.00

A STUDY OF MAYA ART, Herbert J. Spinden. Landmark classic interprets Maya symbolism, estimates styles, covers ceramics, architecture, murals, stone carvings as artforms. Still a basic book in area. New introduction by J. Eric Thompson. Over 750 illustrations. 341pp. 8⅜ x 11¼.
21235-1 Pa. $6.95

A MAYA GRAMMAR, Alfred M. Tozzer. Practical, useful English-language grammar by the Harvard anthropologist who was one of the three greatest American scholars in the area of Maya culture. Phonetics, grammatical processes, syntax, more. 301pp. 5⅜ x 8½. 23465-7 Pa. $4.00

THE JOURNAL OF HENRY D. THOREAU, edited by Bradford Torrey, F. H. Allen. Complete reprinting of 14 volumes, 1837-61, over two million words; the sourcebooks for *Walden*, etc. Definitive. All original sketches, plus 75 photographs. Introduction by Walter Harding. Total of 1804pp. 8½ x 12¼. 20312-3, 20313-1 Clothbd., Two-vol. set $50.00

CLASSIC GHOST STORIES, Charles Dickens and others. 18 wonderful stories you've wanted to reread: "The Monkey's Paw," "The House and the Brain," "The Upper Berth," "The Signalman," "Dracula's Guest," "The Tapestried Chamber," etc. Dickens, Scott, Mary Shelley, Stoker, etc. 330pp. 5⅜ x 8½. 20735-8 Pa. $3.50

SEVEN SCIENCE FICTION NOVELS, H. G. Wells. Full novels. *First Men in the Moon, Island of Dr. Moreau, War of the Worlds, Food of the Gods, Invisible Man, Time Machine, In the Days of the Comet*. A basic science-fiction library. 1015pp. 5⅜ x 8½. (Available in U.S. only) 20264-X Clothbd. $8.95

ARMADALE, Wilkie Collins. Third great mystery novel by the author of *The Woman in White* and *The Moonstone*. Ingeniously plotted narrative shows an exceptional command of character, incident and mood. Original magazine version with 40 illustrations. 597pp. 5⅜ x 8½. 23429-0 Pa. $5.00

MASTERS OF MYSTERY, H. Douglas Thomson. The first book in English (1931) devoted to history and aesthetics of detective story. Poe, Doyle, LeFanu, Dickens, many others, up to 1930. New introduction and notes by E. F. Bleiler. 288pp. 5⅜ x 8½. (Available in U.S. only) 23606-4 Pa. $4.00

FLATLAND, E. A. Abbott. Science-fiction classic explores life of 2-D being in 3-D world. Read also as introduction to thought about hyperspace. Introduction by Banesh Hoffmann. 16 illustrations. 103pp. 5⅜ x 8½. 20001-9 Pa. $1.75

THREE SUPERNATURAL NOVELS OF THE VICTORIAN PERIOD, edited, with an introduction, by E. F. Bleiler. Reprinted complete and unabridged, three great classics of the supernatural: *The Haunted Hotel* by Wilkie Collins, *The Haunted House at Latchford* by Mrs. J. H. Riddell, and *The Lost Stradivarious* by J. Meade Falkner. 325pp. 5⅜ x 8½. 22571-2 Pa. $4.00

AYESHA: THE RETURN OF "SHE," H. Rider Haggard. Virtuoso sequel featuring the great mythic creation, Ayesha, in an adventure that is fully as good as the first book, *She*. Original magazine version, with 47 original illustrations by Maurice Greiffenhagen. 189pp. 6½ x 9¼. 23649-8 Pa. $3.50

SECOND PIATIGORSKY CUP, edited by Isaac Kashdan. One of the greatest tournament books ever produced in the English language. All 90 games of the 1966 tournament, annotated by players, most annotated by both players. Features Petrosian, Spassky, Fischer, Larsen, six others. 228pp. 5⅜ x 8½. 23572-6 Pa. $3.50

ENCYCLOPEDIA OF CARD TRICKS, revised and edited by Jean Hugard. How to perform over 600 card tricks, devised by the world's greatest magicians: impromptus, spelling tricks, key cards, using special packs, much, much more. Additional chapter on card technique. 66 illustrations. 402pp. 5⅜ x 8½. (Available in U.S. only) 21252-1 Pa. $3.95

MAGIC: STAGE ILLUSIONS, SPECIAL EFFECTS AND TRICK PHO-TOGRAPHY, Albert A. Hopkins, Henry R. Evans. One of the great classics; fullest, most authorative explanation of vanishing lady, levitations, scores of other great stage effects. Also small magic, automata, stunts. 446 illus-trations. 556pp. 5⅜ x 8½. 23344-8 Pa. $6.95

THE SECRETS OF HOUDINI, J. C. Cannell. Classic study of Houdini's incredible magic, exposing closely-kept professional secrets and revealing, in general terms, the whole art of stage magic. 67 illustrations. 279pp. 5⅜ x 8½. 22913-0 Pa. $3.00

HOFFMANN'S MODERN MAGIC, Professor Hoffmann. One of the best, and best-known, magicians' manuals of the past century. Hundreds of tricks from card tricks and simple sleight of hand to elaborate illusions involving construction of complicated machinery. 332 illustrations. 563pp. 5⅜ x 8½. 23623-4 Pa. $6.00

MADAME PRUNIER'S FISH COOKERY BOOK, Mme. S. B. Prunier. More than 1000 recipes from world famous Prunier's of Paris and London, specially adapted here for American kitchen. Grilled tournedos with anchovy butter, Lobster a la Bordelaise, Prunier's prized desserts, more. Glossary. 340pp. 5⅜ x 8½. (Available in U.S. only) 22679-4 Pa. $3.00

FRENCH COUNTRY COOKING FOR AMERICANS, Louis Diat. 500 easy-to-make, authentic provincial recipes compiled by former head chef at New York's Fitz-Carlton Hotel: onion soup, lamb stew, potato pie, more. 309pp. 5⅜ x 8½. 23665-X Pa. $3.95

SAUCES, FRENCH AND FAMOUS, Louis Diat. Complete book gives over 200 specific recipes: bechamel, Bordelaise, hollandaise, Cumberland, apri-cot, etc. Author was one of this century's finest chefs, originator of vichyssoise and many other dishes. Index. 156pp. 5⅜ x 8. 23663-3 Pa. $2.50

TOLL HOUSE TRIED AND TRUE RECIPES, Ruth Graves Wakefield. Authentic recipes from the famous Mass. restaurant: popovers, veal and ham loaf, Toll House baked beans, chocolate cake crumb pudding, much more. Many helpful hints. Nearly 700 recipes. Index. 376pp. 5⅜ x 8½. 23560-2 Pa. $4.50

THE SENSE OF BEAUTY, George Santayana. Masterfully written discussion of nature of beauty, materials of beauty, form, expression; art, literature, social sciences all involved. 168pp. 5⅜ x 8½.   20238-0 Pa. $2.50

ON THE IMPROVEMENT OF THE UNDERSTANDING, Benedict Spinoza. Also contains *Ethics, Correspondence*, all in excellent R. Elwes translation. Basic works on entry to philosophy, pantheism, exchange of ideas with great contemporaries. 402pp. 5⅜ x 8½.   20250-X Pa. $4.50

THE TRAGIC SENSE OF LIFE, Miguel de Unamuno. Acknowledged masterpiece of existential literature, one of most important books of 20th century. Introduction by Madariaga. 367pp. 5⅜ x 8½.

20257-7 Pa. $4.50

THE GUIDE FOR THE PERPLEXED, Moses Maimonides. Great classic of medieval Judaism attempts to reconcile revealed religion (Pentateuch, commentaries) with Aristotelian philosophy. Important historically, still relevant in problems. Unabridged Friedlander translation. Total of 473pp. 5⅜ x 8½.   20351-4 Pa. $6.00

THE I CHING (THE BOOK OF CHANGES), translated by James Legge. Complete translation of basic text plus appendices by Confucius, and Chinese commentary of most penetrating divination manual ever prepared. Indispensable to study of early Oriental civilizations, to modern inquiring reader. 448pp. 5⅜ x 8½.   21062-6 Pa. $4.00

THE EGYPTIAN BOOK OF THE DEAD, E. A. Wallis Budge. Complete reproduction of Ani's papyrus, finest ever found. Full hieroglyphic text, interlinear transliteration, word for word translation, smooth translation. Basic work, for Egyptology, for modern study of psychic matters. Total of 533pp. 6½ x 9¼. (Available in U.S. only)   21866-X Pa. $5.95

THE GODS OF THE EGYPTIANS, E. A. Wallis Budge. Never excelled for richness, fullness: all gods, goddesses, demons, mythical figures of Ancient Egypt; their legends, rites, incarnations, variations, powers, etc. Many hieroglyphic texts cited. Over 225 illustrations, plus 6 color plates. Total of 988pp. 6⅛ x 9¼. (Available in U.S. only)

22055-9, 22056-7 Pa., Two-vol. set $12.00

THE ENGLISH AND SCOTTISH POPULAR BALLADS, Francis J. Child. Monumental, still unsuperseded; all known variants of Child ballads, commentary on origins, literary references, Continental parallels, other features. Added: papers by G. L. Kittredge, W. M. Hart. Total of 2761pp. 6½ x 9¼.

21409-5, 21410-9, 21411-7, 21412-5,   21413-3 Pa., Five-vol. set $37.50

CORAL GARDENS AND THEIR MAGIC, Bronsilaw Malinowski. Classic study of the methods of tilling the soil and of agricultural rites in the Trobriand Islands of Melanesia. Author is one of the most important figures in the field of modern social anthropology. 143 illustrations. Indexes. Total of 911pp. of text. 5⅝ x 8¼. (Available in U.S. only)

23597-1 Pa. $12.95

AMERICAN ANTIQUE FURNITURE, Edgar G. Miller, Jr. The basic coverage of all American furniture before 1840: chapters per item chronologically cover all types of furniture, with more than 2100 photos. Total of 1106pp. 7⅞ x 10¾.   21599-7, 21600-4 Pa., Two-vol. set $17.90

ILLUSTRATED GUIDE TO SHAKER FURNITURE, Robert Meader. Director, Shaker Museum, Old Chatham, presents up-to-date coverage of all furniture and appurtenances, with much on local styles not available elsewhere. 235 photos. 146pp. 9 x 12.   22819-3 Pa. $5.00

ORIENTAL RUGS, ANTIQUE AND MODERN, Walter A. Hawley. Persia, Turkey, Caucasus, Central Asia, China, other traditions. Best general survey of all aspects: styles and periods, manufacture, uses, symbols and their interpretation, and identification. 96 illustrations, 11 in color. 320pp. 6⅛ x 9¼.   22366-3 Pa. $6.95

CHINESE POTTERY AND PORCELAIN, R. L. Hobson. Detailed descriptions and analyses by former Keeper of the Department of Oriental Antiquities and Ethnography at the British Museum. Covers hundreds of pieces from primitive times to 1915. Still the standard text for most periods. 136 plates, 40 in full color. Total of 750pp. 5⅜ x 8½.
23253-0 Pa. $10.00

THE WARES OF THE MING DYNASTY, R. L. Hobson. Foremost scholar examines and illustrates many varieties of Ming (1368-1644). Famous blue and white, polychrome, lesser-known styles and shapes. 117 illustrations, 9 full color, of outstanding pieces. Total of 263pp. 6⅛ x 9¼. (Available in U.S. only)   23652-8 Pa. $6.00